World University Library

The World University Library is an international series
of books, each of which has been specially commissioned.
The authors are leading scientists and scholars from all over
the world who, in an age of increasing specialisation, see the
need for a broad, up-to-date presentation of their subject.
The aim is to provide authoritative introductory books for
university students which will be of interest also to the general
reader. The series is published in Britain, France, Germany,
Holland, Italy, Spain, Sweden and the United States.

Frontispiece. *Beliefs of the Old and New Churches* (*c.* 1530),
a print illustrating the fundamental beliefs shared by
Protestants (on the left) and Catholics (on the right).

Henry Kamen

The Rise of Toleration

World University Library

McGraw-Hill Book Company
New York Toronto

This book is dedicated to all those who have
suffered, and still suffer, from religious,
racial and social intolerance

© Henry Kamen 1967
Reprinted 1972
Library of Congress Catalog Card Number: 66-24158
Phototypeset by BAS Printers Limited, Wallop, Hampshire, England
Manufactured by LIBREX, Milan, Italy

Contents

1 The problem of toleration

In its broadest sense, toleration can be understood to mean the concession of liberty to those who dissent in religion. It can be seen as part of the process in history which has led to a gradual development of the principle of human freedom. What should be remembered is that this development has been by no means regular. Even the great English historian Lord Acton, for whom the evolution of freedom lay at the heart of history, was obliged to recognise that toleration has pursued not a linear but a cyclic development; it has not evolved progressively but has suffered periodic and prolonged reverses. The belief that religious liberty is an exclusively modern achievement is of course untrue, and it should cause no great surprise to find that some countries today are further from full liberty than they were five centuries ago. Attitudes are in any case conditioned by social and political circumstances, developing erratically according to their milieu, so that there is no inherent reason why a modern doctrine should be any more progressive than a distant one.

By giving due consideration to the social context of philosophies we can come closer to understanding the contemporary significance of doctrines. It is above all important when studying the protagonists of toleration to realise that they were not merely landmarks in the history of ideas. They were themselves often representative of social forces that cannot be ignored. We may talk of Zwingli and Locke, and yet forget the burgher class in Zürich or the landed aristocracy in England. Rarely indeed do we come across an advocate of toleration as a voice crying in the wilderness; there were some such, no doubt, but they are outnumbered by the voices that represent the vanguard of movements in process of evolution or even dissolution.

Our context is Christian Europe in an age of revolution. To be precise, our geographical unit is what was once Catholic Europe, from Poland to the Atlantic. The age of revolution is capable of differing definitions, many of them imprecise. In the first place there is the economic advance, blurred but unquestionable, in which the increasingly intensive application of new methods of

A third-century painting of the *Agape*, or love-feast, from the catacomb of Priscilla in Rome. This celebration, which accompanied the commemoration of the Last Supper, expressed the early Christians' sense of brotherhood.

production and the growth of a money economy pave the way to the decline of feudalism in western Europe. Allied to this is the growth of a so-called secular spirit in literature, art and politics, as expressed in the Renaissance. The reassessment of both the economic and spiritual place of man in society led initially to criticism and then to revolt. The development of events varied from country to country: in all countries, however, we witness in the sixteenth century, in the era of Renaissance humanism, the rise of a new and more liberal attitude to religion.

Liberalism in religion is not the same thing as tolerance, but historically it was often a prerequisite, and is of considerable importance in helping us to arrive at a general idea of the often vague concept of 'tolerance'. Though the many proponents of toleration were seldom if ever in agreement on general principles, it should be possible to outline the distinguishing features of toleration up to the sixteenth century.

Christianity and tolerance

Catholic Christianity occupies the whole religious background with which we are concerned. 'The Church', Acton claimed, 'began with the principle of liberty, both as her claim and as her rule'. There can be no doubt about this. The liberty proclaimed by the apostles was both external and internal. Internally, the grace of Christ had redeemed and acquitted man, giving him the absolute freedom of the sons of God. A Christian must correspondingly respect others in a spirit of charity based on freedom: the conscience of one's neighbour must not be hurt. 'When you sin against the brethren and wound their weak conscience, you sin against Christ', Saint Paul warned the Corinthians (1 Cor. 8:12). There was to be no forcing of consciences, since the freedom brought by Christ applied to all men. In the Church there was 'no more Jew or Gentile, no more slave and freeman, no more male and female; you are all one person in Jesus Christ' (Gal. 3:28).

Externally, Christians were to be free from political repression

and persecution, since, according to Christ, they were to fulfil all their obligations blamelessly, so as to 'give back to Caesar what is Caesar's, and to God what is God's' (Matt. 22:21). In other words, the spheres of secular government and religion were separate, and the State had no right to force acceptance of religion so long as one fulfilled faithfully all obligations to it. Absolute distinction of Church and State, so unequivocally laid down by Christ, became the charter of Christian claims to toleration under the Roman Empire. As long as Christians, like members of other religions, carried out their secular duties, the State had no right to interfere with the consciences of individual Christians, nor indeed did the State possess any authority in religious matters. For two centuries the fathers of the Catholic Church continued to demand toleration on this basis. 'By both human and natural law', Tertullian protested in the early third century, 'each one is free to adore whom he wants. The religion of an individual neither harms nor profits anybody else. It is against the nature of religion to force religion'.

The intolerance of the early Church to its own members was to be of importance later when the Church had triumphed in Europe. Authorities who favoured persecution would cite the

The idea of the Last Judgement as a harvest
recurs throughout the New Testament. In this
illustration by Hans Cranach for Luther's
translation of the New Testament, apocalyptic
angels are seen gathering in the harvest
and treading the grapes.

11

instance where Saint Peter had struck down Ananias and Saphira
because of their dishonesty. There is little doubt that the discipline
of the Christian communities was often harsh and narrow. Yet the
doctrinal position of the Church in respect of errant members was
clear. The use of capital punishment was totally disallowed. 'The
weapons we fight with are not human weapons' (2 Cor. 10:4),
wrote Saint Paul. Following the advice of Christ, the apostles
made use instead of excommunication as a method of discipline:
'Give a heretic one warning, then a second, and after that avoid
his company' (Titus 3:10). This was often practised, but the discipline was to be charitable, in the spirit of Christ's admonition to
'love one another' (John 15:12). There would certainly be differences
of opinion, but these were not infringements of discipline and
should be borne with. As Saint Paul emphasised, 'parties there
must needs be among you [*oportet haereses esse*], so that those
who are true metal may be distinguished from the rest' (1 Cor.
11:19). With a strict adherence to these scriptural tenets, the early
Church managed to win a reputation for charity and non-violence
of a kind rarely achieved by later heterodox Christian sects. 'See
how these Christians love one another', an observation first made
in the time of Tertullian, became a commentary on their success
and a judgment on their successors.

Texts from the Bible came to be used widely in later controversies on toleration. The golden rule laid down by Christ – 'Do to
other men all that you would have them do to you' (Matt. 7:12) –
became a standard plea for charity among Christians. There were
in addition three texts that played a major part in writings on the
subject. The most famous of them is the parable of the tares
(Matt. 13: 24–30; 36–43). 'There was a man who sowed his field
with clean seed; but while all the world was asleep an enemy of
his came and scattered tares among the wheat'. When this was
discovered, his men offered to weed out the tares. 'But he said,
No; or perhaps while you are gathering the tares you will root up
the wheat with them. Leave them to grow side by side till harvest,
and when harvest-time comes I will give the word to the reapers,

Gather up the tares first, and tie them in bundles to be burned, and store the wheat in my barn'. According to Christ's own explanation of the parable, he meant that the good and bad should be allowed to coexist until the Last Judgment. The common interpretation given to it in later times was that the Church should be tolerant to its own errant children until Christ should come again. Later the interpretation was broadened to mean that Christians should be tolerant to those not of the household of the faith. On either count, it was clear that extreme measures such as the death penalty were not to be applied to heretics or pagans.

The next text, in direct reference to Christ, takes a passage from Isaiah and claims of the Messiah that 'the bruised reed he shall not break, the smoking flax he shall not extinguish' (Matt. 12:20). This was commonly understood to mean that errant sinners ('the smoking flax') would not be cut off by Christ, but would benefit from his mercy. In this, the Church was seen to act in the place of Christ. Several other passages like this, all pointing directly to the extreme mercy of God, were interpreted in the same way, to show that leniency must be practised towards heretics.

A final text concerns the preaching of the apostles in Jerusalem. Their teaching infuriated the Sadducees, who denounced them to the Council and demanded punishment. In Council, however, the rabbi Gamaliel rose and asked for reconsideration. The ground of his argument has become classic. 'If this is man's design or man's undertaking', he said, 'it will be overthrown; if it is God's, you will have no power to overthrow it. You would not willingly be found fighting against God' (Acts 5: 38–9).

Christianity and intolerance

In AD 313 the Roman Empire under Constantine finally gave official toleration to Christians. This achievement of emancipation prepared the way for compromise in the role of the Church. Assimilated into the society of the Empire, Christians adapted themselves to the social norms. The revolutionary philosophy of the Church had brought with it a liberty that extended beyond nation and class: at the *agape* and at the Eucharist all men were equal. But this equality was no more than an accidental achievement of Christian freedom, and when political realities had to be faced the Church became a potentially conservative force, resigned to the inevitable evils of what was, after all, a transitory world, and concerned more and more exclusively with the salvation of souls alone. By the end of the fourth century the Church had grown to accept the exercise of punitive constraint against heterodox Christians, and Catholics looked with approval on the measures taken by the secular authorities against Arians and Donatists. As the established religion, Christianity was drawn irresistibly towards an alliance of interest with the secular power. Despite the regular protests of distinguished prelates, the new Church-State alliance began a programme of selective persecution. The Roman emperors proscribed paganism and pulled down its altars. At the close of the fourth century the noble but vain protests of a few distinguished pagans could still be heard speaking in favour of the liberty of cults. *Uno itinere non potest perveniri ad tam grande secretum* – 'It is not by one path alone', cried Symmachus in the Roman Senate in the year 384, 'that men can attain the heart of so great a mystery!' But the day had passed to champions of an exclusive truth.

Historians have dated the acceptance of persecution to Saint Augustine's campaign against the Donatists of North Africa in the early fifth century. In justice to the bishop of Hippo, it should be recalled that he was an unswerving opponent of extreme torture and of the death penalty. As one who had himself been a Manichean heretic, Augustine was willing to understand the difficulties encountered by Manichees in relinquishing heresy. Moreover, he opposed all coercion which aimed at enforcing belief, and distilled this position in the fundamental principle: *credere non potest homo nisi volens*, man cannot believe against his will. But it remains true that by his appeal to the secular authorities for help against the outrages committed by the Donatists; by the

way in which he wrested the phrase *compelle intrare* from its context in the parable of the supper (Luke 14:23), so as to make it read as a command to enforce the submission of heretics and unbelievers; and by his intolerant exclamation, 'What death is worse for the soul than the liberty to err?' – *Quae peior mors animae quam libertas erroris?* –; he established a precedent which fortified the practice of repression by the mediaeval Church.

The parable of the tares he interpreted to mean that tares should be uprooted if it was clear that no wheat would be uprooted with them. His final position, unbending in its claim to exclusive truth, was uncompromising: 'There is an unjust persecution, which the ungodly operate against the Church of Christ; and a just persecution which the Churches of Christ make use of towards the ungodly ... The Church persecutes out of love, the ungodly out of cruelty'. The bishop of Hippo was to prove a powerful authority for later protagonists of religious intolerance.

The basis of intolerance in the Middle Ages was the alliance between Church and State. The Church on its side taught patient subjection to the powers of the world, and the State stepped in to eradicate religious heterodoxy wherever it reared its head.

Detail from Andrea Bonaiuti's *The Church Militant and Triumphant* (*c*. 1365),
painted for the Dominican church of S. Maria Novella in Florence. In front
of the elevation of Florence Cathedral, representing the Church on earth, the
Pope is enthroned as supreme authority – over Emperor, kings and laity on his
left, and the clergy and religious on his right. The painting illustrates
the Church's view of the structure of contemporary mediaeval society.

Theoretically the ecclesiastical authorities held to the Christian view
that the Church should exercise no undue restraint and have no
recourse to the shedding of blood. In practice they were willing to
resort to the 'secular arm', as the Christian ruler was termed, to
carry out that 'just persecution' of which Saint Augustine had
spoken. The excuse for this lay in the enormous success of Christian
expansion. In the fifth century it was still possible to distinguish
between the relative spheres of the Church and the Empire. By
the eighth century the old Empire was a memory and the Church
had become the unique upholder of civilisation in Europe. The
new Empire of Charlemagne consequently came into being under
the aegis of the Church, whose presence in all the lands of the West
created the concept of an international Christendom embracing
the whole population and both secular and ecclesiastical authorities. The theoreticians of this Christendom were not slow to give
it a theocratic character, and soon prince and bishop became joint
authorities in a sacral society where all authority was divine and
therefore entrusted to the Church.

Pope Gelasius I in the fifth century had taught the duality of
secular and spiritual power in the world, but it was an uneven
duality: 'the world is ruled over by two great powers, that of the
pontiffs and that of the Kings, but the authority of the pontiffs is
far greater, since they must give account to God of the souls of
Kings'. By the time of Innocent III in the late twelfth century
theocratic pretensions were at their peak: 'The royal power',
claimed this Pope, 'derives from the pontifical authority the splen-
dour of its dignity'. In his bull *Unam Sanctam* in 1302 Boniface VIII
claimed that all authority on earth was vested in the Church; two
swords ruled the world, but 'both swords, the spiritual and the
material, are in the power of the Church'.

Fortified by this sovereignty in temporal matters, the Church
did not hesitate to persecute heresies that allegedly threatened the
temporal order. Prelates and lords made common cause against
seditious preaching and rebellion among the lower classes, so as
to preserve the dogmatic and social unity of Christendom. The

The burning of John Hus at Constance in 1415, from a
fifteenth-century manuscript. Hus, who was rector of
the University of Prague, led a revolt that was both national
and religious. Curiously enough the Council of Constance,
which ordered his execution, achieved its most notable
success in reconciling a divided western Christendom.

result was that dissident sects were obliged to reject the coercive
power of the Church in temporal matters, as the only way to
establish toleration for themselves. On occasion the sectarians
placed themselves under the control of some great magnate, in the
hope that his protection would suffice to ward off the vengeance
of the Church. This defensive tactic might imply the political
disobedience of the magnate to his feudal superiors and would call
for retribution on both political and religious grounds. Toleration
in this context could not fail to be a political problem, of which
the thirteenth century crusades against the Albigensians in France
are a classic example.

Society and heresy

Set in political terms, the pattern of mediaeval heresy provides a
continuous development down into the Reformation period.
Conformity in faith implied unity and therefore security in society.
Conversely, to differ in faith meant to threaten the fabric of society.
Both Church and State consequently set their face against ideo-
logical minorities. On their side, mediaeval heretics saw rightly
that in questioning dogmas they must also come to question the
worldly superstructure erected on these dogmas. Not surprisingly,
religious innovators often became social rebels and social rebels
adopted theology as the vehicle of their protest. The religious
Reformation was consequently conditioned by, and in its turn led
towards, social movements which were not necessarily in entire
sympathy with its aims, particularly since the religious changes
of the sixteenth century were often brought about against the
wishes of the mass of the people.

Illustrations of this social background to heresy are provided in
peasant and doctrinal movements of the later Middle Ages. The
influence of the fourteenth-century English heretic John Wycliffe
permeated some of the lower social grades of fifteenth-century
England, and rebels adopted many of Wycliffe's tenets as part of
their economic protest. Doctrine also played a large part in the

Czech communities that adopted Hussite teachings after the death of the great Bohemian heretic John Hus at Constance in 1415. One of these, the Hussite Unity of Brethren, founded by Chelčický, followed a communistic programme that rejected the authority of the State in religious matters and called for a complete separation of the spheres of Church and State. These two principles, later to be adopted as a fundamental feature of Anabaptism, would have secured the Hussites freedom of belief. What the authorities objected to in such a doctrine was, of course, that the Hussites by their own principles made religious liberty dependent on radical alterations in the political structure. The struggle for toleration obviously involved a denial of the whole mediaeval framework of government.

By the early sixteenth century this mediaeval world was being perceptibly transformed. The climate of thought in educated circles; the redistribution of political power among the nationalities of Europe; the expansion of commerce and banking; the rise to power of the bourgeoisie in the Netherlands and their decline in Germany, Italy and Spain; were all part of the process. It is to this period that historians have dated the rise of nation states and the New Monarchy, in which individual realms, by their claim to autonomy, caused the fragmentation of the feudal world-system so long upheld by theoreticians of the papacy and the Empire. The cultural Renaissance, diffused from Italy, made a particular contribution to the reorganisation of social norms, while preachers, pamphleteers and political theorists began to revise and reject the preconceptions of their predecessors.

Although the Middle Ages had not tolerated dissent, it would be misleading to portray this as monolithic intolerance. Non-Christians, for example, were theoretically quite free. Saint Thomas Aquinas had maintained that heretics alone deserve the death penalty, on the analogy that if those who counterfeit money are liable to execution, 'it is far more serious to pervert the faith which ensures the life of the soul than to counterfeit money which is only necessary for our temporal needs'. A different standard of

Panel from *The Veneration
of St Vincent* (*c.* 1465), a
polyptych by the Portuguese
painter Nuno Gonçalves.
The panel shows a monk
presenting a relic of the saint,
a pilgrim and a Jewish rabbi.
The inclusion of the rabbi
in this painting, which
represents the most notable
figures in Portuguese
society paying homage
to St Vincent, is an indication
of the status of the Jewish
community in Portugal at
the time.

values existed for pagans: 'non-believers must not be compelled to believe, because believing is a matter of free will'. On this basis, Catholics could and did coexist peaceably with Jews and Muslims in several parts of the Mediterranean world. It became a common argument in favour of toleration in the sixteenth century that the papacy itself suffered Jews in Rome and allowed them to use their synagogues. Heterodoxy, however, was punished where paganism was not, for the simple reason that heretics had presumably turned their backs on the light and had consequently sinned against the Holy Ghost and against their own conscience. Heretics, Aquinas said, 'must be compelled, even physically, to fulfil what they have promised, and to maintain what they have once accepted'.

The question of toleration, in the form it took at the end of the mediaeval period, may be approached from two principal angles. The issue at stake is the liberty of an individual to dissent from an official truth. Has the State, in its function as an auxiliary of the Church or even in its own right as guardian of the social order, any right to repress heresy? And does the individual – if he appeals to the principle that belief cannot be forced – have any right to freedom of conscience? It was on these two issues that most of the debate turned after the sixteenth century, all other arguments being largely subordinate to these.

The rights of conscience were not explicitly recognised by mediaeval theologians. Error, claimed the scholastics, has no rights; denial of the truth can never coexist with the truth. Certainly it might be objected that those who were sincere in their error necessarily looked on their error as truth. Peter Abelard, for instance, in the twelfth century went so far as to maintain that sin committed in ignorance is not truly sin, because the culprits knew no better. But his views were condemned as heresy, and subsequent theologians came down heavily in favour of the argument that the objective law of God, as laid down by the Church, was the sole criterion of right action, and that a conscience which went against that law, sinned. The duty of someone who saw his own conscience conflict with the law of God, was to reject his conscience, which had obviously been corrupted, and to follow the objective law. This harsh and rigorous position was to some extent modified by Aquinas, who admitted that a conscience in error could plead ignorance of the relevant fact or situation, but he narrowed down the possibilities of invincible ignorance to virtually only the weak-minded and insane, so that in effect his position differed hardly at all from that of his predecessors. Before the sixteenth century there were no influential philosophers to support the cause of the erroneous conscience. This intransigent position continued to be taught in official quarters of the Catholic Church down to modern times. In 1832 Gregory XVI described liberty of conscience as a 'delirium' (*deliramentum*), and in 1864 it was condemned in the Syllabus of Errors.

The power of the State over dissenters had repeatedly been questioned by the most radical mediaeval heretics, especially the Cathars. The Unity of Czech Brethren carried on this tradition during what has been described as the Hussite century in Bohemia. Their protests were based explicitly on the freedom of Christians and their right to liberty in the world. The principle carried with it an explicit denial of part of the State's authority, but very few heretics went so far as to argue logically against all secular power. Both the partial and the total denials of authority were to be utilised regularly as arguments in favour of toleration during the Reformation epoch.

2 The reformation era

Revolutionary as the Reformation was in politics and religion, it is difficult to find any radical departure from tradition in the moral and social thought of the early reformers. The legacy of the Renaissance, with the broadening and deepening of understanding that came with it, was supplemented by the fierce reiteration of religious verities. Some have even viewed the Reformation as a conservative movement – for certainly Luther considered that he was restoring rather than innovating – and have distinguished it from two other movements, radical sectarianism and humanist irenicism, which threatened to carry the reformers off in differing directions. These three streams of development will occupy the next few chapters.

The rationalist impetus of the Renaissance is relevant to the rise of toleration in two ways: firstly, it led to an anticlerical or non-clerical sentiment usually described as the secular or lay spirit; secondly, it led to a search after universal human values and hence to a more kindly attitude to those who differed in point of religion. In a classic study of Rabelais, Lucien Febvre has demonstrated how the first phenomenon, often interpreted as an onset of un-belief, irreligion and indifferentism, was more a decline into a chaos of imprecise ideas, caused to some extent by the inability of the old grammatical terminology to express modern concepts adequately, than a coherent anti-religious philosophy. Literature, and especially vernacular literature, adopted the tone of doubt and mockery, but without specifically rejecting the old orthodoxy. In political literature, the anticlerical content was more specific. Machiavelli's diatribes against papal tyranny were significant not only in that they reinforced the split between organised religion and the exercise of civil power; they were also representative of the views of other thinking Italians, such as Guicciardini. When writers such as these, continuing the tradition of Marsiglio of Padua (1270–1342), explicitly oppose the secular power to institutional Catholicism, we come closer to that separation of Church and State which for many was a prerequisite of religious liberty.

The acceptance of universal moral values could lead to beliefs

Prophetic illustration of the upheavals of the Reformation: a church is upside down, a peasant celebrates Mass, while a nobleman and a monk plough the fields. From a book, published in 1508, foretelling disasters in church and state, by Joseph Gruenpeck, one of Emperor Maximilian I's secretaries.

which were essentially subversive of revealed religion. Typical is the statement once made to Pope Sixtus IV by his tutor, Galeotto Marzio, 'He who lives correctly and acts by the law of nature will enter heaven, no matter to what people he belongs'. Such a concession to unrevealed religion led in a direction not intended by its originators – to scepticism, deism and atheism. Marzio's position is paralleled by that of Montaigne, who claimed that 'though a man be ignorant of Christ, if he faithfully follows the law of nature he can perfect himself. He is even implicitly a disciple of Jesus Christ. He is a Christian without knowing it'. The content of such propositions amounted to a sceptical indifference to organised religion, and a thorough indifference to the Church. As Henri Busson has shown in a penetrating work, this rationalism began to undermine the world of spiritual concepts – miracles, immortality, witchcraft – before it set itself to question the ordinary revealed truths of religion. It bred a naturalism – as in Montaigne, who tended to substitute the word 'nature' for the word 'God' – that led to the rationalism of the eighteenth century, in which toleration was supported not because it was essential to religion

The new vision opened up by the Reformation is shown in this woodcut (1524) by Holbein, showing Christ the True Light expelling the old Church and old philosophies (including Plato and Aristotle) into a pit of darkness.

but because religion itself was unessential. Such a toleration, based ultimately on unbelief, we are not immediately concerned with.

The universalism entertained by thoroughly religious people is of more importance here, because it existed in a world where each religion claimed its own exclusive truth. Those who held these views tended to be non-scholastic humanists, and it is significant that the most serious irenic efforts made during the Reformation era to bring about peace between the contending religions, were the work of humanists. Among the predecessors of this party was Cardinal Nicholas of Cusa (1401–64), a prominent philosopher and churchman, whose wish was to reunite the Greek Orthodox and the Hussites with the Catholic Church, and whose dreams extended even further beyond this, to an ultimate reunion of Jews, Christians, Muslims and Hindus in a joint worship which would secure 'a universal concordat and build a perpetual religious peace'. However unrealistic this dream, and however obviously unacceptable in the prevailing state of the world, it was pursued by other humanists who concentrated more on the philosophic truths common to mankind (for this they leaned heavily on a rediscovered Greek heritage) and less on the purely dogmatic aspects of religion. If a common truth was to be sought, it could only be arrived at by charity and peace, for the composing of differences was a prerequisite of agreement. The humanists were concerned for peace: this was true above all for Erasmus (1466–1536).

The position of Erasmus

'Summa nostrae religionis pax est et unanimitas', Erasmus wrote in 1523. He was then in his fifty-seventh year, already the acknowledged leader of European humanism. All his life had been devoted to the cultivation of 'good letters', which he saw as the decisive weapon in purging the Church of its ceremonial dross and reducing it to a liberal and less dogmatic practice of religion. If at

times in his writings he had descended to vituperation and mockery of his enemies, he remained nevertheless essentially pacific in disposition. Throughout his life he espoused the cause of peace and denounced the resort to war among the princes; himself he described as one 'who never leaves off persecuting war by means of his pen'. He was all the more hurt that both sides in the Reformation controversy refused to solve their theological differences in a spirit of amity.

He had at first looked kindly on Luther, since the Augustinian friar was doing no more than, in the words of Erasmus' enemies, hatching the egg that Erasmus had laid. In 1519 he wrote to Luther and encouraged him 'to continue what you are doing'. The violent methods adopted by the reformers quickly disillusioned him. The Lutherans, he wrote to a friend in 1524, 'have these five words always on their lips: evangel, God's Word, faith, Christ, and Spirit; and yet I see many behave so that I cannot doubt them to be possessed by the devil'. To Luther in 1526 he protested: 'It is this that distresses me, and all the best spirits with me, that with that arrogant, impudent, seditious temperament of yours you are shattering the whole globe in ruinous discord'.

But Erasmus was also strongly opposed to the exercise of force against Luther. No matter how widely the Lutheran heresy had spread, it could not be rooted out by the old inquisitorial methods. He wrote in 1524 to the Duke of Saxony, 'It is not right that an error of any kind be punished by burning unless it is linked with sedition or any other crime which the laws punish by death'. Two years later he was suggesting a sort of political compromise whereby 'in cities where the evil has increased, both parties keep to their quarters and everyone be left to his conscience until time brings the opportunity of some agreement'. This was a foreshadowing of

Erasmus, the doyen of Christian humanism, depicted in his sixtieth year by Dürer. By this date, 1526, the two men were virtually on opposite sides, Dürer a supporter of the Reformation, Erasmus a disillusioned opponent of it.

27

the later *cuius regio eius religio* principle by which Germany was divided territorially according to religion, but few at the time considered such a solution feasible, and time alone proved its necessity.

To support his general position Erasmus put forward his own interpretation of the parable of the wheat and the tares:

> The servants who want to cut out the weeds before the time are those who think that the false apostles and heresiarchs should be suppressed by the sword and by corporal punishment. But the Master of the field does not desire their destruction, but rather that they should be tolerated in case they should amend and turn from tares into wheat.

In urging tolerance towards the Lutherans, Erasmus was by no means adopting a midway position between the parties. By 1524 – the date he published his discourse *On Free Will* against Luther – he had committed himself to the cause of the old Church. What dictated his attitude was an unwillingness to accept coercion in matters of secondary importance. In other words, his firmly pacifist position made it impossible for him to accept that people should be persecuted for doctrines which had not even been dogmatically defined. Nor did he want them to be so defined. The fewer dogmas there were, the greater the likelihood that all Christians would live peacefully together in the acceptance of a few defined truths. 'The sum of our religion is peace and unanimity', went his letter to the archbishop of Palermo in 1523, 'but this can only come about when we define as little as possible and leave the judgment free on many matters; besides, there is the immense obscurity of very many questions'. In general, Erasmus tended to favour the adoption of a few fundamental articles of faith, and the relegation of others to the realm of free discussion. On this basis Luther might well be received back into the Church.

But the error in Erasmus' outlook was that he took too intellectual a view of religious truth. He could never have come to understand the great agony Luther felt before his God, or the passion evoked among the reformers by their rediscovery of justification by faith. Nor could he fully comprehend why Thomas More laid down his life in 1535. 'Would that he had never embroiled himself in this perilous business and had left the theological cause to the theologians!' was his sorrowful comment on hearing of More's execution. The temper of the age eluded him, and he died in July 1536, in a world where the peace for which he longed had been indefinitely postponed.

His great stand for toleration found supporters in the next generation. The unique contribution he made to the diffusion of humanism, the advancement of learning, and the formulation of principles of peace and concord, earn him a primary place in the history of toleration. Yet it should be remembered that for Erasmus, as for other contemporary humanists, toleration was not an ideal; it was only a means towards securing that religious harmony for which all Christians yearned.

In one particular Erasmus seems to have made a contribution of which he himself was not fully aware. Huizinga has pointed out how much the humanist had in common with the Anabaptists: 'a tendency to acknowledge free will, a certain rationalistic trend, a dislike of an exclusive conception of a Church'. Erasmus sympathised with the peaceful tenets of the Anabaptists and their patience under persecution: 'they are praised more than all others for the innocence of their life', he wrote in 1529. His frequent condemnations of the great princes of this world would also have appealed to them. In 1518 he had written to Colet: 'The princes conspire with the Pope against the happiness of the people'. No social revolutionary could have put it more succinctly. True, he was revolted by the excesses of the extreme Anabaptists at Münster, but his general sympathy for their cause transcended the barriers of orthodoxy and social class. This was an important step to have taken in the sixteenth century.

The achievements of Erasmus in the field of religious conciliation were minimal. The reactionary Catholics looked on him with suspicion, and Luther treated him with contempt. His colleagues chose one or other side of the fence; only much later, in the attempts to reach a political settlement in Germany, did any of them play a useful irenic role.

Sir Thomas More (1478–1535), whose reputation for tolerance rests largely on his *Utopia* (1516), is of limited importance in this history. His imaginary pagan state of Utopia is represented as having complete freedom of religion and opinion: the only people to be chastised are those who try to spread their own opinions by force and intemperate zeal. Apart from this, toleration is not granted to atheists and materialists, since they presumably have no moral principles which might govern their social behaviour. More would appear, on the basis of his book, to have been an advanced supporter of toleration. There is evidence that during his exercise of power in England as Chancellor he was not directly responsible for the execution of a single heretic. Yet *Utopia* is an imaginative work, which was not necessarily intended to reflect the author's own views, and in any case More wrote it before the great convulsions of the Reformation. In his *Dialogue Concerning Heresies* (1528) there is no doubt that he, as a lawyer and as a Christian, considered heresy both wicked and treasonable. By that date he had come to appreciate fully the dangers arising from the trouble in Germany. In More's ordinary writings, therefore, there is ample approval given to the use of force against heretics.

Despite its liberal outlook on social and religious questions, Christian humanism proved in the end to be a broken reed. Princes throughout Europe vied with one another to have Erasmus at their courts, but he was not interested in the cultivation of a mass following. Enough for him to be recognised in the great centres of learning, and to have Rome lend a tolerant ear. The way to reform in the Church lay through persuasion of the few and not the many. When the great revolution eventually came it was found that humanism had declined into an elegant creed subscribed to by a powerless minority. The techniques of mass persuasion – the appeal to the people, the use of printing and of the vernacular – were resorted to by others who did not share the same respect for Catholic tradition.

Title of the first edition of Luther's translation of the New Testament, the so-called September Bible, published in Wittenberg in 1522. Luther's translation is notable both as a masterpiece of German literature and as an unqualified success in religious propaganda.

The Lutheran position

Paradoxical as it may be to call the Lutheran reform a conservative revolution, the phrase is inevitable. By re-defining the spiritual position of man Luther did not intend to re-define his temporal position in the world; on the contrary, by the appeal to faith rather than works the great reformer appeared to ignore the social order and to shift the emphasis to spiritual regeneration only. The fundamentally narrow origin of the Reformation has often been obscured by sweeping explanations in terms of political and social factors. However operative these may have been in the long view, Luther's movements began in fact with an appeal to two spiritual principles – justification by faith, and the vernacular Bible – and all other motives, including the reform of abuses, were no more than subsidiary points in the programme. The theology and practice Luther claimed to adopt were those of the early Church; the emphasis on theology, justification, and spiritual practice meant that he was at first quite indifferent to the political context of his struggle. What he did see the necessity for was liberty to allow him to develop his teaching. To this end he was willing to take a firm stand against coercion in matters of religion.

Luther's defence of liberty consisted of a two-pronged attack, first against the compelling of consciences, and secondly against the power of the State to repress heresy.

On the first point he was repeating the traditional Catholic view that belief cannot be compelled, but he liberalised its application. When attacking papal persecution in 1521 he emphasised that 'no man can or ought to be forced to believe, but every one should be instructed in the gospel and admonished to believe, though he is left free to obey or not'. This makes it clear that no external coercion is to be exercised. Luther was careful, however, not to concede a totally unrestricted liberty, and he made some important reservations. What is known as freedom of conscience, he explained in 1521, was nothing other than a freedom 'which frees our conscience from works'. It cannot be absolute freedom, for no one can be free from the obligations of truth. In his work *On the Unfree*

Will (1525) he expressed this by saying that 'the conscience must not be bound by anything, except by the Word of God'. The Scriptures are the direct and sole guide to conscience and belief, and they exercise a constraint of their own which, of course, excludes the application of external force.

On Secular Authority (1523) is Luther's great treatise on the power of the State in religious matters. By attacking the secular power he cut at the root of the mediaeval alliance between Church and State, and attempted to disarm Catholic princes who might intervene against his own doctrines. Heresy, he said, was 'the duty of bishops, not of princes. Heresy can never be kept off by force; another argument is required for that; this is another quarrel than that of the sword'. And again: 'Heresy is something spiritual. One cannot strike it with iron, nor burn it with fire'. Preaching that same year, 1523, on the First Epistle of St Peter, he said: 'If the civil magistrate interferes with spiritual matters of conscience in which God only must rule, we ought not to obey at all, but rather lose our head. Civil government is confined to external and temporal affairs'. These sentiments deny the State any part in religious matters: Luther followed up with the corollary, aimed at the Pope, that religious authorities have no power in secular matters. Both these principles served him well at the time, since they were his

An early portrait of Luther in 1520 by Lucas Cranach the elder. At this period the reformer's development had not yet led to the complete rejection of his Augustinian friar's habit.

theoretical defence against pressure by secular and ecclesiastical authorities. He appears to have himself abided by their practice, for he rigorously abstained from coercion in this early period. In 1522 he put all his authority against the forcible suppression of the Mass in Wittenberg: 'One may speak and write against it, but I do not wish anyone to use compulsion and violence'. Most remarkable of all, he was in favour of toleration towards peaceful Anabaptists. 'Let them preach as they please, for there must needs be heresies', he wrote to the princes of Saxony as late as 1525, quoting St Paul in his support.

It is possible that to some extent Luther's moderation sprang from a sanguine confidence in the ultimate victory of his cause over that of his enemies. Luther was, moreover, still evolving his programme and had hardly begun to accept the need for an ecclesiastical organisation independent of Rome. When at last he realised the extent of his commitments, the embattled reformer was obliged to jettison toleration. Political events played a key part in this development.

Perhaps the most important factor was Luther's reaction to the Peasant War of 1525. The peasants' demands contradicted Luther's basic sympathy with the established social hierarchy and his refusal to mix religion with social protest. Their principal leader, Thomas Müntzer, was understandably angry that Luther's revolution should have been so tepid, and called on him to wake up to the realities of economic life:

Doesn't he see that usury and taxes impede the reception of the faith? He claims that the word of God is sufficient. Doesn't he realise that men whose every moment is consumed in the making of a living have no time to learn to read the Word of God? The princes bleed the people with usury and count as their own the fish in the stream, the birds of the air, and the grass of the field, and Dr Liar says 'Amen!' What courage has he, Dr Pussyfoot, the new pope of Wittenberg, Dr Easychair, the basking syco-phant? He says there should be no rebellion because the sword has been committed by God to the ruler. But the power of the sword belongs to the whole community!

1520

✠ Le premier liure/des nobles et

Excellens faictz darmes/du tresillustre et victorieux duc Anthoine/Contre
les seduyctz et abusez Lutheriens mescreans du pays daulsays/et autres.

FECIT·POTECIA·IN BRACHIO·SVO

CANNI DATA DVPLEX.
Consuit illicitus miracula sessa Lutheri
Vt pius inde viri numina bina regat.

Wider die Mordischen
vnd Reubischen Rotten der
Bawren.

Psalm. vij.
Seyne tück werden jn selbs treffen/
Vnd seyn mütwill/ wirdt vber jn außgeen.
1525.
Martinus Luther, Wittemberg.

Far left. Anthony, Duke of Bar and Lorraine, going into battle against the 'seduced and abused Lutheran miscreants' in Alsace in 1525. Although Luther rapidly dissociated himself from the peasant movement, in the eyes of his opponents they remained 'Lutherans'.
Left. Title page of Luther's tract against the rebellious peasants in 1525. The date and occasion mark Luther's emergence as a conservative on the social question.

Luther was unmoved by such writings. Peasants who had looked to him for support were speedily undeceived. After a mild *Exhortation to Peace*, he issued in May 1525 his pamphlet *Against the Murderous, Thieving Hordes of Peasants*:

If the peasant is in open rebellion then he is outside the law of God, for rebellion is not simply murder, it is like a great fire which attacks and lays waste a whole land ... Therefore let everyone who can, smite, slay, and stab, secretly or openly, remembering that nothing can be more poisonous, hurtful or devilish than a rebel.

The shock of the social revolution so narrowly averted by the victory of the princes over the peasants, confirmed Luther in his growing belief that liberty, particularly in religion, must be restricted when there was danger of sedition. Only a year later, in 1526, he could say through the Elector of Saxony: 'Though it is not our intention to prescribe to anyone what he is to hold or believe, yet we will not tolerate any sect or division in our principality, in order to prevent harmful revolt and other mischief'. At the same time he declared that preachers 'who advocate, preach or hold any erroneous doctrines, are to be told to quit our lands

Print by Lucas Cranach the younger, from a contemporary
Lutheran pamphlet with text by the reformer Matthias
Flacius Illyricus, contrasting the tenets of Christ
(on the left, with Luther in the pulpit) and
Antichrist. The Franciscans seem to be the only
religious order singled out for attack.

in haste, and also that should they return they will be severely dealt with'.

These new formulations coincided with Luther's acceptance of the necessity of an organised reformed Church. Faced by Rome on one side and the left-wing sects on the other, he put out his hands for support to the secular princes. While it is clear that he sought this support particularly after 1525, it should also be remembered that he had tended to move in this direction from the start. His reliance on Frederick the Wise of Saxony indicated where he chose his allies. When the imperial free knights, the noble class whose deteriorating economic and political position led them to conspire against the German princes in 1523, wrote to Luther, pledging their support and asking for his help, the reformer avoided committing himself. He sympathised with the Lutheran beliefs of their leaders, Franz von Sickingen and Ulrich von Hutten, but refused to side with the *Ritterschaft* against the established order. 'I have no desire to fight for the Word with force and violence', he said in his defence. By the mid-1520s, Luther had reached a thoroughly conservative political position. In the words of Engels, 'Not the peasant revolt alone, but Luther's own mutiny against religious and lay authority was thereby disavowed; and not only the popular movement, but the burgher movement as well, were betrayed to the princes'.

Only with the help of the princes could Luther consolidate the gains made for his teaching. And the subsequent foundation of territorial established Churches laid the basis for Lutheran

David killing Goliath; detail from a woodcut border by Lucas Cranach the younger, which was used for the title-pages of Luther's attack on the Turks and of a pamphlet attacking the Münster Anabaptists, for which Luther wrote a preface.

intolerance. The new State supremacy produced by Lutheranism differed very little from the coercive apparatus of mediaeval Christendom. The celebration of Mass was now officially prohibited in Saxony, Prussia, Hesse and other Lutheran territories. When his own past words were quoted against him on this matter, the reformer replied: 'You ask whether the prince should suppress abominations, since no one is to be forced to faith, and the power of princes extends only to externals. Answer: our princes do not compel to faith, but merely suppress external abominations'. In February 1526 he advised Elector John of Saxony that 'a secular ruler must not allow his officials to be led into strife and tumult by contumacious preachers'; and as a corollary he set up a principle which was to have momentous consequences: 'In a country there must be one preaching only allowed'.

This intolerance was social as well as political in character. We have already seen Luther defending intolerance 'in order to prevent harmful revolt'. In this he shared an attitude common to nearly all contemporaries. Given a State Church, it was imperative to preserve the State in order to fortify the Church. In 1530 Luther's colleague, Philip Melanchthon, humanist and conservative, gave his written opinion that the death penalty should be retained for all offences against civil and ecclesiastical order. To this paper Doctor Martin added the words, 'It pleases me, Martin Luther'. He had become an unswerving supporter of the methods he so recently condemned.

One of his firmest admirers, the Landgrave Philip of Hesse, who was famous for his moderation in religious matters, held a position somewhat differing from Luther's. Writing in 1532 to Elector John of Saxony, the Landgrave claimed that 'we cannot find it in our conscience to put anyone to death by the sword on account of religion unless we possess clear evidence of other crimes as well'. True to this principle, the Landgrave became a model of toleration, and even towards the Anabaptists his forbearance was exemplary, since although condemnations against them were published in his territory he never at any time confirmed a death sentence. His

E GRAVE

ENELNBOGĒ

E ZIEGEN

VND NIDDA·

Though a social conservative, the Landgrave Philip of Hesse was notably liberal in religious matters, as shown not only by his notorious bigamy but also by his refusal to use the death penalty for heresy. At his invitation an attempt to reach agreement among the continental reformers was made at Marburg in 1529.

irenic interests were great, and it was at his instigation that a colloquy between the reformed parties was held at Philip's castle in 1529. But this is to look only on the religious side. On the political side, Philip was as ruthless as Luther. He helped to suppress the Knights' rising under Sickingen in 1523, and in 1525 he suppressed the main body of the peasants at Frankenhausen with a ferocity that echoes through history. Luther's comment on the latter event was: 'It is a trifle for God to massacre a lot of peasants, when he drowned the whole world with a flood and wiped out Sodom with fire'.

The Reformation had become both socially and religiously intolerant. Two features of Luther's thought on religious liberty should be categorised here. First, early vacillation had given way to uncompromising intolerance. In 1522 he had opposed the forcible suppression of the Mass; by 1525 he supported it as a duty, since the Mass was public blasphemy of God. In the beginning he had defended the subjective rights of conscience; in 1526 he refused to allow the argument from conscience alone, and instead set up the Scriptures as an objective criterion, for 'a really good conscience desires nothing more than to listen to the teaching of the Scriptures'. In 1528 he had opposed the death penalty for Anabaptists; in 1530 he approved it. In 1523 he had expressed concern for the Jews; in 1536 he approved their expulsion from Saxony, just as in 1532 he advised the ruler of Prussia to expel Zwinglians from his territory because they differed from Lutherans on the theology of the Eucharist. Secondly, Luther had proceeded beyond his initial support of the separation of Church and State. Formerly he had set up the prince against the (Catholic) Church; now he elevated the prince into a ruler of the (Lutheran) Church, so that the public affairs of the Church were to be directly controlled by the secular authority. As he stated in 1536: 'The public authority is bound to repress blasphemy, false doctrine and heresy, and to inflict corporal punishment on those that support such things'. The model of Lutheran government was King David, who had been both chief priest and ruler.

After 1525 and particularly after Luther's repudiation of the popular discontent mirrored in the Peasant War, the Reformation lost a great deal of its pan-Germanic character and its revolutionary appeal. The defeat of the rural lower classes and the defection of many to Anabaptism, meant that Lutheranism came to be the religion of the cities and the landed interest. It was consequently caught up in the political evolution of the anti-feudal and anti-Imperial interests that threatened the existence of the Empire. Luther accepted the position. The Lutheran movement continued to operate at the highest social level, and in Scandinavia the rulers eventually adopted it as their ideology. With State-inspired reformation as the new norm, Lutheranism ceased to accept the necessity for toleration in a world where religious toleration might threaten the security of the State.

The Swiss reformers

The burgher religion of established Lutheranism found its parallel in the achievement of the Swiss pioneer of the Reformation, Huldrych Zwingli (1484–1531). Zwingli arrived at Zürich as a preacher in 1519, and by 1520 had begun to adopt some of the

King David became for Luther and other reformers the model of a
Christian ruler, particularly since his combination of the
functions of chief priest and king (symbolised here by the book
and crown on the cushions beside him) solved the difficult issue
of Church-State relations. The print, by the elder Cranach,
is from the first complete edition of the Luther Bible, 1534.

doctrines propagated by Luther in Germany. From 1521 onwards
Zwingli's influence grew in the upper circles of the city, and in
1523 he managed to make the city reject the authority both of the
bishop of Constance and of the See of Rome. The basis of his
party in the city was the merchant and artisan élite. As one
historian points out, 'the Zwinglian view of the Church reflected
the self-respect of urban citizenry, educated burghers and a
literate artisanry'. The reformer supported Zürich's autonomy
against the demands of external authority and the levying of men
for mercenary service. He demanded that the city should control
its own religious life, and that Church government should be taken
out of the hands of the clergy. Zwingli triumphed speedily because
he was willing to entrust the achievement of reform to the only
competent authorities – the city government. Curiously enough,
therefore, in the same year that Luther published his treatise *On
Secular Authority* (1523), Zwingli was claiming that 'the jurisdiction
which the churchmen have unduly claimed belongs entirely to the
secular authority, provided it is Christian'. The Swiss reformer
antedated his German colleague's position by several years.

The exercise of ecclesiastical jurisdiction by the magistrates of
Zürich need not in theory have led to any threat to religious liberty.
With Christian laws to govern Christian men surely the advent of
true freedom was nigh. Yet Zürich was hardly composed of
Zwinglians only. Coercive measures would have to be adopted
against the stubborn Catholic population. Between 1524 and 1525
the practice of Catholicism was steadily restricted, and finally in
April 1525 the Mass was suppressed.

The old religion, however, was less potentially subversive than
the new sects. The rise of the Anabaptists under Felix Manz and
Conrad Grebel, and their protest against the assumption of civil
authority by Christians, threatened the structure of Zwingli's
burgher reformation. Anabaptist religious practice, together with
their social radicalism, provoked Zwingli's wrath. 'Those who are
so well informed that they know that all things shall be held in
common', he stormed, 'should be fixed to the gallows as a common

The Last Supper (1565) painted by Lucas Cranach the younger as an altarpiece for the Schlosskirche at Dessau. All the figures, with the exception of Christ and Judas, are portraits of leading reformers or members of the family of the donor, Prince Christian of Anhalt. St John, on Christ's right, is Prince George of Anhalt, the 'pious', and next to him are Luther and Bugenhagen. Melanchthon is on Christ's left. The steward in the foreground is a self-portrait.

The Confession of Augsburg, adopted in 1530, gave the Lutheran princes of Germany a religious and political unity. The principal adherents to the Confession are shown in this detail from a print executed in the centenary year 1630 by Johann Dürr.

example for us all'. The Council of Two Hundred which governed Zürich took the appropriate steps. The baptism of children was made compulsory in 1525, and in the following year the death penalty was laid down for the practice of re-baptism (a practice which is discussed in the next chapter, page 58). Under this regulation Manz was drowned in the lake of Zürich, and several others perished at the hands of the authorities. A thoroughgoing theocracy was established, in which the Council was given power over the property, religion and even the morals of all citizens. When objectors to this new regime pointed out that Zwingli had instituted an unrepresentative oligarchy of two hundred to govern a city of over five thousand, the reformer parried by claiming that his oligarchy was ruling according to the Word of God. It was in the name of the same Word that he initiated a bloody persecution of his Anabaptist opponents.

The issue was not simply one of intolerance over the question of baptism. Zwingli himself admitted: 'The issue is not baptism, but revolt, faction, heresy!' The spectre of popular revolt was still to be laid, and his answer, like Luther's, was the uncompromising one of suppression. Only one religion must be tolerated in any one place under his control. Catholics and sectarians must be eliminated. 'Why should the Christian magistrate not destroy statues and abolish the Mass? . . . This does not mean that he has to cut the priests' throats, if it is possible to avoid such a cruel action. But if not, we would not hesitate to imitate even the harshest examples'. Faced by the superior armed forces of the Catholic cantons of Switzerland, and threatened from within by possible religious dissension, Zwingli was driven to accept a stern theocracy as his only guarantee. The clergy were eliminated from the government, and all power resided in the civil magistrates who governed the Church and people. Zwingli welcomed the practice of toleration by Catholic rulers, for it gave his preachers the freedom they required; but wherever Zwinglianism triumphed, religious liberty evaporated. The reformer did not live to see more than partial success for his plans. He died, sword in hand, in battle against the Swiss Catholic cantons, in October 1531, on the field at Kappel.

In the west of Switzerland a new, more fateful, star was already in the ascendant: reformed Geneva. The influences that predominated in the western cantons were French, and it was fittingly a Frenchman, Guillaume Farel, who brought the new teaching to the Alps. A native of Dauphiné, Farel had gravitated from the humanist school to Lutheranism and then to Zwinglianism. His mission to Berne in 1529 coincided with an upsurge of burgher power in the great cities of western Switzerland. Rebelling against the corrupt influence of mercenary service and the political and religious authority of the Catholic bishop, Berne eagerly embraced the programme of reform and set out to destroy Catholic control in the other cities. Thanks to the ruthless methods of the Protestant soldiery and the effective preaching of Farel and his colleagues, Geneva was also won over in 1533, and the Mass was finally suppressed there in 1535. By 1536 the Bernese troops had overrun the western bishoprics and established Protestant rule.

The helmet and sword allegedly used by Zwingli in the fatal battle of Kappel, 1531. Zwingli's reformation of Zürich was threatened from both right and left, by Catholics as well as Anabaptists.

An unusual portrait showing Calvin
as a young man. Creator of the most
dynamic and international of the
Reformation ideologies, Calvin
epitomised the intolerance of
the convinced Christian.

49

Calvinist intolerance

Conversion by force of arms was an inadequate guarantee of lasting success. Farel was accordingly grateful for a visit to Geneva made early in 1536 by a young exile from France named John Calvin. The two men attempted to organise religion according to their own ideas, but the burgher authorities refused to tolerate interference with their dictates. Calvin and Farel were banished in April 1538, the latter going to Neuchâtel, the former to Strassburg. It was in Strassburg – a wealthy trading city that offered tolerance and shelter to victims of persecution; a city moreover which was the parish of the irenic reformer Martin Bucer, who persuaded Calvin to accept a pastoral charge – that the exile from Geneva settled down for three years to think out his doctrinal position. Strassburg produced Calvinism. It was from this city, not from Geneva, that the French reform drew its early inspiration and its methods of organisation. And it was here that, during his exile, Calvin formulated the teachings with which he thereafter set out to transform Geneva and, through it, the world.

In 1536 at Basle Calvin had published in Latin a small volume entitled *Christianae religionis institutio*. The date signposts a crossroad in the religious history of Europe. That year Erasmus died unsung at Basle. At the same time the Pope was sending out letters to summon the leaders of divided Christendom to a general Council of the Church. The voice of the humanist was stilled: that of the Vicar of Christ went unheeded. Nine years were to pass before a general Council would eventually meet, and in that interlude the leaders of Catholicism were obliged to leave the initiative to the secular princes and the reformers. Yet the Reformation itself was an undefined conglomeration of contradictions. Beyond its kernel of religious conviction, which was also accepted by many Roman Catholics, Lutheranism appeared to offer no structural alternative to Rome. Both in Zürich and in Wittenberg the assumption of religious authority by the secular power betokened a political revolution more than a religious one.

POENITENTIAM AGITE.

Bildtnüs eins neu

wen Propheten/auß Franck
reich herbzacht/vnd jetz
erstlich in Deutsche
landen auß
gangen.

Schawe nun/ wahin du gestürtzes
vnnd geworffen bist.

Sihe wie schwer es ist / Gott den
herren / den lebendigen brunnen
verlassen haben / vnd alte cister=
nen graben / die kein wasser hal=
ten mögen.

We dir du stoltze zucht / die du die
gesunde lere nit magst leiden.

We euch ir verkerten kinder / denen
die oren iucken / vñ hauffet euch
lerer nach eweren begirden.

We dem volck das beladen mit vn
gerechtigkeit / das sein gehöre
von der warheit abwendet.

We dir du sündigs volck / das du
dich zü fablen wendest.

We we allen inwohnern der erde /
die nit von lastern abstohn / das
inen ire sünde nicht zügerechnet
würden / vñ der Herre irer vnge
rechtigkeit vergesse.

Bessert euch vñ glaubt dem Euan=
gelio / Vñ/so ir euch nit bekeret /
vñ bessert / werdt ir alle zü hauff
verderben. Vñ / So ir rechtschaf
fen büß thüt / würt euch das hi=
melreich herbei komen / vñ wert
besitzen das land der lebendigé/
inn welchem der könig der herr=
licheit vñ seligkeit / Christus der
best vnd grössist ist.

Sehet / das ir weißlich / vñ wirdig
vor Got wandlet/der euch zü sei=
ner ewigen herrlicheit berüffet
hat/in welche der da heilig / vn=
schuldig / von hertzen rein / vnd
one mackel ist/ein ngehen würt.

Derhalben befleisset euch / das ihr
durch güte werck büß thüt/vnd
euch zü Got bekeret / vnnd euch
ewere sünde außgelescher /vnnd
ewer berüff vnd erwehlung ge=
wis gemacht werde.

Wo ir euch nit bekeret / hat d Herr
sein schwert gefasset / sein bogen
gespannet / dz er in euch schiesse.

lere.

lere.

parts
ex B
ta, p
tm
s. ed
mo.

Apo.
Eze.
Psal.
Ro.4

Mat.
Luc.
Luc.
Mar.
Pf. 1

Eph
Colo.
Pf. 2
et. 1

a.Pe.
Act.

Psal.

Dis ist die bildnüs vñ controfeitung eines heiligen mans/seines alters sietzig järig/der sich jetze
belter zü Monpelgart/ein stat in Deutschland/gelegé acht meilen von Strasburg. Diser man
aber ist gerad von leib/hat ein grawen bart/der im bis vff den gürtel reicht. Gehet gar nach bloß/
prediget/vnd haltet täglich ein Messe/desgleichen thüt er auch vil wunderzeichen/aus welcher
verwunderung/bekeret er zum glauben die verderbte ketzer/vñ sinlosen Lutheraner.

Mit begnadigung.

Ist feil zü Paris inn S. Jacobs gassen zum guldenen morselstein/
bei Vivian Gautherot. 1530.

Placard issued by Calvin in 1539, during
his residence in Strassburg, to put the
public on their guard against a
self-styled Lutheran prophet, 'free from
all sin', who travelled through France
and Germany preaching repentance.

51

Calvin recalled the Reformation to its proper mission. In
opposition to the practice of the other reformers, he emphasised
the complete independence, and yet interdependence, of Church
and State. The State was no longer to assume sole direction of the
Church of God. On his return to Geneva in 1541 Calvin persuaded
the authorities to accept his Ordinances as the form of government
in religion. By these new rules, a ministry was set up largely
independent of control by the State, and doctrine and Church
discipline was discussed by ministers and elected laymen rather
than by secular authorities. This theoretical autonomy of the
Church was in some measure deceptive. The State still intervened
in religious discipline through lay members of the Consistory,
which governed the Church but had no coercive jurisdiction; and
in political matters the city Council had a pre-eminence. Moreover
the independence of the Church failed completely to bring about
that religious liberty which a proper separation of Church and
State might have effected. Calvin claimed that his ministers had
the right to exercise 'spiritual police powers' over the morality
and conduct of citizens. So began, with the aid of the State
authorities, a system of religious regimentation which turned
Geneva into a by-word for intolerance and, at the same time, a
model for other reformed Churches which sought to set up the
Kingdom of God on earth.

The Consistory, it is true, was explicitly denied civil jurisdiction
and was only given the right to excommunicate in extreme cases.
But, as the Ordinances state, when severe punishment is called for,
the ministers in the Consistory 'must represent the whole case to
the Council, which will consider their report, ordain, and judge
according to the merits of the case'. There was clearly to be close
cooperation between Church and State, despite their theoretical
autonomy. The initiative in prosecution lay generally with the
Consistory, which therefore assumed a superior position in the
disciplinary life of Geneva, punishing immorality, prostitution,
gambling, swearing, and the use of Catholic religious practices.
In one case a woman was prosecuted for kneeling by her husband's

The Birth of Antichrist, from
The Depiction of the Papacy
(1545), a series of woodcut
caricatures by Lucas
Cranach the younger, with
scurrilous verses by Luther.

grave and saying 'Requiescat in pace'. Under Calvin's influence
the Council also initiated several proceedings touching religious
matters, such as the enforcement of the rules about attending
sermons. Civil and ecclesiastical authority therefore combined to
crush religious nonconformity.

At a later stage in Geneva's evolution, by about 1557, cooperation between Church and State was for all practical purposes
replaced by the dictatorship of the Church under Calvin, even
though the constitutional distinction between the two was explicitly upheld by the New Ordinances of 1561. In Mackinnon's
words, 'the grand adjunct and instrument of the theocracy is the
Consistory, which now becomes all-powerful and with which the
Council energetically and deferentially cooperates in the policy
of establishing the rule of God in the republic'. The rigour of
Calvinistic discipline is illustrated by the number of excommuni-
cations, which rose from only 80 for the four years 1551–4, to over
300 in 1559 alone. It was this regime that an enthusiastic John
Knox, then a minister to Geneva, called 'the most perfect school of
Christ that ever was in the earth since the days of the apostles'.

The intolerance of the Swiss Reformation is explained largely
by the theological opinions of the Protestant reformers. But some
influence must be attributed to the oligarchic structure of the Swiss
cities, and their unyielding social conservatism. Zürich, Geneva
and Berne were in common in representing the interests of political
factions impatient of foreign tutelage, but intolerant also of radical
movements. Each city had its outstanding victim – Manz in Zürich,
Servetus in Geneva, and Gentile in Berne, the last of these having
escaped from Geneva only to be executed at Berne in 1566 for his
anti-Trinitarian beliefs. Over and above the conservatism of the
burgher classes, however, loomed the vast formulations of Calvin.
In re-assessing the basis of Protestantism he constructed a new
orthodoxy which increased the militancy of the Reformation,
rejected all compromise (he denounced the 1548 Augsburg interim
in Germany, which was supported by Melanchthon), and projected
the religious struggle on to an international arena.

Was the Reformation essentially intolerant?

The three principal theorists of the official Reformation had rejected the concept of religious liberty. Their intolerance, however, was not only anti-papal and anti-sectarian. Under the weight of political events in Europe, it became mutual. The high pressure of theological controversy exploded, as we shall see, into the era of religious wars.

It is hardly necessary to add that in Scandinavia and in England, where the State initiated a Reformation, intolerance was the order of the day. Under Henry VIII of England, both papal adherents (like Sir Thomas More) and sectarians were executed. In Denmark, Frederick I declared at the Diet of Odense in 1527 that he would tolerate both Catholics and Lutherans until a general council of the Church should decide. 'Both parties believe that they are in the right', he announced, 'but as yet there is none to judge. His Majesty is king and judge and has power over life and property in this kingdom, but not over souls'. But long before Frederick's death in 1533 the position of the Catholic Church had become untenable, and the new king, Christian III, instituted a rigorous State Reformation in 1536, which was subsequently extended to Norway. The Swedish Diet of Västerås, held under Gustav Vasa in 1527, legalised Lutheranism in the north and prepared the way for further inroads into the power of Swedish Catholicism. In 1544 the Diet, again sitting at Västerås, declared the kingdom Lutheran and banned the practice of the Catholic religion.

The inevitable use of force by religious revolutionaries, and their ready reliance on the help of the State, are easily understood by the need for self-preservation. But was intolerance an essential component of their practice? The English critic Hallam claimed in the nineteenth century that 'persecution is the deadly original sin of the Reformed churches'. The language used by the Scottish reformer John Knox drove the nineteenth-century liberal historian Lecky to describe him as 'this great apostle of murder'. Lord Acton in a famous essay claimed that 'Protestantism set up intolerance as an imperative precept and as a part of its doctrine, and it was forced to admit toleration by the necessities of its position, after the rigorous penalties it imposed had failed to arrest the process of internal dissolution'. The actions of the great reformers give ample warrant for these judgments. But it is difficult to admit their justice. Despite the reformers, the Reformation brought greater religious liberty. Luther and his colleagues might base their persecution on Holy Scripture, but Scripture was by their own teachings liable to private interpretation, and this interpretation came rapidly to discover fallacies in the old arguments for repression. As Lecky rightly points out, 'toleration, however incompatible with some of the tenets which Protestants have asserted, is essentially a normal result of Protestantism, for it is the direct, logical, and inevitable consequence of the due exercise of private judgment'. This conclusion is not as obvious as it may appear today, for everywhere in the sixteenth and seventeenth centuries Catholics were in the vanguard of the movement for toleration. Catholic humanists and Catholic politicians were actively concerned in the promotion of religious liberty both in Europe and, eventually, in America. They were, however, always a minority; and their efforts were soon overshadowed by the contributions of those who drew from the first principles of Protestantism the definitive formulations of religious freedom.

3 The radicals and toleration

As Luther, Zwingli and Calvin developed forms of organisation which closely identified Church and State and shut the door to religious and social dissidence, the individualism of other reformers who had looked to the Reformation for greater liberty of the spirit expressed itself in open discontent and even rebellion. The conservative reformers, far from breaking clear of the intolerant notion of an established Church, had reasserted it with greater vigour as the correct counterbalance to religious and political insecurity, and had lent their support to the concept of theocracy. Those who differed from their ideas refused to believe that the final answer had been reached by this obvious compromise with the established order.

Against the dominating 'Church' there had in mediaeval Christendom periodically existed small groups of opposition which organised themselves as 'sects'. The distinction between 'sect' and 'Church', made famous by the German historian Troeltsch, is a useful one to employ in studying the evolution of heresy. Between the two concepts the ethical differences are enormous, but often it was only by accident that would-be sectarians (like Saint Francis of Assisi) remained within the official Church. To illustrate the differences between the two we can do no better than follow Troeltsch in defining as sectarians those who sought for 'personal achievement in ethics and in religion, religious equality and brotherly love, indifference towards the authority of the State and the ruling classes, dislike of technical law and of the oath, separation of the religious life from the economic struggle by means of the ideal of poverty and frugality'.

In the great ages of the Catholic Church, these sects distinguished themselves by their appeal to the pure and primitive spirit of the gospel, and by the support they received among the poorer and humbler classes in the population. The Protestant reformers, despite their conservative attitude to the social order, contributed to the reaction that created a new flowering of sectarianism among the lower classes, who gave the first real impetus to the formulation and practice of positive toleration in the age of the Reformation.

This print by the younger Cranach emphasises the
continuity of mediaeval and Reformation heterodoxy.
It shows Hus and his successor Luther giving communion
simultaneously to the German princes. Protestants
felt themselves part of a great tradition of
protest which went back to Wycliffe and beyond.

Luther was one of the great links. At the debate held between him and Johann Eck at Leipzig in July 1519, he was accused by Eck of following the errors of Wycliffe and Hus. Luther did some quick research into the proceedings of the Council of Constance, which had condemned Hus, and professed openly that 'among the articles of John Hus I find many which are plainly Christian and evangelical, which the universal Church cannot condemn'. A few months later, in February 1520, Luther was able to say: 'We are all Hussites without knowing it'. By identifying his rebellion with that of the Bohemian leader, Luther accepted the inspiration of the pre-Reformation sectarian opposition to Rome. By this sympathy, he also helped to universalise his cause. From this time the leaders of the Reformation were to look with sympathy on the heresies that had preceded them, and grew to accept the international dimensions of the revolt against the Church. The Waldensians in Italy, the Bohemian Brethren in central Europe, the Wycliffite tradition in England, were accepted, respected and tolerated because of their pioneering rebellion against Antichrist.

There the sympathy ended. Had the old sects ever come into close contact with Luther or Calvin, the reformers would speedily have disowned or suppressed them. The motive would have been the religious and social radicalism of the sectarians, a radicalism which also exploded in the very heart of the Reformation, in the form of Anabaptism.

The rise of the Anabaptists

The name Anabaptist, or Re-baptiser, refers to one who rejects the necessity or validity of infant baptism and (re-) baptises adults in the belief that baptism should follow, and not precede, a personal confession of faith. The term was used very loosely to cover a variety of religious opinions, and was often applied to those who did not re-baptise at all but merely practised adult baptism. Despite this imprecision, it is a useful term if taken to describe particularly those who opposed child baptism. The first organised group in the Reformation to adopt this as a belief appears to have been the 'prophets of Zwickau', a circle of illuminists who moved from Zwickau to Wittenberg in 1521. Their most forceful associate was Thomas Müntzer (1491–1525), a fiery priest who became a Lutheran pastor in 1519 and was given a temporary post at Zwickau in 1520. Müntzer did not accompany the prophets to Wittenberg; instead he wandered through Bohemia and Saxony before eventually joining the Peasant War. The presence of the prophets in Wittenberg, their attacks on the doctrine of child baptism, and their communistic social doctrines, moved Luther to make a personal stand in the town against their influence. The expulsion of the prophets from Wittenberg and Müntzer's corresponding alienation from the Lutheran cause, mark the definitive break between the official Reformation and its left wing.

The first known practice of rebaptism, and the first Anabaptist community, can be located in Zürich. Zwingli's reform of the city had not lacked opposition from even more radical spirits who objected to the dependence of Church on State and the resultant lack of autonomy and liberty in religious matters. The most prominent of Zwingli's opponents was Balthasar Hubmaier (1481–1528) who, together with Grebel and Manz, formed a dissident group of 'Swiss brethren' who began the practice of rebaptism in January 1525. The first Anabaptist congregation was established in the neighbouring village of Zollikon. Zwingli, as we have seen, viewed the dissidents as a threat to his regime; in March the death penalty was decreed against Anabaptism, and several executions followed, including that of Manz in January 1527. In the indictment of Manz it was claimed that the Anabaptists 'disturb the general peace, brotherly love and civic concord, and provoke every kind of evil'. How true was this?

The fact is that the Swiss brethren and kindred Anabaptists were dangerous principally because of their support among the humbler sections of the population and also among the artisans and commercial classes. This was even truer after they had been expelled from Switzerland and had scattered through the cities of the

TOMAS MVNCER PREDIGER ZV ALSTET IN DVRINGEN.   BALTHASAR HVBMOR DOCTOR VON FRID•

Empire. Of civil disturbance there was little or no evidence. The Anabaptists were complete pacifists and withdrew deliberately from intervention in public affairs. Theirs was a passive social nihilism which rejected the concept of a State Church and refused to participate in the activity of the State. All violence was condemned. As Grebel put it in 1524:

Neither the Gospel nor those who stand by it should be protected by the sword ... On the contrary, faithful Christians are like sheep in the midst of wolves, like sheep that are led to the slaughter. They use neither the temporal sword nor war, because they are forbidden to kill.

At the same date the gospel of toleration was being preached unequivocally by Hubmaier. His *Concerning Heretics and Those who Burn Them*, written that year, is probably the earliest plea for complete toleration penned in Europe. For Hubmaier heretics are simply those who oppose the Scriptures:

One should overcome them with holy knowledge, not angrily but softly ... If they will not be taught by strong proofs or evangelic reasons, then let them be and leave them to rage ... The law that condemns heretics to the fire builds up both Zion in blood and Jerusalem in wickedness ... This is the will of Christ who said, 'Let both grow together till the harvest, lest while ye gather up the tares ye root up also the wheat with them'.

The inquisitors are the greatest heretics of all, since, against the doctrine

Three famous sixteenth-century heretics: Müntzer and Hubmaier (*far left*), representatives respectively of the violent and pacific wings of Anabaptism; and Servetus (*left*), an early proponent of anti-Trinitarianism. Of the three only Hubmaier was a supporter of toleration; he was martyred by the Catholics, while Servetus met his death in Calvinist Geneva, and Müntzer was executed by Lutherans.

and example of Christ, they condemn heretics to fire, and before the time of harvest root up the wheat with the tares. For Christ did not come to butcher, destroy and burn, but that those that live might live more abundantly.

The existence of contrary beliefs, according to him, serves to provoke and strengthen one's faith, so that heresy even has a useful purpose. The tract ends with Hubmaier's characteristic slogan: Truth is immortal, *die göttliche Wahrheit ist untödlich.*

Complete separation of Church and State, indifference to the secular authority, and rejection of the use of force – these tenets made the Anabaptists a nuisance certainly, but not an explicit threat to the State. This at least was recognised by Philip of Hesse. But nearly all other religious and lay rulers were agreed on the employment of death against them. Their attitude seemed to be justified by the participation of revolutionary and non-pacifist Anabaptists in the Peasant War, and by the use of rebaptism by some rebels. Hubmaier himself in 1525 apparently helped to draft the Twelve Articles of the Swabian peasants. He was not essentially a social agitator: 'With us neither tax nor tithes has ever been spoken against with the least word', he claimed later. But the authorities held him guilty of both heresy and treason, and he was burnt at the stake in Vienna in 1528. Three days later his faithful wife had a stone tied round her neck and was thrown into the Danube. Hubmaier's successor as a leader of the Anabaptists, Jacob Hutter, was likewise burnt in 1536. Altogether several thousand martyrs to the cause could be numbered by the 1530s. And this was in Germany alone.

The universal detestation in which these sectarians, or *Schwärmer* (enthusiasts), were held in the sixteenth century make them the touchstone for any proponents of religious toleration. By this test all the major figures of the age, with the possible exception of Erasmus, must fall. The Anabaptists themselves, despite a sectarianism that was often too exclusive and sometimes fanatical, laid the foundations of religious liberty by their rejection of the traditional doctrine of baptism and their 'spiritual' view of religion. In all the major religions the practice of child baptism committed an infant to a certain faith before he had even begun to reason about it. In Anabaptism alone, the child was free of any obligation to accept religious dogma until his voluntary faith had made him assent to baptism at an adult age.

In this picture of repression it is worth recalling that some limited freedom was granted to the sects in exceptional circumstances, more often than not for economic reasons. Many Dutch Anabaptists, for example, were allowed into Prussia in the late 1520s by Duke Albert, to help repair the destruction caused by the Polish–Prussian war of 1519–21. When Luther urged the Lutheran Duke to expel the sectarians, he received a reply in June 1533 refusing the request on the grounds that the land would grow 'even more desolate' if they left. The Anabaptists were in fact expelled more than once after this, particularly after the Münster episode, but they seem to have been regularly allowed back. In neighbouring Elbing, and in the environs of Danzig, the authorities were also driven by economic motives to allow the settlement of refugees, mainly Mennonites (followers of Menno Simons, who is discussed below), from western Europe. Further south, in Moravia, the Anabaptists achieved the greatest degree of toleration allowed them anywhere in Europe. The principal reason for this

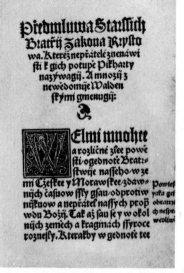

Opening page of a manifesto of the Unity of Brethren, published in Moravia in 1536. The beliefs of the Brethren provide a link between Hus and the Anabaptists.

was the determination of the very independent nobility of Moravia to develop their estates without regard to the religion of their labourers. Even after Münster, therefore, we find the Moravian Diet at Znaim in 1535 affirming that expulsion of the sects would create economic hardship for the lords and reduce royal income from taxation. The same arguments were put forward at the Diet of Olomouc (Olmütz) in 1540 and that of Brno in 1545. Partial expulsions occurred, but a large Anabaptist community continued to exist up to the time of complete toleration under Maximilian II.

The mystical Anabaptists

Indifference to the sacramental character of baptism, and an emphasis on the purely 'spiritual' nature of the religious life, also lay at the root of beliefs held by a few thinkers who stood outside the Anabaptist tradition. Of these, adherents of the German school of mysticism, we may take Sebastian Franck (1499–1542) and Caspar Schwenckfeld (1489–1561) as representatives. Both of these men began as supporters of the Lutheran Reformation but turned against it in disgust at its conservative trends and its denial of religious liberty. Franck, an ex-priest who became a Lutheran in 1527, abandoned his new religion after a year in

John of Leiden (1536), leader of the Anabaptist community in Münster, by Heinrich Aldegrever. The drawing, which shows John with the orb of kingship, is believed to have been made from life after his capture. The Münster episode made toleration of Anabaptists impossible.

favour of a more individualistic and libertarian faith. Like Schwenckfeld, a noble from Silesia, and a Lutheran since 1521, he went in 1529 to Strassburg, then an oasis of toleration in Europe, and met sectarians who attracted him further away from orthodox religion. Both these men placed absolute freedom at the heart of Christianity, in accordance with St Paul's statement: 'Where the Lord's Spirit is, there is freedom' (2 Cor. 3: 17). Freedom from dogma and outward observances not unnaturally led to belief in a completely invisible Church. But both men went further than the concept of a merely *Christian* invisible Church. For Schwenckfeld, 'the universal Christian Church extends in all directions; it consists of all saintly and faithful men from the beginning of the world to the end'. So strongly did he hold to an invisible Church that he abstained from all existing denominations. In 1534 he wrote to Philip of Hesse:

Although ... I have not joined any party or Church to partake of the sacraments, and I cannot submit to men who would dominate my beliefs, I do not scorn any Church, man, authority or pastor ... I only ask to be a brother and a friend to anyone who has the zeal of God, loves Christ with all his heart, clings to the truth and is devoted to piety.

For Franck, writing in 1539, the noble concept of the brotherhood of all men before God is expressed in immortal words:

To me, anyone who wishes my good and can bear with me by his side, is a good brother, whether Papist, Lutheran, Zwinglian, Anabaptist, or even Turk, even though we do not feel the same way, until God gathers us in his own school and unites us in the same faith.

Let no one try to be master of my faith and to force me to follow his belief; he must be my neighbour, and become my well-beloved brother; even if he is Jew or Samaritan, I want to love him and do him as much good as in me lies.

I reject no one who does not reject me.

In worldly matters Schwenckfeld was quite clear about his position. Church and State were for him absolutely separate and 'the civil power, even if it is Christian, has no right whatever to interfere in the affairs of the Christian faith'. This view assumed that Christianity was essentially a spiritual religion without outward signs that might concern the civil authorities, and could obviously not have been held by any member of the principal Churches. Adopting the same spiritual view of religion, Schwenckfeld spoke out openly against persecution of the Anabaptists, who would, he maintained, 'be more easily persuaded by gentleness than by violence. Even if they refuse to change their mind, they should be separated from devout people not by the stake but by excommunication and by exposing their errors'.

It was not an easy matter to speak for tolerance from a mystical and thoroughly undogmatic position. In the dangerous years of the Reformation considerable courage was required to proclaim one's freedom from sectarian prejudice. The spiritual writers were not moving in a visionary world. They were participating in a great movement to carry the Reformation further towards true liberty, and in that cause they risked their lives.

Attitudes to the radicals

Even among adherents of the official Reformation there remained a few supporters of tolerance. Strassburg, as we have seen, was a notable case. In the first half of the sixteenth century this city offered asylum freely to the principal leaders of the reform movement in Europe, to Lefèvre d'Etaples, Calvin, Beza, Farel, Denck, Schwenckfeld, Servetus, Melchior Hofmann and Sebastian Franck. Protestants of all persuasions were accepted, not so much however from a positive practice of toleration as from the desire of the rulers of Strassburg to promote Christian reunion. In this effort the central figure was Bucer.

Martin Bucer (1491–1551), who joined the Reformation in 1518, came to Strassburg in the 1520s and became the principal religious leader of the city. Most of his life was spent trying to reach agreement with Lutherans and Zwinglians, particularly over the doctrine of the Eucharist. His irenic journeys took him to Marburg,

Advice on Christian Authority, published by Bucer
in 1539, was a notable appeal for toleration of Jews
at a time when Luther in the Germanic world was adding
to the abuse of them. Though hostile to Anabaptists,
Bucer was generally irenic towards fellow Christians
and remarkably tolerant in principle of non-Christians.

Jr Jacob Sturm der Meister vnd der Rath zů Straßburg thůn khundt: Nach dem sich diser zeit zů uerhinderung vñ abwendung des göttlichen beuelchs/ vil Secten vnd prasit lerer erheben vnd erzügen vnd nämlichen mit etlichen personen/ die vns rauffer gnant/ so vnder jren schein/ vor andern Christen ein frøö leben fůssieren für geben/ Aber dobey zůwider aller göttlicher vnd Euangelischer geschrifft die oberkeit/ so den alten iß schuty/ vnd den bösen iß straff/ von Gott ingesetzt Christlich lassen/ allein mit bekennen/ sonder auch darnechen etliche vngegründe böse fürnemen mit tegen den Artickeln/ so iß vnderhaltung gemeine nutze lieb seid vnd einigkeit dienstlich/ vfgesetzt/ vnd von Gottz zůthan mit verboten sindt/ fürhaben/ vnd als zertrenner/ vnd beleydiger einer Christlichen vnd einhelligen wesens/ vff jren hartnäckigk köpffen beharren vñ keiner vnderwysung sich settzig wöllen lassen. Dwil nun vns als einer fürgesetzten oberkeit solchem vngegrundten strafflichen zwissendem handel/ von Gott vnd ampts halb vns zů lassen/ gebürt zympt vnd beuolen iß. Demnach so gepieten wir mit hohem ernst/ allen vnnd yeden vnsern Burgern/ hinder sessen/ angehörigen vnd verwandten/ Geistlichen vnd weltlichen/ in Stadt vnd lande/ das sy sich solcher leren/ vñ der heiligen geschrifft widerwertige versuerung verbieten/ der widerteuffer oder jrer anhenger sich entschlagen/ deren einen noch keinen bey jnen hausen/ herbergen/ etzen oder trencken/ noch vnderschleiff geben. Sonder die selbigen/ alß so zyrgezeigen synne mit gestrafft oder vnderwysen wöllen werden/ abwysen. Dann welcher das mit thäte/ er wer fremd oder heymisch/ niemandes vßgeschlossen/ vnd sich mit den selbigen vnd jr geschädlichen fürnemens vermischen/ sie vnderhalten/ oder gemeinschafft mit jnen haben/ oder jrer schädlichen meynung/ stadt geben/ vnd anhangen würde/ Den oder die wöllen wir mit ernst/ der gepür nach/ vngestrafft mit nit lassen/ Das wir einyeden warnung wyse sich vor schaden haben zůchieten/ mit wöllen verhalten/ Actum et decretum vff Sampstag den xxvi. July Anno. M.D.xxvi.

Kworich zů am 29 September ao ē 1530.

Above. Jacob Sturm, chief magistrate of Strassburg until his death in 1553.   69
Under him the city became a centre of culture, often transcending religious
differences, and also a principal shelter for refugees from persecution.
Below. A decree dated 27 July 1527 against Anabaptists in Strassburg.
The decree was issued by Sturm and the city council. The Anabaptists were
the most notable exception to the city's general policy of tolerance.

Wittenberg, Basle and Zürich; he also participated in discussions
with Catholic theologians at Worms and Regensburg. His approach
to Church unity was governed by his conviction that agreement
could be reached on essentials, and that one could differ on other
beliefs. He supported the free circulation of contentious literature,
even if it were Catholic or Muslim, and did not object to unrestricted discussion. Towards the Anabaptists his attitude was
generally harsh, but he and other Strassburg theologians were
discerning enough to distinguish between seditious and peaceful
sectarians.

Equally significant, perhaps, was Jacob Sturm, chief magistrate
of Strassburg for twenty-five years. His dream was to create in the
city a centre of learning which would attract both Catholics and
Protestants, and it was in recognition of this lofty aim that Erasmus
described him as 'the noblest among nobles for his knowledge,
sincerity, honesty and wisdom'. Despite the high ideals of the rulers
of Strassburg, they were unwilling to extend their benevolence for
long to the public exercise of Catholicism or to Anabaptists. The
latter were discouraged by stern legislation and finally in 1540
by the institution of the death penalty against their adherents.
This legislation occurred despite the opposition of tolerant clergy
such as the reformer Matthew Zell, whose wife wrote in defence
of the Anabaptists that 'these poor folk accept the Lord Jesus
with us and agree in all the essentials over which we separated
from the papacy. As to salvation in Christ, they are in accord with
us. But because they differ at other points, are they then to be
persecuted and Christ in them?' Zell's wife also attacked all coercion
by the authorities: 'He who does evil, him shall the government
punish, but it shall not compel and govern faith. It belongs to the
heart and the conscience and not to the external man'.

Among German Lutherans a few stood out for clemency to the
Anabaptists. The reformer of Württemberg, Johann Brenz, published in 1528 an enquiry into whether Anabaptists and other
heretics should be persecuted. His conclusion, utilised later by
Castellio, was that to repress heresy by force was to do the devil's

work for him. Brenz subsequently changed his opinions on this matter. Other Lutherans in the 1530s were also hesitant about intolerance: one of these, Johann Forster, maintained that 'heresy is something spiritual and can only be exterminated by spiritual weapons'.

In 1531 several south German Lutheran towns drew up what became known as the Memmingen Resolutions. In these they pleaded that:

on account of the Anabaptists, we wish very sincerely that they be treated as tolerantly as possible, for we have hitherto seen very clearly that the much too severe and tyrannical treatment exercised toward them in some places contributes much more toward spreading them than toward checking their error. It is contrary to the right of Christian government to force faith upon the world with the sword and other violent compulsion and to uproot evil therein, which should be resisted alone through the mighty Word of God, and the person erring in faith should not be suddenly knocked down but should be tolerated in all Christian love as a harmless person.

These sentiments, which coincided precisely with those of the Anabaptists, were unhappily not widespread. To a great extent distrust of the Anabaptists was occasioned not by their radical theology so much as by their social origins and their identification with the lower classes. A majority of them were drawn from agricultural areas, since the movement had been driven out of the towns, particularly in Switzerland and Germany. But where there was an urban nucleus, as in parts of south Germany and in the Netherlands, they were drawn from the labouring population, principally those engaged in textile production. They were generally accused of subverting authority and of preaching community of goods. Such, for example, were the accusations levelled against Hans Denck, known as the 'Anabaptist pope', who was expelled from Strassburg in 1526 and from Worms in 1527. Denck, like others of his sect, was a moderate and peaceable man, and hardly a threat to the civil power. The moderates were soon to be replaced by others in favour of the immediate and violent establishment of the kingdom of God.

Violent and peaceful radicals

The radical movement in southern Germany and Switzerland was an heir to the official Reformation and a reaction against it. The situation was quite different in northern Germany and the Netherlands, where the radicals were in the vanguard of the reform movement, and Sacramentarian and Melchiorite preachers were active in the late 1520s. The leader of the latter group, Melchior Hofmann, was the pioneer of Anabaptism in the Low Countries. He was responsible for the conversion of two visionary Dutchmen, John Matthijs, a Haarlem baker, and John Beukels of Leiden, an ex-tailor. After preaching an apocalyptic gospel throughout the country, these two were eventually in 1533 invited to the city of Münster, which under their influence fell rapidly into Anabaptist control. The communistic regime they imposed on Münster justified all the fears of secular authorities in Europe.

The enthusiasts of Münster betrayed their own cause by their lack of discretion. The beginnings were hopeful. Bernard Rothmann, who had originally won the city over to Lutheranism, was a firm proponent of Christian communism. News of this attracted the poor to the city. 'Dutch and Frisians and scoundrels from all parts ... flocked to Münster and collected there', reported a hostile contemporary. After Rothmann's conversion to Anabaptism and the advent of the two Johns in 1534, there was a further immigration of Anabaptists and poor people. Matthijs, who soon became leader of the city, expelled all the Catholic and Lutheran population, enforced a general rebaptism of all the remaining inhabitants, and set up a regime in which all things were held in common. A manifesto issued by Münster in 1534 for distribution to neighbouring towns, claimed that 'everything which has served the purposes of selfseeking and private property, such as buying and selling, working for money, taking interest and practising usury, or eating and drinking the sweat of the poor (that is, making one's own people and fellow-creatures work so that one can grow fat) and indeed everything which offends against

The surviving leaders of the Anabaptist
episode at Münster were in 1536 sentenced
to be exposed until death, in cages
suspended from the tower of the church
of St Lambert. The photograph shows the
same cages as they are today.

love – all such things are abolished among us by the power of love
and community'.

Matthijs died in a foolhardy sortie out of the city against the
besieging forces of the Prince-Bishop of Münster early in 1534, and
his place was taken by John of Leiden, whose genius and fanaticism
transformed the city into an absolute theocracy. The death penalty
was decreed for sins as varying as blasphemy, disobedience,
spreading scandal, and even for complaining or scolding one's
parents. Polygamy was instituted against bitter minority opposition, and John, who soon assumed royal powers, was granted a
harem of fifteen wives, all but one of whom were aged under
twenty. The aberrations of his rule, notably the institution of a
wealthy royal court with a well-stocked banquet table, at a time
when Münster's citizens were starving and dying under the
pressure of the siege, destroyed the popularity of the regime. In
June 1535 the city fell to the investing troops and most of its
inhabitants were put to the sword. This tragic episode signalled
the end of any moderation towards Anabaptists, who were thereafter, and with few exceptions, hunted throughout Europe as a
danger both to religion and to the social order. The reaction was
unfortunate, since the majority of post-Münster Anabaptists were
even more peaceable than before.

The spokesmen of peaceful Anabaptists were, in particular,
Menno Simons (1496–1561) and David Joris (1501–56), both
natives of the Netherlands. The former was shocked at the blind
and futile policy pursued by Anabaptists at Münster and elsewhere. A firm believer in moderation, he assumed the leadership
of several Anabaptist congregations in the northern Netherlands,
and after his death his followers assumed the name of Mennonites.
Like his predecessors, Menno taught a religion of the spirit. The
elect are those who have chosen, on the basis of their faith, to
receive adult baptism. Mennonites rejected any secular control
over the Church, but unlike the extreme Anabaptists, they recognised the authority of the State. As Menno described his followers:
'They are children of peace . . . who know nothing about war.

They render to Caesar what is Caesar's and to God what is God's'. By emphasising the pacifist beliefs of his followers, Menno disarmed those critics who tried to identify them with the tradition of Münster. At the same time, by distinguishing sharply between the spheres of Church and State, he supported thoroughgoing toleration. The State, in his view, had no coercive power or jurisdiction over religious matters. Within his own sect Menno believed in the imposition of rigorous discipline, but as between religions his position guaranteed complete civil tolerance.

With Joris the plea for toleration was even more explicit. Dissatisfied with the other Anabaptist movements, he founded his own sect, the Church of David. More mystical in character than his coreligionists, Joris was able more easily to rise above the conflicts inherent in traditional forms of religion. His denial of secular authority over religion was expressed in several outspoken protests against persecution. For him, as it was for Hubmaier, the true Church 'is not the one that persecutes, but the one that is persecuted'. This striking remark was later to become the common property of radicals in their struggle against intolerance. In 1553 Joris protested against Calvin's condemnation of Michael Servetus, in words that show how universal his own personal tolerance had become:

How many men would remain on earth if each had power over the other according to their mutual estimation of heresy? Turks or Jews consider Christians to be heretics, and Christians treat each other as such. Papists and Lutherans, followers of Zwingli and Anabaptists, Calvinists and Adiaphorists, all excommunicate one another. Must men hate and kill each other because of this difference of opinion?

Joris himself was not to receive the tolerance he sought for others. In 1544, after bitter persecution, he went underground and turned up in Basle under a pseudonym. When after his death in 1556 in that Protestant city it was discovered that he had been the notorious Anabaptist heretic, his body was dug up, judged, and publicly burnt. Among those who witnessed this degrading ceremony was a man named Sebastian Castellio.

The sad fate of the Anabaptist movement was that while it progressed through the fury of the Peasant War and Münster to a gospel of peace and tolerance, its opponents in high places (and they included both Catholics and Protestants) systematically developed methods of repression against it. Because of their association with violence and social radicalism, and perhaps even more because of their fundamental appeal to the lower classes, the Anabaptists were never given an opportunity to prevail in the councils of princes, so that their immediate practical contribution to toleration was nil. In the German- and Dutch-speaking countries, the vast majority of Christians executed on religious grounds in the sixteenth century were Anabaptists. By 1530, according to Sebastian Franck, more than two thousand Anabaptists had been executed in Germany. In the Netherlands two-thirds of the recorded victims of persecution in the sixteenth century, or 617 out of 877, were Anabaptists. These tragic figures underline the hostility of Catholic and Protestant Europe to left-wing heresy. At the same time they make the attitude to Anabaptism one by which to judge alleged supporters of toleration. Pre-eminent among these supporters was Castellio, who springs to prominence in the case of Michael Servetus.

Calvin, Castellio and the execution of Servetus

The greatest controversy on toleration in the sixteenth century centred round the condemnation of Michael Servetus. Servetus (1511–53) was a distinguished and brilliant Spaniard whose interests, as befitted a man of the Renaissance, ranged from medicine, geography and law to theology. Born at Villanueva in Aragon, he studied in Toulouse and travelled in Europe. In his twenties he adopted firm anti-Trinitarian views and published two works developing his ideas, but was forced by the possible consequences to retire into less public life under a pseudonym. Later he began to correspond with Calvin, whom he alarmed with his theological views. The reformer made it clear that he was no friend to Servetus. Proof of this came in 1553 when one of Calvin's friends, with his active help, supplied material to the Inquisition of Lyons informing against Servetus. The latter was arrested, but escaped a few days later. Some months after, he turned up in Geneva, where he was recognised and promptly arrested. Condemned as a heretic by the city Council at Calvin's instigation, he was burnt to death at the gates of Geneva. In modern times a group of Calvinists have set up an expiatory column near the place where he was executed.

The general reaction at the time was one of approval. The leaders of the Reformation confessed that they would not have acted otherwise. Bullinger, then at Zürich, approved. Melanchthon wrote, in October 1554: 'I entirely concur with your judgment'. The greater part of the Protestant Churches signified their approval. The protests were few. The most significant of them, penned before Servetus' execution, came from Basle, from the hand of the man we know to have been David Joris. He appealed to Calvin: 'I hope that the bloodthirsty counsel of the learned will not weigh with you. Consider rather the precepts of our only Lord and Master, Christ, who taught not only in human and literal fashion in Scripture, but also in a divine manner by word and example, that we should crucify and kill no one for his faith, but should rather be crucified and killed ourselves'.

Calvin acted in accordance with the dictates of the time and of his own conscience. Blasphemy against the Trinity was universally abhorred among Christians, and in the case of Servetus an impetuous temperament was added to the holding of heretical opinions. By his zeal for controversy, Servetus virtually handed himself over to be burnt. At the same time, however, little can be said in extenuation of Calvin. The martyrdom of Servetus set the seal on his reputation as an intolerant leader. One historian has said of him: 'as a man he was not cruel, but as a theologian he was merciless; and it was as a theologian that he dealt with Servetus'. Though Calvin never doubted the correctness of his decision, he allowed himself to be drawn into controversy over the burning.

The principal attack directed against him came in March 1554, in a little book called *De haereticis, an sint persequendi*, published under the pseudonym Martin Bellius.

The author of the *Concerning Heretics* was quickly recognised to be Sebastian Castellio, a French Protestant and former pupil and colleague of Calvin. By his writings Castellio was to prove himself one of the foremost apostles of religious liberty. As early as 1551, in a preface to a version of the Bible he had translated into classical Latin, Castellio pointed to Scripture, the sacred rule of the reformers, and noted how obscure many of the doctrines in it were; yet there were those who were willing to shed innocent blood for the sake of a doubtful interpretation. Religious truths, he maintained, were not necessarily clear to everybody. 'We ought certainly, however much we may think we know everything, we ought, I say, to fear lest in crucifying thieves justly we crucify also Christ unjustly'.

The execution of Servetus brought Castellio back to the theme of toleration. His book was a compilation of passages from several distinguished authorities, among them Calvin. Each passage was chosen to illustrate an argument made by the author in favour of toleration, and the sources ranged from the earliest Church Fathers to Castellio himself, who was cited under a pseudonym. In his preface Castellio appeals for a rejection of the concept of 'heretic'. A heretic is simply one with whom we disagree, and 'there is practically no sect which does not hold all others for heretics'. He objected to the fact that heresy or doctrinal disagreement was treated as being more reprehensible than moral crimes such as murder and adultery.

Among the writers cited by Castellio in defence of his thesis, the most striking was Sebastian Franck. Like Castellio, Franck had emphasised the uncertainty of truth and the futility of dogma in a religion where 'the cross alone is the Christian's theology'. Our knowledge is imperfect, Franck held: 'We know in part. Socrates was right, that we know only that we do not know. We may be heretics quite as much as our opponents'. By adopting a spiritual, undogmatic religion, there would be complete liberty: 'Where the spirit of God is, there is freedom – no constraint, tyranny, partisanship or compulsion'. Castellio quotes Franck's fine peroration:

My heart is alien to none. I have my brothers among the Turks, Papists, Jews and all peoples. Not that they are Turks, Jews, Papists and Sectaries or will remain so; in the evening they will be called into the vineyard and given the same wage as we.

In his own text, Castellio pursued the term 'heretic' and found that 'the name "heretic" is found only once in the Scriptures, in the Epistle of Paul to Titus, the third chapter: "A man that is an heretic, after the first and second admonition reject" '. This passage showed to Castellio's satisfaction that excommunication was the only form of chastisement permitted to Christians when dealing with heresy. Apart from that, the heretic was not to be troubled. The one thing worse than heresy, Castellio maintained, was hypocrisy. To be forced to profess what one believed false was to sin against conscience through hypocrisy, whereas the 'heretic' should be allowed to hold to what his conscience dictated. Servetus, he claimed, had been killed for preferring his own truth to that of Calvin. Would it have been better to coerce him into living what he felt was a lie? Here Castellio penetrates to the core of the question about the rights of an erroneous conscience, and upholds it against the then accepted idea that the objective divine law was to be put before subjective opinions.

Castellio's toleration did not extend to atheists. This limitation was common to all the religious radicals. But within the company of believers in God, Castellio did not shrink from advocating universal toleration:

Let not the Jews or Turks condemn the Christians, nor let the Christians condemn the Jews or Turks, but rather teach and win them by true religion and justice, and let us, who are Christians, not condemn one another, but, if we are wiser than they, let us also be better and more merciful. The better a man knows the truth, the less is he inclined to condemn.

To further this attitude he appealed to the civil power to refrain from supporting ecclesiastical tyranny. 'O princes, do not heed those who counsel you to shed blood for religion. Do not serve as their hangmen . . . Evil will never be overcome with evil. There is no remedy against murders than to stop committing murder'.

Even before the appearance of Castellio's work, Calvin had attempted to forestall criticism by publishing in January 1554 his *Declaratio orthodoxae fidei*, which was issued both in Latin and in French. This work, described by Lecler as 'one of the most frightening treatises ever written to justify the persecution of heretics', was an unrepentant defence of the most extreme intolerance. The person and doctrines of Servetus were covered with abuse, and total obliteration of heresy was advocated. The powers that be were ecstatic at Calvin's brilliant apologia, and Melanchthon told the author that the Church would forever be in his debt. Among the few dissenting voices was that of Nicholas Zurkinden.

Zurkinden (1506–88), chief magistrate of Berne, was a friend and correspondent of Calvin, Beza and other leading reformers; at the same time he was a friend of radicals like Lelio Curio and Castellio. Zurkinden was by no means an opponent of the death penalty for heresy: during his term of office several Anabaptists were executed in Berne, and although he disapproved of Servetus' death he was willing to allow its necessity. His moderation in theological matters made him disagree fundamentally with Calvin's attitude on predestination and his intolerance to dissidents; but his temperament prevented him progressing further than this towards a fully tolerant position. He is interesting primarily as an example of a conservative who thought seriously about the evil effects of religious repression. In 1554 he described to Calvin the reasons which governed his attitude. To illustrate his case he recalled an execution he had witnessed in 1538:

It is not only the lessons of antiquity which turn me against the use of force, but also the incredible examples of the persecution of Anabaptists in our own days. I witnessed here an eighty-year-old woman and her daughter, a mother of six children, being led to death for no other reason than that, after the known and customary teaching of the Anabaptists, they had refused to have the children baptised. And that only at their own peril, since it was hardly to be feared that two old women would be able to corrupt the whole world with their false teaching. This one example out of many is enough. It impressed me deeply, and I greatly fear that the authorities may not keep within the bounds you assign them, namely that they should inflict the death penalty only on the most abominable destroyers of faith and religion.

Another reason (he went on to say) why I shrink from bloodshed lies in the observation that the sword proves effective only against individuals, and is powerless against a multitude. I dislike any law over life and death which is sharp against individuals but blunt against the many.

In other words, he believed, one might execute individuals *ad infinitum* but never begin to solve the problem of mass heresy. Indiscriminate persecution was no answer to the problem.

Since Calvin's defence had preceded Castellio's contribution, another combatant entered the fray against the latter. That same year 1554, Theodore Beza, later to be Calvin's successor at Geneva but then the professor of Greek at Lausanne, issued his *De haereticis a civili magistratu puniendis*, directed principally against Castellio, who was now professor of Greek at Basle. Beza's work was a systematic attack on the doctrine of toleration, which he was to describe a few years later as 'diabolical' (*vere diabolicum dogma*). Unshaken by this blast, Castellio returned to the fight with a book which was not published during his lifetime and which appeared in print only in 1612, in Holland. This work, *Contra libellum Calvini*, was a crushing indictment of the reformer. Taking selected passages from Calvin's *Declaratio*, Castellio provided a commentary in the form of a dialogue between himself and Calvin. To the claim by Calvin that 'kings are commanded to protect the doctrine of piety by their support', he gave the short and unanswerable reply: 'To kill a man is not to defend a doctrine, but to kill a man. When the Genevans killed Servetus they did not defend a doctrine, they killed a man'.

Castellio died in 1563. The arguments which he and the moderate circle at Basle had used, fell on barren soil, and Calvin's ethic pressed forward to greater triumphs in Europe. The controversy was, however, important for several reasons. Although Servetus himself was not a notable supporter of toleration, his martyrdom in the cause of anti-Trinitarianism was to have an impression on other eminent anti-Trinitarians who developed their own doctrines of tolerance in retaliation against the bitter persecution to which they were subjected. And though Castellio had little influence on the thought of his generation, later thinkers were careful to make use of his ideas, and his stature in the history of human freedom is indisputably great.

The Italian anti-Trinitarians

That the death of an anti-Trinitarian should lead to a profound debate on liberty is singularly apt, for it was the anti-Trinitarians more than any other single sect who stood in the vanguard of the struggle for toleration. It was in 1531 that Servetus had published his *De Trinitatis Erroribus*, a frank and honest attempt to discuss rationally the doctrine of a triune God: coming as it did in a period of acute theological strife it disgusted the Catholics and alarmed the Protestants. For the leaders of the Reformation there were some issues that remained beyond the range of discussion: of these the trinity of God and the divinity of Christ were the principal ones. But Servetus' book struck deep roots, particularly in Italy where, as Vergerio informed Bullinger in 1554, 'the Servetian plague is spreading'. Even the Anabaptist communities in that country began to adopt Unitarian beliefs. Out of Italy, as a result of these influences, emerged the greatest leaders of tolerant Protestantism in Europe.

A few words should be said of one Italian follower of Servetus who was also a victim of the Calvinist regime. This was Giovanni Gentile, who came from Italy to Geneva in 1556. Thanks to the system of espionage at Geneva, Gentile was soon betrayed into giving voice to his Unitarian opinions. In 1558 he was arrested and made to do public penance: bareheaded and barefoot, wearing

SATANAE STRA-
TAGEMATVM LI-
ber Primus.

D Satanæ cognofcēdas artes cōmodifsimus fit aditus: fi, quis omnium cōfiliorum eius finis fit, infpexerimus, atq; is q̄dem in promptu eft. fiquidem ex eo quod dicatur homicida fuiffe iā inde ab initio: quē alium hunc effe finem credamus, quàm ho-

only a shirt and with a lighted torch in his hand, he abjured his errors. Shortly after this he fled the city. He wandered through eastern Europe and returned to Switzerland after Calvin's death. He was arrested and imprisoned in Berne, tried for heresy under Beza's regime, and executed in 1566. The absence of public protest at his death was a measure of the triumph of intolerance in Protestant Europe.

Foremost among the Italian humanists who defected to the Reformation was Bernardino Ochino (1487–1565). At one time General of the Observant Franciscans, he resigned from the order to join the more austere Capuchins, a newly-founded order of which in 1538 he became General. His fame for preaching was equalled only by his reputation for sanctity. Even the stones wept when he preached, reported one contemporary. But the authorities soon discerned unorthodox trends in his sermons, and in 1542 he fled Italy in the company of the humanist Peter Martyr Vermigli. His defection created an enormous sensation. He eventually settled down in Zürich as a pastor, but through his writings he fell foul of the watchful eye of Bullinger. The Council of Zürich objected to sections in his *Dialogues* (1563) which appeared to

Part of the first page of Acontius'
Satan's Stratagems, from a 1565 edition.
Acontius was by this date living in
England, but his European interests led
him to publish the first edition of his
work in Latin at Basle in 1564.

favour polygamy and Unitarianism, and expelled him. Now an old man of seventy-six, he was forced to set out in a wintry December with his four small children, whose mother had recently died. His wanderings took him through Germany to Poland and Moravia, where he died in the Anabaptist colony at Slavkov, a prey to the same plague that had by then carried off three of his children. Himself a victim of persecution, Ochino was a firm opponent of intolerance. In his *Dialogues* he rejected the interference of the magistrate in religion, and the resort to capital punishment. Even the most serious errors should be tolerated for the sake of charity, he maintained, citing the parable of the tares and Gamaliel's exhortation to the Jews.

The year before Ochino died, another expatriate Italian, Jacob Acontius (*c.* 1500–67), who had known Castellio, published at Basle his *Satanae Stratagemata*. This became one of the most influential works on toleration written in the sixteenth century. A French translation came out in 1565 and an English one in 1648. Translated into all the major languages of modern Europe, it played an incalculable role in the growth of a spirit of tolerance among Protestants. A pioneer anti-Trinitarian, Acontius drifted through several countries before settling down finally in England in 1559. Although *Satan's Stratagems* was not translated into English until much later, it exercised a great influence through the Latin version, and helped to rear a whole generation of liberal theologians in England.

Acontius' wide experience of sectarian conflict led him to look on all discord as a stratagem by which Satan succeeded in sowing error and confusion among Christians. He condemned the use of violence to defend truth, as wrong and self-defeating. The Church certainly has disciplinary power to be exercised over its own members, but neither it nor the magistrate can use coercion in religion. Acontius allows the magistrate a legitimate authority in Church affairs, but denies that he has the power to use force. Conflict in religion could be reduced if men would only reach agreement on a number of fundamental articles, among which the doctrines of the Real Presence and the Trinity are not included. This important point of agreement on essentials, first proposed by Erasmus and his humanist followers, was for Acontius the beginning of wisdom in ending strife.

He went further than merely opposing violence: he supported complete liberty of choice in religion. He conceded that such liberty would lead at first to a proliferation of opinions and hence to contradictions and confusion, but out of this chaos, he believed, would emerge agreement on the common principles of truth, and in this way Satan's schemes would be foiled. Heretics are of some benefit, he claimed: 'By them godly men are stirred to search the Scriptures much more carefully and diligently, who otherwise would give themselves up to sloth and would gradually sink into a state of general ignorance'. So libertarian an attitude was clearly optimistic in the extreme, but Acontius was undaunted. Turning his back on the past and on all tradition, he maintained that the Word of God alone should be our guide for the present and future, and that the pretensions of so-called authorities and past interpreters of the Bible must be rejected. He had accordingly relied in his work only on citations from the Bible and had not quoted earthly 'authorities'. Once free enquiry had been allowed and all coercion of the conscience removed, the truth would emerge triumphant. Acontius was not afraid of granting freedom to error, for the erroneous conscience had as much right to liberty as any other. 'Although it should be your aim that he who disseminates errors should not escape just and merited chastisement, yet he who deceived others, being himself deceived, should be treated far otherwise than he who did it maliciously . . . If you are wroth with him, it will appear that you are wroth not so much with him as with God, who has not furnished him with a better judgment'.

The readership Acontius acquired in western Europe, particularly in England and Holland, the two most dynamic Protestant countries, make him one of the most important precursors of a more liberal approach to religion. On the other side of Europe, in Poland, his influence was surpassed by that of another Italian who was to give his name to the whole anti-Trinitarian movement, and whose authority led to the formulation of one of the first manifestos of toleration in European history. This was Faustus Socinus.

The Sozzini (Latinised as Socinus) were one of the leading families of Siena. Lelio Socinus (1525–62) was the first of its many members to go over to the Reformation. He journeyed widely in Protestant Europe and made the acquaintance of Calvin, Melanchthon and other reformers, including the radicals Castellio and Acontius. He died at Zürich in 1562, leaving his numerous manuscript writings to his nephew Faustus. The latter (1539–1604) seems never to have been a convinced Catholic, thanks to the strong heretical influences in his family, but he remained in Italy until 1574, when he left his native land forever. His first residence was in Basle, where he wrote his principal theological study, *De Jesu Christo Servatore*. The work remained in manuscript until 1594, when it was eventually published in Poland, but long before then the author's religious opinions had become notorious. Towards the end of the century Socinus went to live among the Anabaptist communities in Poland, and it was there that his influence was most felt. Although he never joined the communities formally, he became their accepted leader, and from him the Unitarian radicals derived the name of Socinians. His death in 1604 marked only the beginning of his fame, which in the next generation or so spread throughout Europe. In a later chapter we shall examine his thought in the context of events in Poland.

4 Humanists and irenicists

The first generation of the Reformation continued to be un-reconciled to the spectacle of a divided Christendom. As it had been Erasmus' vain desire to see all the parties agree at last in a common charity, so it became the burning concern of others in the humanist tradition to find a basis for eventual unity. On the political side, there was considerable concern that religious fragmentation would lead to anarchy in the Empire, dissolution of the established social order, and a weakening of defences against the Turks. On the religious side, there seemed every reason to consider unity feasible: theologians had differed before, the dogmatic differences between the sides were not too clearly defined, and the common philosophic and historical inheritance of both sides allowed a basis for discussion. The attention of everyone was focused on Germany. It was there that the split had begun and there, God willing, that it would be healed. The great work of reconciliation was undertaken by the exponents and then by the heirs of Erasmian humanism.

Although the irenicists in general were socially conservative and less inclined to look with favour on the great number of novel heresies that followed from the Reformation, their role was of cardinal importance for two reasons. First, their charitable moderation made them prepared to approach opponents and heretics in the spirit of peace. Secondly, their unanimous search for as narrow as possible a dogmatic basis for reunion made them bring into relief the doctrine of 'fundamentals', one which has since become the foundation of ecumenical movements among the Protestant denominations. The best statement of this position was made by a Lutheran theologian of the time, Peter Meiderlin (1582–1651), who drew up the now famous formula, derived ultimately from a phrase of Augustine: *In necessariis unitas, in non necessariis libertas, in omnibus caritas.*

Nothing is easier than to imagine that with Luther the Reformation came *tout court*, a clear-cut alternative to Catholic orthodoxy. Lutheranism developed away from the old Church only very gradually. In its early years few even considered it heretical.

It was a practice of the reformers to contrast the simplicity of early Christianity and the luxury of the papal court. This print, one of a series on the *Passion of Christ and Antichrist*, executed by Hans Cranach in 1521 and with a text probably written by Luther, compares the humiliation suffered by Christ with the adulation given to the Pope.

CHRISTVS.

ilites plectentes coronam de spinis, impofuerunt capiti eius, & veste urpura circundederunt eum. Iohan: XIX.

ANTICHRISTVS.

Imperator Conftantinus tradidit nobis coronā Imperialem: Phrygiū chlamydem purpuream: uunicam coccineam: & imperialia indumē̄ & fceptra. c. Conftantinus. xcvi, dift. Eiufmodi mendacia ad tuendaṁ tyrannidem fuam confinxerunt: contra omnes & hiftorias & annales Neq̃ m̄ vnquam in morefuit Romanis Imperatoribus tales geftar coronas.   A ij

Certainly the Pope in 1520 issued the bull *Exsurge Domine* and described Luther as a 'son of iniquity'. But Rome's stock was low in the Catholic world. By its moral corruption it had forfeited its claim to speak for the Church of Christ, or so its opponents claimed. 'The sacred authority of the Roman pontiff', wrote Erasmus in 1519, 'is so abused that the godly cannot see it without a sigh'. There were many like Luther who had visited Babylon and shaken its dust off their feet. The disputes of the conciliar

The trade in indulgences did more to discredit Rome in the eyes of opponents than many other failings. The illustrations show (*right*) an indulgence issued in Constance in 1521, and (*above*) a satirical print attacking John Tetzel, the Dominican whose sale of indulgences occasioned Luther's initial protest.

epoch of the early fifteenth century, when many theologians declared that the papacy was in some matters subject to a general council of the Church, and the degeneration of the pope into a warlike secular prince like any other princeling, completed the disillusion. With the voice of Rome discredited, there was no authoritative voice to condemn. Theologians and kings went their way with impunity. In Germany there were many like prince George of Anhalt, who regarded himself as a Catholic but whom the Lutherans, no doubt more accurately, claimed as one of themselves. The lines of division therefore remained consistently blurred, and the party of the humanists could hope for nothing better, for in that incertain atmosphere lay the seeds of toleration and the hope of eventual unity.

An illustration from an account of Luther's appearance before the young Emperor Charles V and prelates at the Imperial Diet of Worms in 1521.

All the auguries at first favoured the moderates. In 1526 it appeared to Mercurino Gattinara, the Erasmian Chancellor of the Emperor Charles V, that Erasmus led a third party which interposed between the papal and Lutheran factions. The Emperor himself, no friend to the political pretensions of the papacy, was an ardent admirer of Erasmus. Everywhere in Europe for almost a generation thereafter the Erasmians were represented. On the Catholic side, such advisers of Ferdinand I (Emperor since 1558) as Johann Faber, bishop of Vienna since 1530, were devoted Erasmians. It was claimed in 1536 that among the prominent bishops belonging to this party were those of Gniezno, Basle, Augsburg, Olomouc, Chełmo and Durham. These and others were important more because of their personal standing and their political influence than because of their numbers. The chief princely courts of Germany had their core of humanists. In Saxony there was the chancellor Simon Pistorius, Julius Pflug, and George Witzel. In Cleves there was Conrad von Heresbach. At Cologne, Heidelberg and Koblenz, whether the courts were Catholic or Protestant, humanists were in positions of influence. Even at the papal court the eminent diplomat Gaspar Contarini represented moderation at its best.

Three principal efforts were made in the sixteenth century to arrive at a solution to interdenominational conflicts. First, in concert with the secular powers a policy was followed of holding colloquies or conferences between the disputing parties in order

This print by Erhard Schoen, *The Devil's Bagpipes* (1521), showing Luther as the instrument of the devil, was typical of the propaganda that embittered religious feelings on both sides.

to settle outstanding differences. This was attempted mainly in Germany and in France. Secondly, the Protestant reformers tried to unite through the same method of colloquies. Finally, individuals working from either side, sometimes with the support of the Pope or the Emperor, tried to carry into practice the teachings of Erasmus.

The main field of their activity was Germany. It was there that the revolt had begun and there that its greatest support remained. Not that it was purely a religious problem. The great difficulty arose with the political support that different sections of the population gave to Luther. The Dukes of Saxony befriended Luther, and other princes, notably the Margrave of Brandenburg, went over to the Reformation. The lesser nobility under Hutten and Sickingen gave their voice for his cause. 'Three things', wrote Hutten, 'are hateful to Rome: a general Council, the reformation of the Church, and the opening of German eyes'. It was before German eyes that the drama to win religious peace and liberty was now played out.

The policy of colloquies in Germany

What made colloquies at all possible was the fact that neither Rome nor any other authoritative voice had pronounced on the issues. Among the humanists, and indeed among most Christians, it was felt that only a general Council of the Church could command the requisite authority. Until that Council pronounced otherwise, some of Luther's views were held to be perfectly tenable by Catholics. Whenever orthodox theologians phrased their arguments, they appealed back to tradition; the reformers appealed forwards, to a Council. In the words of the historian of the Council of Trent, 'the fixed star of the Council still shone in the sky'. The Protestants certainly had no intention of accepting the authority of any Council, but so long as they claimed to want one some hope of compromise remained. The humanists were given a few years grace to attempt their solution. The 'dialogue' between differing faiths,

resorted to with profound hope in the twentieth century, was already being tried in the sixteenth.

The first significant debate between opponents was held on the Protestant side. It was a time for compromises. When the Diet of Nürnberg at its final session in 1524 adopted the formula that each prince in his own territory should enforce the Edict of Worms

The signatures of the chief participants at the Marburg Colloquy in 1529. All the leaders of the German and Swiss Reformation attended this conference in Philip of Hesse's castle at Marburg. Agreement between the Germans and Swiss was reached on fourteen major points of doctrine, but on the fifteenth, that concerning the Eucharist, agreement was impossible.

according to his capabilities, it was obvious that the Lutherans would be given a respite. The significance of the gains that political arrangements like this could give Lutherans was not lost on leaders like Philip of Hesse. At the second Diet of Speyer in 1529, he led the princes in their protest (hence the name 'Protestant') against the unequal political settlement granted to Lutherans. Philip dreamed of an international alliance of Protestants which would present the Church with a united front. This at least was the political excuse for the Marburg Colloquy of 1529. The principal leaders of the European Reformation came to Marburg: Zwingli from Zürich, Luther and Melanchthon from Saxony, Bucer from Strassburg, Oecolampadius from Basle. That they failed to agree was not entirely the fault of their intransigent theological positions. Luther, certainly, is said to have despaired of Zwingli's salvation; but he was also concerned about the efforts of Melanchthon to find some *modus vivendi* with the Catholics, and was not anxious to throw such a settlement over for the sake of agreement with the Swiss.

The most prominent humanist on the Lutheran side, Melanchthon did his utmost to heal the breach with Rome. At the Diet of

Augsburg in 1530, he made concessions that failed to move the Catholics. His last attempt was the Confession of Augsburg, a statement of faith which expressed Lutheran dogma but aimed to conciliate Catholic sentiment. The acceptance of the Confession by all the Protestants, save the Swiss and Strassburg, gave Lutheranism at last a unity and a programme it sorely needed. At the same time, it cut the Lutherans off from Catholicism as surely as the Council of Trent was to cut Catholicism off from the Reformation. By accentuating the division, it destroyed all hopes of reunion. Because of this, it has been claimed that the Diet of Augsburg 'ended the Erasmian dream'. The Erasmians at the time were not so sure.

With the unity of the Church and the political stability of Germany at stake, it was necessary to attempt all possible means to secure a peaceful settlement. The policy of discussions now adopted by the Emperor was not congenial to conservatives, who saw in it only a confession of weakness. All factions nevertheless took part, including the papacy.

The first great colloquy was intended by Charles v to be held at the Diet of Speyer in the spring of 1540. In May this Diet was moved to Hagenau because of the plague. The Emperor intended to make the proceedings into what the Lutherans had long desired – a Christian Council of the German nation; but differences among the parties made failure almost certain. The conference was thereupon suspended, and a new one, a 'Christian colloquy', was summoned to Worms for October that year, to be followed by an Imperial Diet. At Worms the representative of the Emperor was the Erasmian Cardinal Granvelle. The Pope was represented by the nuncio Campeggio and other prelates. Discussions did not begin until 14 January 1541. Four days later, after the two sides had reached agreement on the doctrine of the Trinity but not on that of original sin, the assembly was adjourned to the Diet at Regensburg. The failure of two attempts at compromise was serious. 'If no agreement is reached at Regensburg it is all over with Germany', observed a contemporary.

At Regensburg all hopes centred on the figure of the papal legate – Cardinal Gaspar Contarini. One of the most eminent diplomats of his time, revered by liberals both inside and outside the Church, he was appointed Cardinal in 1535 although a layman. His arrival at Regensburg in March 1541 aroused the most sanguine hopes in Germany. He himself was inspired by a profound optimism. In February 1541 we find him writing, 'As I have often told the Pope, the disagreements on essentials were not so serious as many supposed. Would to God that many had never taken up their pens on behalf of the Catholic cause, doing thereby more harm than good'. In April the chief disputants on either side were nominated. They included the principal Erasmians and moderates. For the Protestants there were Melanchthon, Bucer and Pistorius; for the Catholics, Johann Gropper, Pflug and Eck, of whom the last was included only at the instance of the papal representatives. The basis for discussion was a special moderate document called the 'Book of Regensburg', drawn up mainly by Gropper.

It was Contarini's moderate conduct that carried the discussions along. As Pastor observes: 'All his behaviour to those who differed from him in religion was founded on mildness and conciliation. With a scrupulousness which almost amounted to anxiety he endeavoured to avoid everything which might hurt the feelings or rouse the animosity of those severed from the Church'. The fruits of this moderation, and of the common inheritance of Erasmus, were revealed in the agreement reached by both sides on 2 May over the doctrine of justification. This astounding success on a point of cardinal importance was not followed up. Some agreement was reached on minor points, but on issues such as transubstantiation and penance the gulf was unbridgeable. Despite the desire of Granvelle and the Emperor to compromise on these points, Contarini was adamant that a false agreement was worse than none. Further concessions would have meant a surrender of dogma. Contarini had done his best and failed. 'I am vexed to the soul', he wrote sadly, 'to see things thus hurrying on the road to ruin'. Despite his personal moderation and tolerance, it is of

interest to see that he was not tolerant by principle. On the dissolution of the Diet of Regensburg in July, Charles v ordered the
discussion of disputed articles to be suspended until a General
Council. Until that time, toleration of such articles was decreed,
and warfare between the religions was forbidden. Contarini
disapproved of such a toleration, which for him was 'illicit and
damnable' and threatened the security of the Catholic religion.

In May the same year invitations to the Council of Trent were
issued by Rome. Here at last was the General Council so long
dreamed of. But it was four years before the Council officially
opened, and by that time the political situation in Germany was
virtually irreparable. A subsequent attempt at a colloquy, at
Regensburg in 1546, failed completely, and the Emperor was
induced to find a military solution for his problems. After Charles
v's victory over the Protestants at Mühlberg in 1547 he decided
to make his own settlement, regardless of the papacy. The result
was the Interim of Augsburg, of 1548. Drawn up as a compromise,
with the Erasmian Pflug prominent in its drafting, the Interim allowed
the marriage of priests and communion in both kinds – two demands
fundamental to the Protestants. Purely religious concessions of
this sort were not enough for the dissident princes, who initiated
another war in Germany that led to the treaty of Passau in 1552
and an eventual general settlement at Augsburg in 1555.

The Peace of Augsburg offered a temporary solution to the
religious problem by perpetuating the practice of intolerance. The
principle enshrined in the peace was a Lutheran one, namely that
it is the secular ruler who decides what religion should be observed
in his territory, and that in any one territory there should be only
one religion: this policy was summed up in the phrase *cuius regio,
eius religio*. By inflating the role of the prince against the power
of the Church, Luther concentrated both secular and ecclesiastical
power in the same hands. It was to these hands that the administration of the Peace of Augsburg was now entrusted.

The essential feature of Augsburg is that it was an agreement
among German autocrats. Toleration was denied to everyone save

to the princes, who were given the freedom to uproot vast numbers of their population who refused to accept the religion laid down for them by the State. Only Catholicism and Lutheranism were made a party to this agreement: all other faiths were excluded.

Far from being recognised for what it was, a compromise, Augsburg was assumed to be a settlement. Only the short-sightedness of politicians could have allowed such a conclusion. It was a negation of what the irenicists had fought for all along. Even when the political settlement of 1555 was followed by the lengthy, and invariably conservative, deliberations of the Council of Trent, the Erasmians refused to recognise defeat. But by now their influence was minimal and could not divert the princes of Europe from the impending era of religious wars. Those who tried to bridge the gap between the two parties were scorned by both and their projects rejected. The principal irenicists on the Catholic side were George Witzel and George Cassander.

A satirical print from Magdeburg, probably of the same date as the Interim of Augsburg (1548), attacking the compromise in the style of the psalm *Beatus vir*: 'Happy is the man who puts his trust in God and rejects the Interim.'

Two influential Catholic irenicists

Witzel (1501–73) was a priest who in 1524 left the Church to marry and become a Lutheran, only to return to Catholicism nine years later. Never a man of partisan mind, he devoted his efforts to finding some common ground for a dialogue between the factions. In the early 1530s he was an ardent Erasmian and an orthodox Catholic who looked for disciplinary reform to a future Council and to the German princes. Some of his schemes for reform were extremely radical, but, despite this, in the hopeful atmosphere of the thirties he found support at the court of the Duke of Saxony. From 1541 to 1552 he stayed with the liberal abbot of Fulda, after which he moved to Mainz. In this later stage of his career Witzel became a friend and confidant of the Emperor Ferdinand I, for whom he drew up plans for ecclesiastical and disciplinary reform. In his *Via Regia*, which was addressed to Ferdinand and published only after his own death, he outlined the royal way of reform by compromise, which included radical modifications to Catholic belief and practice. 'No longer, dearest brothers', he pleaded, 'should we hear the words: I am of Paul, I of Apollo, I of Cephas; or, as we hear these days: I am of the Pope, I of Luther, I of Zwingli, I of Calvin. Is Christ divided? Was the Pope crucified for us? Were we baptised in the name of Luther, or Zwingli, or Calvin?' This appeal for reason was accompanied by a firm rejection of coercion in matters of religion. The issue, moreover, must be settled peaceably and soon. The book ends with words of hope: 'Now is the time for talking: the time for silence is past. May that be done which is good in the Lord's eyes'.

The most outstanding humanist and irenicist to follow Witzel was Cassander (1513–66), an ardent Erasmian and a native of the Netherlands. His independent ideas led to his dismissal from the University of Louvain and he eventually settled down in Cologne. Like Witzel, Cassander directed his writings to the secular powers, in an effort to secure through them the unity which churchmen and colloquies did not bring. His principal work, *De officio pii ac publicae tranquillitatis vere amantis viri in hoc religionis dissidio*

(1561) is notable more for its attempt to find common ground between the Christian sects than for its advocacy of toleration. Since Cassander, like Witzel, was a convinced Catholic, he could find no possible reason to tolerate the antidogmatism of the Anabaptists and other extremists. But he rendered later generations an inestimable service by his efforts to base eventual unity on the common acceptance of certain 'fundamental articles' of religion. The basis of this approach was the fifth-century formula: *quod semper, quod ubique, quod ab omnibus*; the essentials, in other words, are just those articles that have always and in all places been commonly accepted. So long as Christians agreed on their beliefs about Christ as a person and as head of the Church, all other differences were to be tolerated in a spirit of charity as nonessential.

Those therefore who seek nothing but the glory of Christ and the restoration of his Church, and who work wholeheartedly for peace and unity, and who despite some difference in rite and belief are bound to the rest of the Church by charity, these I am unable to separate and cut off from Christ our head and from his body which is the Church; even if there are some who, out of thoughtless zeal or personal animosity, reject any restoration or reform, and traduce and condemn them as heretics, schismatics and enemies of the Church.

Those from whom we differ must, he emphasised, be treated with love:

If they are evil heretics, and you burn with true charity, do not abandon them: but even if they are in the worst error go to them, weep, admonish, argue. Just because we have to bear the burdensome and almost insupportable weight of the Roman Curia, do we therefore flee and give up? Far from it. We pray and we advise, but we do not break the unity of the spirit; nor let us endanger that unity, knowing that charity overcomes all things.

A few years after this work Cassander issued his *De articulis inter Catholicos et Protestantes controversis consultatio*. This was addressed to Ferdinand I and, after him, to Maximilian II. Cassander dealt with the Confession of Augsburg article by article and attempted to reconcile it with the fundamentals of Catholic doctrine, in an effort to reduce the two creeds to a common basis. He ended this work on a note of hope, looking forward to a solution based not on force but on peace, 'so that at length the grave wounds of the Church may be cured by legitimate and timely remedies rather than by those violent and untimely methods so far unhappily used through imprudent advice, methods which have not merely aggravated the ills of the Church but have even made them incurable'. With these words the treatise ends.

Despite his peaceable irenic approach, Cassander was essentially a conservative, as all the humanists tended to be. It would therefore be unwise to consider him a supporter of absolute religious liberty. In the controversy between Castellio and Calvin he expressed sympathy for the former, but, as he stated in 1562, he was of the opinion that 'moderate constraint can be useful, as long as it is medicinal and not penal. In this way the guilty may be brought to reflect on the evil they suffer from and to look for remedies instead of resting comfortably on their errors'.

Though Witzel and Cassander did not secure their main objectives by these writings, the Emperors who encouraged them were actively committed to finding a compromise that might bring peace to Germany. It was in the Erasmian tradition to look to the prince for an implementation of reforms. What differentiated the Erasmians from the Lutherans, who also relied on the prince, was of course the Lutheran belief that the prince could exercise absolute coercion in matters of religion. Because of this distinction, and the opposition of Erasmians to the death penalty in religion, we may rightly view men like Cassander as exponents not only of irenicism but also of limited toleration.

Humanism in the Habsburg lands

In Spain, where the existence of the Inquisition produced a special brand of intolerance, Erasmian humanism was slowly crushed out in the course of the 1530s. It has consequently been assumed that

protagonists of religious liberty ceased to exist in a country which very soon became a by-word for persecution. There were, however, always a few voices to protest against the methods of those in authority. The seventeenth-century Jesuit historian Juan de Mariana testifies that as early as the late fifteenth century there were many who opposed the use of the death penalty for heresy. Fray Luis de Granada (1504–88), a devout Catholic and a supporter of the Inquisition, went on record in his *Introduction to the Creed* as saying:

Christian charity and zeal for the salvation of souls oblige me here to say a word in warning to those who, out of a mistaken zeal for the faith, believe that they do no sin by inflicting evil and harm on those who are outside the faith, be they Moors or Jews or heretics or Gentiles. They deceive themselves greatly, for these too are brethren, like those of the faith.

Another Spaniard, Alonso de Virués, preacher at one time to the Emperor Charles v and eventually bishop of the Canary Islands till his death in 1545, suffered at the hands of the Inquisition in the 1530s because of his Erasmian views. He expressed a deep abhorrence of the use of coercion in religion, and condemned those 'who spare neither prison nor whip nor chains nor the axe; for such is the effect of these horrible means, that the torments they inflict on the body can never change the disposition of the soul'.

A print of 1571 from Strassburg by Tobias Stimmer showing the Emperor Maximilian II at the Diet of Speyer in 1570. Of all the Emperors of the Reformation era, the irenic Maximilian is the only one to have been seriously suspected of Lutheranism.

These quotations are nevertheless only flickerings in the darkness, and by their paucity emphasise the general triumph of intolerance in Catholic Spain.

In Catholic Germany, where the Habsburgs also ruled, a completely different approach was being adopted. The Emperor Ferdinand I initiated the policy of religious compromise which his successor Maximilian II brought to perfection. In June 1562 Ferdinand's envoys handed to representatives of the Council of Trent a so-called *libellum*, containing proposals for Church reform. The major part of the document dealt with reform of abuses, and asked for a moderate attitude to be adopted towards Protestants. Where Ferdinand's proposals alarmed Rome was in two demands which for him, as for other German Catholic princes such as Duke Albert of Bavaria, were fundamental: the granting of communion under both kinds (that is, both bread and wine), and permission for clerical marriage. Two years later the Pope eventually allowed the clergy of Germany to distribute communion under both kinds. This was the only success of Ferdinand, who died shortly after, in July 1564, his life having been spent in a sincere and tireless effort to promote reunion. 'Unite all Christians by the bond of peace, that the fear of God and mutual charity may flourish among us', went a prayer he composed and recited during the last weeks of his life.

His son Maximilian II was equally devoted to unity. Unfortunately, his Catholicism was so superficial that he was suspected of being, and distrusted as, a Lutheran. Whatever the truth, his vacillation in religious matters led to the beneficial and positive profession of the principles of tolerance. In his proprietary lands in Austria he allowed the Protestant nobility complete and statutory toleration, thereby becoming the first German, or Catholic, prince to practise civil tolerance in defiance of the terms of the Peace of Augsburg.

This concession is notable in three respects. It was a Catholic prince who had put it into effect, just as it was subsequently to be Catholic princes and countries that generally led the way in

Eighteen months after Rudolf II had in July 1609 reluctantly granted
toleration to the Bohemian Estates, his cousin Archduke Leopold invaded
Prague, probably with the Emperor's connivance, but was defeated by the Estates –
the corporate oath of the two armies is seen here. The Estates then deposed
Rudolf in favour of his brother Matthias. The events of 1609–12 in Prague show
the political pressure exerted by influential groups who demanded toleration.

establishing civil toleration. Secondly, the measure was taken on
principle, but it also very significantly assured the political loyalty
of a section of the nobility professing a different religion, so that
in this as in subsequent measures of toleration we must admit
that political commonsense helped to dictate policy. Thirdly, the
toleration granted to the aristocracy was intended to apply to them
personally and not to the population as a whole. This was also to
be the policy in Poland, and led to the ironical result that depend-
ants of the nobles might feel obliged to desert their Catholic
religion for the sake of their masters, whereas a more universal
toleration would have assured each individual the right to his
own religion and so have protected the Catholic lower classes.

The tolerant policy of Maximilian was becoming increasingly
out of date in the fierce world of the Counter-Reformation. The
intrusion of militant Calvinism into the Empire and its adoption
by one prince after another led to an expansion of the religious
conflict into one between three Churches rather than two as of old.
In state after state the ruler – whether Catholic, Lutheran or
Calvinist – began to enforce religious uniformity according to the
strict interpretation of the Peace of Augsburg. In only two parts
of the Empire were the principles of toleration extended – Brandenburg and Bohemia. Everywhere else the political tension in Germany led to uncompromising intolerance.

In Imperial Bohemia the Hussite revolution had destroyed the
power of the old Catholic Church. Despite some recovery of
property and authority, the Church in the sixteenth century was
still a minority religion. The Emperor Rudolf's efforts to reinforce
Catholicism in his hereditary lands were vitiated by political
rivalry between himself and his brother the Archduke Matthias.
Profiting from this situation, the Bohemian Estates met at Prague
in 1608 and demanded guarantees for the Bohemian Brethren and
Lutherans. The following year the Bohemian Diet met and
induced Rudolf to sign a compromise known as the Letter of
Majesty. By this the Emperor agreed to recognise the Bohemian
Confession which his predecessor Maximilian had recognised in

1575. At the same time the Protestant and Catholic deputies to the Diet signed an agreement by which they guaranteed each other full liberty of worship, and conceded that both faiths should enjoy full freedom on Crown lands. Together, all these written guarantees established for the first time substantial religious liberty in a European country. Even the rights of individuals were theoretically recognised, for peasants and tenants were not obliged to follow the religion of their lord, as they were elsewhere in Germany by the *cuius regio* terms of the Peace of Augsburg. Unhappily the Bohemian solution was short-lived. The increase of German

This contemporary relief from a Roman church shows the Pope investing the Duke of Cleves in 1572. Cleves and Jülich became, at the opening of the seventeenth century, the scene of a short-lived exercise in religious toleration on political grounds.

influence; rivalry among the nobility and even among the Protestants; the immense resources of the Catholic minority, who could always rely on Imperial support; were among the factors undermining political stability. When a disgruntled clique of Protestant nobles attempted to reclaim their rights by launching a coup in 1618, they precipitated a conflict that sparked off a European war.

Decline of toleration in the Empire

In Brandenburg events were less remarkable. John Sigismund, Elector of Brandenburg from 1608–19, was converted from Lutheranism to Calvinism in 1613 and attempted to enforce his new faith on his territories, according to his clear rights. Faced, however, by the opposition of the Estates of Brandenburg in what was an overwhelmingly Lutheran country, John Sigismund was obliged to compromise, and in 1615 guaranteed freedom of worship to the Lutherans. Other political reasons also forced the ruler of Brandenburg to make civil toleration a cornerstone of his government, without ever subscribing to the actual principle of tolerance. When in 1611 the king of Poland had granted Brandenburg the duchy of Prussia in fief, one of the conditions of the new territorial accession was that Catholics in the duchy should have complete religious and civil liberty and equality. With possessions stretching across all northern Europe from the Rhine to the Niemen, Brandenburg acquired commitments that cut through confessional affiliations. An example of how this situation might promote religious toleration is given in the dispute over the Cleves–Jülich succession.

The Rhine duchies of Cleves, Mark, Jülich, and Berg were united under one head in 1521 and remained so until the last duke died without a male heir in 1609, after which the duchies were by international treaty and after several political crises divided among different claimants. Although the dukes of the territory remained Catholic after 1521, the individual duchies, situated on the Rhine and consequently exposed to the varying cross-currents of the

Reformation period, became bitterly divided in point of religion. The religious conflict seriously impaired both the political stability and the economic prosperity of the region. In June 1609 the two chief claimants to the succession, the rulers of Brandenburg and Neuburg, signed the Treaty of Dortmund, by which they agreed to administer the duchy jointly till a solution was reached. The Treaty guaranteed freedom of religion for both Catholics and Lutherans, and also, by an important concession, for Calvinists. This was probably the first occasion that Calvinism, not officially recognised in the Peace of Augsburg, was solemnly guaranteed equality with the other religions in a German treaty. When Cleves–Jülich was officially partitioned by the Treaty of Xanten in 1614, the guarantees of religious freedom were reinforced for both sections of the duchy. The settlement did not last long. John Sigismund, tolerant as he had to be of the Catholic majority in Prussia, was intolerant of the Catholic minority in his new acquisitions of Cleves and Mark. In Jülich and Berg Protestants were likewise persecuted. The later history of the duchies is one of confusion, repression and intolerance.

Nowhere in the Empire at the beginning of the seventeenth century was toleration established in principle, with the possible exception of Bohemia (up to 1620) and the Brandenburg territories, where some limited freedom was granted for political reasons only. In the age of the Counter-Reformation, the doctrines of peace and compromise had all but vanished. It was not simply a war between Catholic and Protestant. The venomous diatribes exchanged between Calvinists and Lutherans up to the outbreak of the Thirty Years War are unsurpassed in their bitterness. To a very large extent this bitterness centred on the Rhine Palatinate, where the dynamically Calvinist regime had set itself up as a centre of international propaganda and subversion, and had taken the lead in the militant Protestant policies that disrupted the peace of the Empire and led eventually to war.

The bitter military struggles of the sixteenth and seventeenth centuries left little room for irenic discussions in Europe. Catholics and Protestants moved farther apart in their aims and methods, and the latter found it expedient to group together as the menace of Catholic absolutism loomed larger in the shape of the Habsburg monarchy. The advent of the Thirty Years War, and the gradual realisation among Lutherans and Calvinists that their common political interests overrode sectarian prejudice, awoke a new irenicism, principally among Protestants. On the Catholic side the methods of intolerance were everywhere sanctioned by theologians, with two important modifications. In the first place, as we shall see when we come to examine Poland and France, civil toleration was expressly guaranteed by two of the leading Catholic nations of Europe. In the second place, the charitable moderation preached by many individual Catholics, of whom Saint Francis de Sales is one of the most prominent, is evidence of the new and growing belief that more flies could be caught with honey than with vinegar.

Two seventeenth-century humanists

Although Protestant irenicism was often rigidly intolerant of Catholicism and of non-Christian religions, it made the greatest advances in the seventeenth century to understanding among the reformed churches, and should consequently be noted here. Characteristically a tolerant irenicism was not displayed by convinced adherents of either of the major Protestant Churches, save when exclusively political considerations dictated it, and it was left to an Independent Protestant – Oliver Cromwell – to make the first real effort to promote evangelical reunion in Europe. Among the most distinguished exponents of religious peace in the early seventeenth century was Jan Komenský (1592–1670), better known as Comenius. A refugee from his native Bohemia after Habsburg troops had defeated Bohemian nationalism at the battle of the White Mountain in 1620, Comenius spent the rest of his life in various European countries, expounding his theories on education and working hopefully for a reunion of the Protestant sects. His classic *Labyrinth of the World* (1623, published 1631) is notable not only for its concern about religious disunity but also for its almost total absence of hatred for his Catholic persecutors. In the *Labyrinth*, the author is conducted by a guide who points out the various Christian sects, and to his question, 'Do all agree as to their faith?' answers 'There is indeed some difference; but all have the same foundation'. The author was indignant that despite this common foundation the different sects (described as 'chapels') continued to differ:

> Some foolish ones took up at random any doctrine that came in their way; others more cunningly entered or left the divers chapels according to what appeared to them advantageous . . . I was displeased by the confusion and wavering among these dear Christians.

The rest of his life consisted in an attempt to right this confusion by promoting a unity which he considered would be universal among all Christians, including no doubt Catholics, though he seems never to have made a serious attempt to approach the Catholic position, so that his writings should more properly be taken to refer only to Protestant reunion.

A slightly older contemporary of Comenius, and like him a refugee from persecution in his native land, was Hugo Grotius (1583–1645). Narrowly escaping death in 1619 at the hands of the anti-Arminian party in Holland, whose controversies we shall outline in a later chapter, Grotius spent the rest of his life as an honourable guest of several European States. Repelled by the exclusivism of predestinarian Calvinism, Grotius sought in all the Christian Churches some common principles and heritage which would lead to unity and toleration. His initial efforts met with encouragement in France and England, and for a time in 1635 he cooperated with John Dury (1596–1680), the energetic advocate of Protestant reunion and colleague of Samuel Hartlib. At this period, when Dury's declared aim was unity for 'the great advancement of the Gospell, and preservation of it from the incroachments of Popish superstition', Grotius' interests did not really

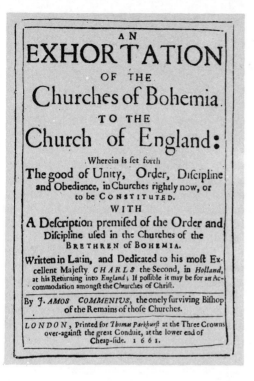

A N

EXHORTATION

OF THE

Churches of Bohemia

TO THE

Church of England:

Wherein is set forth

The good of Unity, Order, Discipline and Obedience, in Churches rightly now, or to be Constituted.

WITH

A Description premised of the Order and Discipline used in the Churches of the Brethren of Bohemia.

Written in Latin, and Dedicated to his most Excellent Majesty *CHARLS* the Second, in *Holland*, at his Returning into *England*; If possible it may be for an Accommodation amongst the Churches of Christ.

By *J. AMOS COMMENIUS*, the onely surviving Bishop of the Remains of those Churches.

LONDON, Printed for *Thomas Parkhurst* at the Three Crowns over-against the great Conduit, at the lower end of Cheap-side. 1 6 6 1.

After his escape from Bohemia in 1621, Jan Comenius, the famous educationalist and minister of the Moravian Brethren, became an ardent advocate of 'an Accommodation amongst the Churches of Christ', as shown by this irenic appeal to his Anglican friends, whose country he visited in 1641.

embrace reunion with Rome. Gradually, however, he came to realise that the largest Christian Church called for special consideration. By 1641, in his *Annotata ad Consultationem Cassandri*, which took the form of a commentary on Cassander's famous work, Grotius had come to a position hardly distinguishable from that held by the subject of his annotations. Papal leadership he came to accept as necessary: 'Protestants can only be united among themselves', he wrote, 'if they join up all together with those who are linked with the See of Rome, that See without which there is no hope of any common government in the Church'. In accepting the traditions of the early Church, he had come to accept the dogmatic structure of Catholicism, although he never actually joined the Church. At the same time, he continued firmly to reject the use of extreme penalties against heresy, and took his stand for toleration on the parable of the tares.

Comenius and Grotius are distinguished examples of the impulse to unity in the spirit of tolerance. For this reason they should be considered in a category apart from ecumenical workers like John Dury, who, despite his work for reunion, constantly displayed illiberality not only to Catholics but also to fellow Protestants. As late as 1652, when Dury and his colleagues presented the English Parliament with a list of fifteen fundamental articles meant as the basis for Christian union, the wording was so designed as to exclude all Anglicans, Catholics, Quakers and Unitarians.

By the end of the seventeenth century it is no longer possible to consider irenicism – in the sense of charitable dogmatic compromise – as a moving force in the growth of toleration. While official Catholicism remains in adamant opposition to religious liberty, official Protestantism is everywhere losing ground to, on one hand, a spiritualising and subjective pietism, and, on the other, a philosophic and rational indifferentism. The threads of this development we shall resume later in our narrative.

5 Social classes and toleration

The great spark that ignited the Reformation came from Luther's intensely individual concept of justification. But long before Luther there had been revolutionary tinder in Europe. The assertion of God's saving power and man's powerless sinfulness, a doctrine rather than a revolt against organisational abuses, lay at the core of Luther's programme and was responsible for its success. Among his followers, however, there were those for whom the personal doctrine of salvation was only a step towards a radically new orientation of religion. In the person of Müntzer, whom we have already encountered, the illuminist circle known as the 'prophets of Zwickau' found a spokesman who began to reinterpret Luther along increasingly revolutionary and visionary lines. Disowned by Luther, fleeing from Zwickau to Prague and then to Allstedt in Saxony, Müntzer and his colleagues preached a violent and apocalyptic form of Anabaptism. In his celebrated sermon before the leading officials of Saxony in 1524, Müntzer warned the German princes that their duty was to exterminate all godless unbelievers, but that if they refused to take up the sword and identify themselves with the people of God, the sword would pass from them to the people. At this point the German Reformation, in the person of Müntzer, for the first time makes contact with the cause of the common people. The long struggle of the peasant classes in Germany coincided with the revolutionary tenets of the apocalyptic Anabaptists, and the social and religious upheavals complemented each other.

The importance of these converging movements is amply illustrated by the coincidence, particularly during the Reformation period, of the cause of the common people and that of toleration. Intolerance was a weapon entrusted almost exclusively to those who wielded power, the ruling circles and nobility, and where liberty was granted it was inevitably restricted to the upper classes of society. Only with the growth of democratic movements – whether religious or secular – do we get any progress towards the attainment of a universal toleration, so that freedom in both is interconnected. This was nevertheless slow in developing, particularly since the identification of Anabaptists with both the Peasant War and Münster discredited civil toleration of those who were religiously radical.

The identification, if there is any, between popular movements and heterodox theology, is not directly relevant here. Certainly the political and social promise of Protestant theology may have contributed to the emancipation of individualism and to a new social ethic. What we are concerned with, however, is the narrower issue of how far intolerance reflected class divisions, and how far anxiety for social stability influenced the intensity of persecution. One cannot fail to be struck by the humble origins of the vast majority of early Protestant martyrs. To deduce from this that Protestantism was largely a lower-class movement would clearly be absurd. Yet the fact remains that victims were chosen from virtually only one class. Figures available in the Paris region for those who fell victim to the Chambre Ardente, the State Inquisition set up in 1548 by the French government under Henry II, show that they were virtually all of plebeian origin, with few or no nobles, some few functionaries, several priests and a great many monks and artisans. Yet the backbone of support for the Huguenots came from the bourgeoisie, and, later, the nobility, rather than from the artisans and labourers. The Paris figures are indicative of a general trend in persecution: some prominent individuals were sacrificed as an example, but most martyrs were drawn from the common people. The Anabaptists, who were drawn largely from humbler callings, were particularly vulnerable to this technique.

The Peasant War

Despite class origins that were often the same, the aims of religious sectarianism and the programme of social revolt were essentially different. The social rebels shared in much of the nihilism of the religious revolutionaries, but they looked farther. For this reason it is unwise to emphasise too closely the identity between the

Anabaptists and the peasants in revolt. The practice of rebaptism was adopted by some of the rebels only after the outbreak of the main rising, and the practical demands of the peasantry went well beyond the visionary aspirations of the Anabaptists. For all that, the religious ideals of Müntzer and his comrade Henry Pfeiffer provided the evangelical and crusading spark to light a social conflagration.

Religion played a cardinal role. In Skåne, in Danish Sweden, the year 1525 witnessed a peasant revolt comparable in its origins and extent to the German one of the same year, but as in Germany it was ruthlessly crushed by nobles who were themselves anti-clerical. The 1517 programme of the German Bundschuh, the peasants' rebel organisation, was patently influenced by Hussite ideals and anticlericalism, and to this extent could be identified with religious heterodoxy. Similarly the moderate Twelve Articles of the Swabian peasants in March 1525 based themselves expressly on the Word of God, each article being copiously justified by Biblical citations, and could have attracted the support of the Reformation. Social and religious factors complemented each other in the articles. Every congregation, they demanded, should have the right to dismiss its own pastor. Tithes were to be limited to grain and produce and not to include livestock and dairy produce. Serfdom should be abolished, 'seeing that Christ has redeemed and ransomed us all by his precious blood, the lowest as well as the highest, without exception'. The eleventh article demanded an end to the death penalty often exacted by lords, and the twelfth submitted all the articles to the test of Holy Scripture. The document ended with the words, 'The peace of Christ be with us all', and the peasants' Union agreed upon in May decided not to resort to force. Since, however, the only way for the articles to be put into effect was through force, the peasants took up arms and the princes retaliated in kind. At Frankenhausen in May 1525 Philip of Hesse annihilated the main body of the revolt. We have, as Engels points out, the spectacle of the so-called tolerant Landgrave resorting to social intolerance on a vast scale.

The massed but ill-disciplined hordes of rebellious peasants are strikingly depicted in this contemporary illustration. At the battle of Frankenhausen in 1525 an estimated 600 peasants were captured and 5,000 massacred by troops under Philip of Hesse. The peasants' uprising was a vast movement which was not confined to Germany alone. Anabaptist inspiration was predominant among the leaders of the movement.

The victors of the revolt were the princes. The peasants lost all chance of their case being heard, Luther by his immoderate language lost support among the rural masses, and the Anabaptists by their identification with Hubmaier and Müntzer lost all hope of toleration. Just as the failure of the colloquies led to the initiative for a religious settlement falling into the hands of the secular princes, so the failure of social protest led to greater reliance on the nobles as guardians of the political order. It became accepted, and was reinforced by the Lutheran attitude to

A drummer and ensign on the rebel side
during the 1525 Peasant War.
From a contemporary engraving by Beham.

political authority, that the will of the prince alone should prevail.
In practice as well as in theory the peacemakers were driven to
accept the rights of the princes, the noble class, and the Reformation State. The religious liberties of the population were subordinated to the religious whims of their rulers, and when, as in
the Palatinate, the princes alternated between Lutheranism and
Calvinism and arbitrarily decreed changes of religion throughout
the principality, it became obvious that toleration had become
a political convenience available only to the ruler.

Persecution in England and central Europe

This trend was most marked in countries where the Reformation was brought about politically by the King's *fiat*. Of these the most prominent was England, where prosecution of heresy displayed a continuous pattern of class repression. The heretics of the sixteenth century were principally working-class people, and had their origins notably in the clothworkers' trade, among the independent artisans who continued the Lollard (Wycliffite) tradition of protest. Between 1527 and 1532 the inquisitions around London collected 218 heretics, most of them from the cloth industry. Urban heretics, however, were of less concern to the government than religious and social dissidents in agricultural areas. The identification of peasant risings with religious radicalism was taken for granted by ministers who were already conversant with events on the continent in 1525, and people like Cranmer, who had spent several months in Germany, were careful to point out the dangers of tolerating sedition. The notes for a sermon he preached in London in July 1549 against the western pro-Catholic rising, contains precisely the same doctrine as was now accepted in the Empire, namely that only the prince has rights in matters of religion: 'In Germany for their sedition were slain almost in one month about two hundred thousand . . . Though the magistrates be evil, and very tyrants against the commonwealth, and enemies to Christ's religion; yet the subjects must obey in all worldly things, as the Christians do under the Turk'. Certainly the archbishop does not say explicitly that subjects must also adopt the religion of the magistrate, but this was effectively implied in his rebuke to the Catholic Cornishmen. The religion of the State was the official one, and dissidents whether of the left or the right, whether Anabaptist or Catholic, must conform or be punished, as occurred under Henry VIII.

The reign of Edward VI began in 1547 with a respite after the persecutions of his father. Lord Protector Somerset, a political and religious moderate, attempted to restore civil concord to the country by enforcing a truce on religious controversy. Although personally inclined to Protestantism, he considered peaceful methods more conducive to success. Under his regime only two people, neither a Catholic, were sentenced to death for heresy. Some influence may have been exercised on him by his chaplain and physician William Turner, a hater of Papists but a hater also of the use of coercion, even against Anabaptists. Writing in 1551 against Anabaptism, Turner affirmed that 'it were most meet that we should fight with the sword of God's word and with a spiritual fire against it, or else we are like to profit but a little in our business'. (Unhappily he later became a steadfast supporter of coercion in religious matters). Somerset was at the same time attempting to pursue a conservative agrarian and social policy, and in 1548 he instituted a Royal Commission to take measures against the enclosure of land by the gentry. Among the landed classes this dual policy against persecution and against enclosures appeared to threaten social stability. When the Protector's efforts blew up with a peasant revolt in 1549, the lords on the Council of State issued a proclamation against him, claiming that he had incited the people to rise against the nobility and gentry of England. Somerset in reply issued an appeal to the people to protect him and the king against those who had always oppressed the commons. Both Catholics and Protestants combined to overthrow him. The Earl of Warwick, who had suppressed Kett's agrarian revolt in Norfolk with unsurpassed ferocity, assumed leadership and signalled the end of Somerset's era of toleration by sending Joan Bocher to the stake in 1550 for denying the Incarnation, and George van Paris in 1551 as an Anabaptist.

Under Mary Tudor the repression reached its peak. During her brief reign of five years 273 people were burnt for heresy. Of the ninety or so whose occupations are known, almost eighty can be classified as tradesmen or artisans, principally weavers, fullers, tailors, labourers and the like. Generalising from this, it seems likely that most of the Marian victims were from the labouring class. The incredible feature of this situation is that almost a generation had passed since Henry viii's Reformation, and that

prominent sections of the gentry and clergy had participated in the heresy of that period; yet apart from a few prelates the only people to be victimised were members of the social class who had least understood the consequences of their heresy. As on the continent, however, pleas for toleration from this social stratum were unlikely to be accepted so long as sectarian heresy lacked adherents in high places.

In eastern Europe social and religious issues were even more closely intertwined than in the rest of the continent. The Hussite movement of the fifteenth century in the Czech lands provided the inspiration for post-Reformation radicals. The founder of the Hussite Unity of (Bohemian) Brethren, Chelčický, had taught the complete separation of Church and State, the licitness of conscientious disobedience, the immorality of the temporal wealth of the Church, the wrongfulness of the death penalty and torture, and the evil of war. A doctrine of this sort obviously contained the necessary basis for the practice of toleration. The example of the

Foxe's *Book of Martyrs*, from which this print
showing the martyrdom of seven Protestants is taken,
established its author as an opponent of religious
tyranny, particularly that of the Catholic Mary
Tudor. Foxe's countrymen omitted to note that he
also hated persecution when exercised by Protestants.

Unity was followed after the Peasant War by large groups of
Anabaptists who withdrew to Moravia and there set up a community called the Moravian Brethren. They adopted a rigorous
communistic way of life and favoured a form of pacifism which
was almost indistinguishable from anarchism. Many of their
members carried wooden swords as a sign of their total rejection
of methods of coercion. The most eminent of their leaders was
Hubmaier who, despite his active role in the Peasant War, was a
firm opponent of persecution. As we have seen above, he believed
that heretics should be won over by spiritual means only.
There is no contradiction between Hubmaier's resort to force in
the struggle for social justice, and his thorough toleration in religious matters. For him the separation of Church and State was
absolute, so that while force must be employed to repress crime
in civil affairs, in the field of religion it cannot be employed without
endangering the voluntary character of faith. From the foregoing
it will be seen that Hubmaier was not as extreme a pacifist as some
of his colleagues, whose social nihilism made them withdraw from
any participation in secular affairs.

The establishment of toleration in Poland

The whole tradition of political life in Bohemia and Moravia had
been anti-German. The Hussite programme in the fifteenth century
had become a national one very largely because of this hostility
to the advance of German domination. Like Bohemia, Poland was
part and parcel of the German frontier, and the anti-German
sentiment of the Poles made them receptive to the extension of
Hussite influence. By 1557 the Unity of Brethren had about thirty
churches established in Great Poland. The Reformation, in so far
as it destroyed the old structure of German power, also advanced
towards the east. In 1525 the secularisation of the Teutonic Order
gave the Lutherans their first large extension of territory. But by
1540 Calvinism had begun to supplant Lutheranism among the
noble and gentry class, the *szlachta*, who took the lead in furthering

the Reformation. The peculiar constitutional structure of Poland, where the monarchy was elective, gave the aristocracy considerable autonomy. This they exploited to the full. From 1552 to 1565 the Protestant nobility dominated the Diets and brought about the repeal of all punitive edicts against heresy, so that thanks to their efforts religious liberty was speedily established in Poland. The attitude of the two kings Sigismund was particularly helpful to the Protestants. When Sigismund I was implored by Johann Eck in 1526 to follow the example of the King of England and take a stand against Luther, he replied, 'Let King Henry write against Luther, but allow me to be the king of sheep as well as goats'. His successor Sigismund II Augustus (1548–72), who had a Calvinist queen, was even less inclined to be the Catholic champion. When asked by the Pope to exterminate heretics, he replied: 'I fear that in trying to pull up the tares I might uproot the wheat also'. And at a Diet in 1569 he declared, 'Let no one think that I shall ever use force to bring someone to the faith or that I ever force anyone's conscience'. After the brief rule of Henry of Anjou the throne was given to an inflexible Catholic, the great Stephen Báthory (1576–86). Though he was committed by oath to tolerate all religions, according to the terms of the Confederation of Warsaw, Báthory was in fact a sincerely tolerant ruler. His famous saying, 'I am king over peoples, not over consciences', is on a par with his declaration in the 1581 Edict of Pskov that 'we do indeed desire with all our heart that all citizens and inhabitants of our kingdom, whatever class they belong to, adore the one true God and profess the one and ancient Catholic faith. But as God forewarned us that at the end of the world there would inevitably arise scandals and heresies, we want none to be compelled to accept the faith'. Throughout most of the sixteenth century, therefore, and for the first half of the seventeenth century under Báthory's successors, religious liberty was protected in Poland. Much of the credit for this belongs to the Protestant nobility.

The consolidation of *szlachta* power on the land and in the State is a predominant feature of the late fifteenth century in Poland.

Their consequent struggle against ecclesiastical privileges and land-holding was a decisive factor in the success of the Reformation. As one historian puts it, 'the Polish religious reformation was a class movement. It was accepted, adhered to, and championed by the upper classes of Polish society; in the cities by the commercial population, and throughout the country by the nobility, the large magnates and the well-to-do gentry'. Both Lutherans and Calvinists found their principal support among the upper classes. In 1570, by the Union of Sandomir, these two sects joined the Bohemian Brethren to make common cause and defend Protestant interests. Profiting by the troubles after the death of Sigismund Augustus, they managed to gain the acceptance of all parties, including Catholics, to a pact of Confederation at Warsaw in 1573. Of the 98 signatories of the Confederation, 41 were Catholics. The operative clause on religious liberty stated that the

dissidentes de religione bind ourselves for our own sake and that of our posterity in perpetuity, on our oath, faith, honour and conscience, to keep the peace among ourselves on the subject of difference of religion and the changes brought about in our churches; we bind ourselves not to shed blood; not to punish one another by confiscation of goods, loss of honour, imprisonment or exile; not to give any assistance on this point in any way to any authority or official, but on the contrary to unite ourselves against anyone who would shed blood for this reason.

This famous agreement consolidated the gains of religious toleration for nearly a century, and overshadowed in importance any earlier agreements of mutual tolerance, as had for example been made in 1564 between Lutherans and Calvinists in Transylvania or in 1568 in the Austrian possessions of the Emperor Maximilian II. Thanks to the Confederation, whose terms the kings of Poland had subsequently to swear to at their accession, political and religious toleration was assured, and Poland – Catholic Poland – became the first great European country to recognise religious liberty in its constitution.

It must be emphasised, however, that as in previous attempts at toleration, the interests of the nobility alone were guaranteed by the Confederation. A subsidiary clause of the Confederation professed not to derogate from the authority of the lords over their dependents, and this, when interpreted to give Protestant nobles a free hand over their largely Catholic peasantry, meant an intensification of persecution among the lower classes. One other weak point in the Confederation is of importance. Being an agreement among Trinitarian Christians, it was gradually interpreted so as to exclude anti-Trinitarians from its operation, so that members of this last sect were in time subjected to the intolerance of both Catholics and orthodox Protestants. Finally, the Confederation at no time gave explicit formulation to any principle of religious liberty, so that at best it was only a truce between contending parties, and crumbled in the late seventeenth century before the onset of triumphant Catholicism.

Long before the Confederation, Poland had witnessed a concrete expression of tolerance in the doctrines of an anti-Trinitarian group which had sprung up within the Calvinist Reformed Church. In 1565 this group broke away from the parent body and formed the Minor Reformed Church, known generally as the Polish Brethren or, more simply, as Arians. The social composition of the Minor Church seems in particular to have disturbed orthodox Protestants. The Arian leader, Peter Gonesius, advocated pacifist and communist doctrines, and had adopted the Anabaptist usage of wearing a wooden sword to signify opposition to violence. 'They deny any authority to magistrates, extol Christian freedom, and introduce community of all property; they abolish also all distinction of classes in Church and State, so that there may be none between king and people, between rulers and subjects, between the nobility and commoners', reported one horrified official in 1567. The fear had some basis. The greater Protestant Churches were aristocratic in membership and attitude, whereas the Arians, particularly at their chief centres in Kraków and Lublin, were democratic. In 1569 the radicals founded a new town called Raków, which in time became their religious capital. Raków was despised by the upper classes. One noble wrote, 'The very scum of humanity are joining this sect, but few of the nobles and so far as I know none of the magnates'. Nobles were certainly members, and there were those like Jan Przypkowski who in 1572 gave up his lands, freed his serfs and joined the sect to work the soil himself. The difference between Raków and the Protestant Churches was that in this haven of refuge and centre of communal democracy, class counted for little, and all were respected. A Scottish visitor, passing through in 1612, reported that 'whereas elsewhere all was full of wars and tumult, there all was quiet'. The basis of concord in the community was tolerance, and for this the Minor Church owed much to Faustus Socinus.

Faustus Socinus and his followers

Socinus, who made his way to Poland in 1579 and died there in 1604, was the most prominent friend and supporter of the Arians, though he was never actually accepted into membership of the Minor Church. It was his teaching that became the basis of the so-called Rakovian Catechism, the Unitarian confession of faith drawn up in Polish in 1605 and in Latin in 1609.

Socinus held an essentially positive and not negative doctrine of toleration. Writing to a friend in 1584 he said, 'I do not condemn the other Churches and in no way despise them, for I recognise as true Churches of Christ all those in which is heard the voice of the teaching of Our Lord Jesus Christ'. Going further than this, Socinus granted that the true doctrine of salvation could be discovered by reason in most Churches or even, perhaps, without resorting to a Church. The truth was for him not a body of dogma given once for all: it was arrived at through a range of development, through direct and continuous revelation. As Luther had corrected the old Church so others had corrected Luther, and still others would in time correct these, until the final truth was eventually brought to light. To this undogmatic attitude Socinus added a stern pacifism which rejected completely all resort to force, above all in religion. The sword was not Christian,

CATECHESIS
Ecclesiarum

Quæ in Regno Poloniae, & magno Ducatu Lithuaniæ, & aliis ad istud Regnum pertinentibus provinciis, affirmant, neminem alium, præter Patrem Domini nostri Iesu Christi, esse illum unum Deum Israëlis : hominem autem illum Iesum Nazarenum, qui ex virgine datus est, nec alium, præter aut ante ipsum, Dei Filium unigenitum & agnoscunt & confitentur.

Ante annos quatuor Polonicè, nunc verò etiam Latinè edita.

Ose. 14. ult.
Rectæ sunt viæ Iehovæ, & justi ambulabunt in eis: prævaricatores verò corruent in eis.

Racoviae,
Anno Domini, 1609.

Title page to the first Latin edition of the Rakovian Catechism, the original edition of 1605 being in Polish. The town of Raków, capital of the Socinian community in Poland, was eventually destroyed by intolerant officials in 1638.

therefore under no circumstances could a Christian resort to it. Capital punishment, particularly for crimes against property such as theft, was illegitimate, and Christians must never take life. The pacifism of the Arians was later modified after extensive discussions, and many members condescended to fight in the royal forces in the early seventeenth century, in an effort to discountenance charges of lack of patriotism. But the opposition to violence in matters of religion still remained.

In 1605 the Socinians issued their first great confession of faith, the Rakovian Catechism. The preface to the 1665 edition of this document guaranteed complete toleration and religious freedom on principle, and constitutes a landmark in the evolution of liberty in matters of faith:

In composing this Catechism we give no orders to anyone. In expressing our opinion, we oppress nobody. Let everyone be free to express his judgment in religious matters, provided we too be allowed to express our opinion on divine things without injury or insult ... In so far as we are concerned, we are all brothers, and no power, no authority has been given us over the conscience of others. Although among brothers some are more learned than others, all are equal in freedom and in the right to affiliation.

The importance of the Catechism is limited by the fact that the group expressing these sentiments was a very small minority in a divided country. Raków, moreover, did not have an entirely successful history. A prey to the hostility of Catholics as well as Protestants, the town was destroyed in 1638 by a recrudescence of intolerance on the part of the authorities. A protest against the destruction order was signed by Arian leaders, as well as by several Calvinists, Catholics and Orthodox, but their liberal influence was restricted. Finally in 1658 the sect was banished from Poland by order of the Diet.

Among the earliest exiles was Samuel Przypkowski (1592–1670), who made his way to East Prussia. There he drew up his *Apologia afflictae innocentiae*, which pleaded for understanding and tolerance for his sect. Using a political argument of some force, he maintained that liberty of conscience was the basis of civil liberty, since respect for individual rights was at the root of the one and contributed to the other. Error cannot be put down by force but only by spiritual weapons. During his subsequent travels he published in Holland in 1628 his *De pace et concordia ecclesiae*, which based the practice of tolerance on absence of dogma. He subscribed, like other Socinians, to the belief that agreement on fundamentals of religion was alone necessary, and that in any case theological formulae were of less importance than the necessity of leading a good and moral life. This stress on moralism went beyond Socinus' original rejection of dogma. 'We must not', Przypkowski wrote, 'impose spiritual censures on anybody, for each of us has a right to his own individual evaluation ... We do not grant anyone the liberty to violate, in private or in public, the freedom of conscience, nor the liberty to propagate religion by force and violence'.

Among the other Socinian defenders of liberty was John Krell (1590–1633), whose *Vindiciae pro religionis libertate* went through many editions in several European languages. Krell was concerned to convince members of other faiths that their own principles often supported the case for toleration and that violence should not be used against heretics. Like Przypkowski, he stated that civil and

religious liberty were interdependent. Civil tolerance should rightfully be granted to all peaceful subjects, regardless of religion: 'All those who contribute to the existence of civil society and do not disturb the peace of others cannot in justice be excluded from civil society, and no one is in any way entitled to prevent them from living in peace'. Church and State are to be completely separate, and plurality of religions should be recognised as harmless, for religious ills in the past have come about largely through attempts to enforce unity rather than through the toleration of disunity.

The non-sectarian persuasions of Socinus and his followers are

Print from a Czech book of
1616 savagely attacking the Arians
and Socinians as the 'true
progeny of the Mahomedans'.

127

reflected in the work of Daniel Zwicker (1612–78), an anti-Trinitarian from Danzig who published at Amsterdam in 1658 his *Irenicum Irenicorum*. Zwicker claimed to be free of all loyalty to any particular sect:

> I am not a Lutheran nor a Calvinist nor a Remonstrant nor a Greek nor a Papist nor a Socinian nor a Mennonite nor a member of any of today's sects; but although I hold no communion with any of them, yet I desire that all and every one of them should, according to the divine truth of which alone I claim to be an adherent, be reformed both in teaching and in manner of living ... Until then I scorn no ecclesiastical body or sect of Christians; and I shall frequent them all to the extent that I find some good in each of them.

> I hold all the Christian sects of today, without any exceptions, to be Churches of Christ, in so far as they all believe equally in Christ and receive and confess Christ as the Son of God, their Head and their Lord.

The writings of Zwicker bear some affinity to those of Acontius; like the latter, he professed a kind of anti-Trinitarianism but at the same time recognised belief in Christ, the Son of God, as the one essential of all Christians.

The history of the Bohemian and Moravian Brethren, and of the Polish Arians, illustrates how the more radical doctrines of non-Catholic Christianity appealed to the humbler classes in society, and how the intolerance from which sectarians suffered was often as much social as political or religious in inspiration. But while it was the sectarians who led the way in formulating positive principles of religious liberty, the main credit for this should not be given to the fact that they were the primary victims of persecution. More important, without any doubt, is the consideration that their non-dogmatic theology reduced the number of articles on which Christians could conceivably differ. Secondary in importance is the factor that, thanks to their extreme distrust of the apparatus of the persecuting State, the sectarians at first rejected all participation in the machinery of civil government; this enabled them to live a religious life in a community where the coercion normally exercised by a magistrate was totally absent.

Sometimes, as had happened in past history, sects travelled down the dangerous road to that fanatical exclusivism which had been the mark of radicals through the ages. This danger was a real one in the case of the Anabaptist communities of central Europe, and led to some hard thinking among the Polish Arians when it was suggested in the 1560s that they should have closer relations with the Anabaptist Moravian Brethren. Both sects appeared to have much in common, since the latter also drew their support from the humbler classes, rejected State interference, and led a communistic life. The Moravians, however, were Trinitarians. In addition, those Arians who had visited them in order to examine their way of life found their discipline too rigorous and austere, their doctrines too opinionated and exclusivist, and their much vaunted communist regime in fact a patriarchal dictatorship where elementary freedoms were not observed. The Poles therefore returned home convinced that their own gentler regime was more Christian.

Not surprisingly, the Socinians contributed very little in practice to the extension of religious freedom. Even in Poland, their great historical home, they were no more than a small minority, and after their dispersion in 1658 they were active only as particles of leaven in the vast European loaf. Apart from Holland and England, the two countries where they exercised most influence, their importance was small. The significance of Poland as a pioneer in toleration therefore springs less from the principles of the Minor Church than from the Confederation of 1573 and the sober policy of the Catholic rulers of the sixteenth and seventeenth centuries.

6 Religious war and nationalism

We have so far been considering toleration as a product of Reformation heterodoxy and the acceptance of a division between Church and State. The radical and proletarian aspect of Protestantism played a leading part in this process. No less important a part was played by the development of aggressive Calvinism, for it was as a result of the armed conflict provoked in western Europe by the Reformed Church (as Calvinism was generally termed), that a moderate degree of religious liberty was forced on several countries by political necessity.

It is unnecessary to emphasise that the so-called religious wars of the late sixteenth and early seventeenth centuries were not merely or even primarily religious, and that they were caused partly by the emergence of factional interests and partly by the political problems inherent in the formation of a strong national State. In these quarrels religion was the essential and vital bond of unity, but often only a subordinate motive for action. Consequently, when settlements for civil peace were being discussed, they were placed in a political rather than a religious context. In France, Germany and the Netherlands, supporters of mutual toleration as the basis of peace began to argue from political necessity rather than from principle, and thereby shifted the debate about religious liberty on to more secular grounds. This development is probably best outlined by discussing each country in turn.

The religious conflict in France

The early Reformation movement in France was Lutheran in influence and Erasmian in personnel. Arising from an unease similar to that felt in Germany, it claimed among its earlier sympathisers such great humanists as Lefèvre d'Etaples and queen Marguerite of Navarre. In the 1520s the relative moderation of measures taken against Lutheranism can be attributed to Marguerite's influence. As in Germany, there remained a reformist Erasmian party, which included the brothers du Bellay and Guillaume Budé, proponents of a pacifist policy in the face of provocation from both right and left. Thanks to advisers like these, Francis I was willing to abstain from extreme measures of repression. The provocation by Lutherans in the affair of the Placards in 1534, when inflammatory anti-Catholic posters were set up in public, led to the beginning of open and bloody repression. On 29 January 1535 a decree ordering the extermination of heretics was issued. Five years later, on 1 June 1540, the Edict of Fontainebleau initiated the great period of persecution of Protestants, a persecution all the more reprehensible because jurisdiction over heresy was entrusted largely to the secular tribunals, the *parlements*. Among those who perished in these savage years were the unfortunate Vaudois of Provence: in the year 1545 alone they were proceeded against by armed forces, a thousand or more were massacred, and their houses destroyed.

Calvin was by now on the scene. In 1536 the first edition of his *Institution* was published at Basle. In 1544 his books were burnt by order of the Sorbonne. The year after that, the year of the Vaudois massacres, witnessed the opening of the Council of Trent. All the elements of a vigorous conflict were now present. Henry II, who succeeded Francis I in 1547, was determined not to tolerate the existence of heresy in Catholic France. The most extreme persecution was carried on, aided by the establishment in 1547 of the Chambre Ardente. Despite bloodshed, or because of it, the Reformation increased in strength, and Calvinism began to supplant Lutheranism not only among the lower classes, where Calvin's supporters had been and where the Chambre Ardente found most of its victims, but also among the highest nobility, the most eminent adherent being Antoine de Bourbon, king of Navarre. Almost imperceptibly, the Reform in France became a religion less of the common people, among whom it had been largely burnt out, than of the bourgeoisie and nobility, who alone were capable of granting it the protection it desperately needed. In 1559, the year after Bourbon's conversion, Francis II succeeded to the throne. With his accession the religious wars may be said to have begun.

The bloody conflicts of the next forty years were superficially religious in character, but the alignment of parties along dynastic lines, with the Bourbons and Châtillons on the Huguenot side and the Guises on the Catholic, made confessional allegiances progressively unreal. In particular, the difficult position of the Crown, which under the remarkable influence of the Queen Mother Catherine de Medici attempted to reach a satisfactory civil pacification that would not leave either dynastic party supreme, put the political aspect of the wars in the forefront of the picture. As early as the 1560s there also came into existence a so-called third party consisting of members of both religions who believed that the conflict between faiths was of less consequence than the danger to the State implicit in civil war: by placing political stability at the head of their programme, they earned the title of *politiques*.

Humanism in France: the Chancellor L'Hospital

In this setting the proponents of tolerance appear under various guises. For our purposes, they may be divided into two broad categories. Firstly, there are the heirs of Erasmian humanism who by and large preceded the civil wars. Secondly, there are the advocates of religious coexistence, the *politiques*.

Several of the French humanists developed away from orthodox Christianity. Lefèvre d'Étaples compromised himself with the Reformation, but Étienne Dolet, executed for heresy in 1546, in fact progressed beyond the Reformation towards a completely non-Christian attitude of mind. Rabelais, even more notably, had been, though falsely, suspected of atheism. Montaigne expressed himself in a rationalism that led to naturalism and tolerance, and his approach arouses suspicions about the religious basis of his beliefs; but he remained fundamentally Catholic in outlook. It is worth noting that he was aware of the issue as to whether a conscience in error deserves punishment: his comment on this was that 'our nature has saddled us with so much imperfection and weakness that many people think that we can hardly be blamed

Anti-clerical caricatures, attributed to Rabelais, from the *Songes Drôlatiques de Pantagruel* (1565). Rabelais, who was a priest and secretary to Joachim du Bellay, was one of the leading Catholic humanists to attack the abuses of the Church. The caricatures satirise the worldliness of priests and monks and the suppression and destruction of books.

for acting against our conscience; some base partly on this the opinion that capital punishment for heretics and unbelievers is to be condemned'. Other humanists of the period, particularly Catholics like Ronsard and Joachim du Bellay, were likewise convinced of the necessity to forego methods of violence if religious and civil peace was to be restored.

One unusual figure who deserves some mention is the humanist Guillaume Postel (1510–81), whose irenic endeavours consisted in attempting to discover the good in all religions, as the basis for a simplified and renovated Christianity. His outlook was thoroughly tolerant, relying explicitly on the belief that only God can judge error and that man cannot presume to judge innermost intentions. 'Let us excuse all our brethren', he was writing in the 1540s, 'above all those whom till this day we called heretics. Is it not our sins that have given them a pretext for their opinions?' Differences on unessentials should be left to the scrutiny of God, whose purpose

is at the end to enlighten every one, not just those from one faith 'but all and each one in particular, whether he be a Catholic, a heretic, a Jew, a pagan, or an Ishmaelite'. To arrive at this liberal position, however, Postel was obliged to adopt a very indifferent attitude to dogmatic truth, with the result that he was not surprisingly suspected by both Catholics and Protestants and was confined for a time by the Inquisition. In his later years he travelled in the Middle East and began to look favourably on Islam as being a religion which was not only tolerant of others but was also monotheistic and recognised the significance of Christ.

The most prominent of the defenders of toleration to emerge during the civil wars can be classified both as humanist and as a *politique*. Michel de L'Hospital (1503–73), Chancellor of France from 1560 to 1568, was a humanist of the Erasmian school and an uncompromising supporter of civil and religious peace. Non-dogmatic in religion, to the extent that his Catholicism has been, unjustifiably, called in doubt, L'Hospital was principally concerned with moral reform rather than with institutional change. His ideals were in perfect accord with the plans of Catherine de Medici, who was concerned above all to secure for her sons a secure Crown in a peaceful France. Among L'Hospital's earliest acts in office was an order, dated 1560, to governors and other local officials to keep the peace 'without proceeding by way of punishment against any of those suspected of heresy, but only against those who rise up in arms and create sedition'. The prosecution of heresy was therefore officially suspended, and this was confirmed by government edict in February 1561. In April 1561 L'Hospital issued an edict forbidding Frenchmen to abuse each other 'by the names of Papist, Huguenot or others like them; or to destroy crucifixes or images, break into temples, attach placards, pillage or sack houses, under the pretext of discovering illicit assemblies'.

The tenor of L'Hospital's tolerance may be gathered from some of his public speeches. Of these the most famous is his address to the Estates General which sat at Orleans from December 1560 to January 1561. In the course of this discourse he said:

The cause of God does not need to be defended with arms: *Mitte gladium tuum in vaginam*. Our religion was neither started, nor maintained nor preserved by force of arms ...

Hitherto we have acted like bad captains who assault their enemies' fort with all their forces, but leave their own quarters stripped and defenceless. We must in future clothe ourselves in virtue and good conduct, and then assault them with the weapons of charity, prayer, argument and the Word of God, which are the proper arms in such a battle ...

A good life, as the proverb says, is more persuasive than exhortations. The knife is of no use against the spirit, if not to destroy the soul together with the body ... Mildness is more beneficial than rigour. Let us get rid of these diabolical words, the names of parties, factions, rebellions: Lutherans, Huguenots, Papists; let us leave unchanged the name of Christian.

In August 1561, at the Estates held at Saint-Germain, L'Hospital again emphasised to the assembly that their task was not to discuss religious differences but to settle the kingdom:

Right. This striking contemporary portrait of Michel de L'Hospital by an unknown painter brings to life one of the greatest sixteenth-century exponents of religious coexistence. His efforts to win civil reconciliation, though unsuccessful, prepared the way for the eventual pacification achieved under Henry IV.

Below. Illustration of the meeting of the Estates General at Orleans in 1560–1. The Queen Mother, Catherine de Medici, is enthroned beside the young King Charles IX; on his right, beside his younger brother, is the King of Navarre. Sitting on the dais below King Charles is the Duc de Guise, with the Chancellor L'Hospital on his left.

The King does not wish you to enter into disputes about which opinion is the better, for there is no question here *de constituenda religione, sed de constituenda republica*; and it is possible for people to be *cives, qui non erunt christiani*, for even an excommunicate does not cease to be a citizen.

Towards the end of that year, in September, L'Hospital was called upon to pronounce the opening discourse at the famous Colloquy of Poissy. The Reformed leaders were present, under Beza; against them were arrayed the French hierarchy under the Cardinal of Lorraine, and other theologians including the General of the Society of Jesus. L'Hospital began by reminding both sides that they were agreed on fundamentals. Speaking of the Protestants, he pointed out that 'their only difference is that they wish to reform the Church along the lines of the early Church. Yet they still believe in God, in the Trinity, recognise Holy Scripture, and look for no other salvation than in Jesus Christ as God'. Finally, he arrived at one of his most important arguments. To try to crush the Protestants, he said, would be to endanger society, for 'the majority of the evangelicals are people of substance, and nobles, who, as everyone knows, serve as columns to uphold the king'. He went on:

The conclusion then is that while it seems for the best to proceed with mildness and put an end to the normal prosecutions, as much for the ease of conscience of the king's subjects as for the good of his service; there is need for a further and fuller settlement through a good council which will not set itself against the evangelicals but will have an eye only to avoiding rebellion and to preventing riots among the people, who are the sole cause of rebellions.

L'Hospital may justifiably be called a *politique*, but the term itself needs to be defined precisely. It could refer to those who, impelled only by secular and temporal motives, put the interests of the State above all else. Alternatively, it could refer to those who, despite their own religious convictions, felt that purely party interests must admit of compromise when they threatened the security and integrity of the State. On either count, a *politique* would tend to accept a greater emphasis on the power of the Crown, and would therefore support absolutism rather than anarchy. L'Hospital certainly moved in this direction; he approved, in J. W. Allen's words, 'of a national government without legal limitation to its powers: a government not independent of religion, for the king holds authority from God; still less indifferent to religious opinion, but seeing in the maintenance of peace, order and justice its essential function and owning a duty to secure as far as possible the welfare of all its subjects, irrespective of creed'. It was because of this belief in royal authority that L'Hospital worked conscientiously for eight years with Catherine de Medici, a woman who, if she was a *politique* at all, should be classified in our first category.

The tragedy of Saint Bartholomew

From the very beginning Catherine had accepted as the basis of her policy some sort of tolerant coexistence between the Catholics and Protestants, her aim being, however, not so much the preservation of civil peace as the maintenance of the authority of the Crown. The moderate Edict of Amboise (1560) initiated her policy, as did the appointment as Chancellor of L'Hospital. In September 1561 the famous Colloquy of Poissy took place between the two religions. This was Catherine's attempt at a national Council to achieve agreement. The colloquy broke up in failure after only four weeks. As in Germany, colloquies were inspired by humanists and destroyed by the rise of Calvinism. Thereafter the queen was obliged either to play off the parties against each other or to support one side alone; the third alternative, of granting some autonomy to the Protestant princes, would threaten the unity of France and the authority of the king. Unfortunately, the policy of conciliation to Protestants, now adopted by Catherine and encouraged by L'Hospital, led to the increase in power of the Reformed party. The edict of tolerance issued in January 1562 by Charles ix strengthened Protestantism and intensified the wars of religion. A year after this the government introduced a temporary pacification in the second Edict of Amboise (1563). This guaranteed liberty of conscience, but restricted the exercise of open worship to the principal families in the countryside. As had happened before in Germany, toleration in France accepted a class division and the lower classes were excluded from its enjoyment. By accepting compromise on such terms, the Reform and its aristocratic leaders began to lose the mass support which might have won them France. The Huguenots also lost Catherine's sympathy in 1567, when Condé rashly attempted to promote the Reformed cause by seizing the Queen Mother and her son Charles IX; Condé failed, and precipitated another war. From this time Catherine appears to have despaired of her policy of reconciliation and, despite momentary tolerance in the Edict of Saint-Germain (1570), she became steadily convinced that only destruction of the Protestant leaders would restore peace and protect the Crown. The inevitable result was the Massacre of Saint Bartholomew in 1572.

The bloody massacre of Protestants signalled the failure of Catherine's policy, and the initiative for a settlement thereupon passed to other hands. Pleas for tolerance had not been lacking, particularly on the Catholic side. Prelates as eminent as Charles de Marillac, archbishop of Vienne, in 1560 warned the Royal Council that only extremists profited from religious divisions, and that timely reforms and the calling of a national council were necessary in order to restore peace and unity. Jean de Montluc, bishop of Valence, claimed that persecution only aggravated and did not cure the situation. After the Estates General held at Orleans in 1560–1 the abbot of Bois-Aubry spoke up in favour of tolerating two religions in one kingdom, not indeed for the reason adduced by *politiques*, namely to preserve peace in the State, but for the humanist reason of respect for conscience: 'There is no sense in wanting to use force in matters of conscience and religion, because conscience is like the palm of the hand, the more it is pressed, the more it resists'. Adopting a frankly tolerant position, the abbot went on to say that 'it is better that a man be a Christian in one way or other, good or bad, than that he become an atheist, that is to say, a man without God, without religion and without conscience'. This discourse is extremely modern in its premises and argument, and reflects honour on those members of the French Church who felt that ethical grounds, even more than political, demanded the practice of tolerance as a prerequisite to order in the State.

On the Protestant side a few voices were raised in favour of a more liberal policy. At the Estates of Saint-Germain in 1561 the orator of the Third Estate, Jacques Bretagne, a Calvinist and mayor of Autun, pleaded for toleration of his co-religionists until a national council could settle the state of religion. Though the request was in favour of his own religion, the principle Bretagne expressed could well have applied to all minorities: 'From all rational creatures the Eternal demands principally the heart and internal affection, which cannot act or be offered up when it is constrained'.

The triumph of the politiques

In the savagery of the civil wars, however, it was the political argument that gained the most support. Some, like Castellio in his *Conseil à la France désolée* (1562), denounced the fratricidal strife because it was based on 'the forcing of consciences'. He, like the Catholics Michel de L'Hospital and the abbot of Bois-Aubry, was morally and in principle opposed to persecution. Others, not fortunate enough to begin with the same conviction, arrived at it through their concern at the wars. Consisting for the most part of orthodox Catholics, these began to be known in the late 1560s as the party of *politiques*, led initially by the Montmorency family. The tolerant Edict of Saint-Germain in 1570 reflected the interests both of the *politique* party and of Catherine de Medici, but the latter's vengeful policy, which ended with the Massacre, broke the association and drove the *politiques* into opposition as another group opposed to the Crown. In 1575 Protestant and Catholic *politiques* together set up an independent and tolerant government

François Dubois, who himself narrowly escaped the
massacre of Saint Bartholomew, illustrates clearly in this
painting the savagery of which both sides were equally
guilty during the French wars of religion. An estimated
three thousand Huguenots perished in Paris on this occasion;
the total throughout France has been put at 20,000.

in Languedoc. They swore 'not to cause any actual detriment to
each other's religion in this present association, so that each will
on this point enjoy entire freedom of conscience'. This agreement
can be compared with the 1573 Confederation of Warsaw. Both
were treaties of mutual tolerance agreed upon between the principal religions in the name and person of noble representatives.
The cause of the *politiques* was immeasurably advanced by the
favourable terms granted to Protestants in the 1576 Edict of
Beaulieu, which, while excluding Huguenots from Paris, granted
them freedom of worship everywhere else in France. Subsequent
concessions, even the Edict of Nantes, were not as generous as
this; and the gains of 1576 were wiped out by the intolerant edict
of Henry III in 1585. But it was clear that a large and powerful
group supported official toleration. The aged Marshal Tavannes
sneered at the Catholic *politiques* as men who preferred the realm
to be at peace without God than at war for him; but with the
adherence to their side of the tolerant king of Navarre, later
Henry IV, the *politiques* were poised for victory.

Only the religion of the king of Navarre stood in the way of his
acceptance as king by France. Among many *politiques*, however,
even his religion was satisfactory, provided he respected consciences. The distinguished Huguenot war-veteran François de la
Noue, an ardent supporter of Henry of Navarre, was certain that
Henry as king would maintain the principles of tolerance by which
he had lived. The sceptics were in the majority, and Henry was
forced to realise that only his conversion would unite France.
Accordingly in May 1593 the king of Navarre became a Catholic.

The proliferation of *politique* literature favouring the toleration
of two religions in one state, reached its peak in the years between
the accession of Henry III (1585) and Henry IV's conversion in
1593. It should be made clear, however, that most of the *politique*
arguments were based on political compromise, and that the aim
of religious unity was seldom lost from sight as the better ideal.

Two Frenchmen of consequence in the political life of France
should be introduced here. Maximilien de Béthune, Duke of Sully

(1559–1641), chief minister of Henry IV throughout his reign, is a perfect example of the *politique* for whom toleration was a political necessity. He remained a nominal Protestant throughout his life, as though to illustrate the possibility of a Catholic king governing with a Calvinist prime minister. But his own convictions were undogmatic. In his memoirs he claimed to look on 'all religions as indifferent which agreed in essentials', and confessed that 'I never had the bitter and furious zeal which is inspired by a difference in religion'; the Protestant teaching that the pope is Antichrist, he called a 'ridiculous tenet'. His main interest lay in stopping the civil war and establishing a strong, absolutist monarchy; to achieve this he was prepared to advise Henry IV to abjure his religion and become a Catholic.

Jean Bodin (1530–96), the greatest political theorist of sixteenth-century France, was an important supporter of civil toleration. The six books of his famous work on the *Republic* were published in 1576: in them he pays little attention to the questions on religion posed by the civil wars, and what he does say is very guarded. His main concern is the preservation of public order, and for this he proposes that one official religion should be upheld by the State. If, however, a minority religion becomes powerful, it should be

A figurative portrayal of Henry IV's
reception into the Catholic Church. The
actual abjuration and conversion took
place in 1593; it was in 1595 that the
Pope granted him absolution and recognised
him officially as King of France.

treated with gentleness and caution rather than with oppressive force. 'The more a man's will is forced, the more it rebels', so that coercion would only aggravate civil war. Besides, it is likely that force will create not converts but atheists, and 'just as the greatest tyranny is not as wretched as anarchy, so the greatest superstition in the world is not nearly as detestable as atheism'. Politically, therefore, Bodin in 1576 was tolerant in practice but not expressly in principle. His allegiance during the civil wars varied with fortune, but it is certainly fair to consider him a *politique* by inclination. What his religion was, is less certain. By the time of his *Heptaplomeres* (1593), a Latin work which remained in manuscript until the nineteenth century, he seems to have drifted far from his early Catholicism into a kind of deism. The result is that in the *Heptaplomeres* Bodin treats all religions as equal, and argument about religion as futile. Toleration is only a side issue. The proper course is, like that of the seven representatives of different religions whose discussion occupies the whole book, to live in peace and charity regardless of denomination. Such a conclusion was no doubt part of the reaction against the meaningless carnage of the civil wars in France.

The guarantees and terms of pacification offered by Henry IV to his Huguenot supporters were embodied in the 1598 Edict of Nantes. By this famous decree freedom of conscience was established throughout France, and freedom of worship was granted to Protestants in certain areas and under specified terms. This toleration was bitterly resented by the extreme Protestants under Agrippa d'Aubigné, who had hoped for complete and legal equality between the two religions. On the Catholic side there was strong opposition, but Henry denounced this in forthright terms: 'There must be no more distinction between Catholics and Huguenots, but all should be good Frenchmen. Let the Catholics convert the Huguenots by the example of a good life'.

By the end of the sixteenth century, therefore, France had achieved constitutional toleration after a volume of bloodshed which Poland had happily avoided. The spectacle of these two

These illustrations by Frans Hogenberg, from Eytzinger's
De Leone Belgico (1585), depict two key developments in the Dutch
revolt. In one (*above*) the Prince of Orange. on a white horse,
attempts to pacify the fury of the Calvinist mob in Antwerp in
1566. The other shows the executions carried out in Haarlem by
the Spaniards on orders from Alba's Council of Troubles.

predominantly Catholic countries as the first in Europe to establish
legal toleration is a phenomenon of some importance. Unlike all
Protestant States, which practised rigorous intolerance towards
dissenters, these countries allowed their religious opponents
freedom not only of conscience but also of worship, and, what is
even more significant, free access to most public offices short of
the Crown. Against the objection that this toleration was dictated
exclusively by political compromise, it could be pointed out that a
large and influential body of Catholic opinion in both countries
voluntarily and conscientiously accepted the moral and political
rightness of religious liberty. The reality remains, however, that
Catholic opinion in most of Europe was still doctrinally intolerant,
a position shared by Protestants. The Warsaw Confederation owed
more to the balance of power among the *szlachta* than to any
blossoming of freedom; and the Edict of Nantes, for all its inspiration by the *politique* party and a *politique* king, arose out of an
apparently insoluble conflict among political and dynastic factions.
The absence of a strong Catholic opposition in Scandinavia,
Britain and the United Provinces, and the monopoly of the machinery of Church and State by a Protestant caucus, may explain why
the countries of the Reformation did not make comparable
progress towards religious liberty.

The national struggle in the Netherlands

In the Netherlands, or what is roughly modern Holland and
Belgium, events bore some resemblance to those in France. As in
France, the advent of Calvinism after the 1540s intensified religious
divisions and provoked national conflict. What differentiated the
Netherlands was that it was a nation subject to Spanish rule, and
that Philip II's arbitrary policies drove it into a revolt which tended
to equate religious rebellion with the national cause. On both the
Dutch and the Spanish side, extremism produced one of the
bloodiest wars of independence in European history.

The country of Erasmus could be said to have fathered the

Reformation, and Lutheranism and Anabaptism took early root there. By the time of the religious wars in France, the Netherlands Calvinists were a powerful minority, and threatened the peaceful operation of government despite the severe heresy laws already in existence. In 1563 the Prince of Orange, William of Nassau, reported to the Duchess of Parma, then regent of the Netherlands, that even in his own principality of Orange (in France) the heretics had grown so strong that he had been compelled to come to a compromise and tolerate them, since he disapproved of persecution. In the Netherlands the Reformed Church was also rampant, but could not rally any support among the higher nobility; and, as Orange and his two colleagues the Counts of Egmont and Hoorn informed Philip II in 1562, 'were it not for the zeal which the principal seigneurs, the nobility and other gentry have for the faith, matters would not still be in such tranquillity and peace in these countries'. Orange and the Catholic lords opposed a policy of persecution, partly because they felt that an extension of initiative by their

Superior Protestant propaganda acquainted Europe with the atrocities committed by Spaniards. Here a contemporary print depicts the other side of the picture: the equally horrifying massacre of Observantine friars in the Dutch provinces in 1580.

Spanish rulers in ecclesiastical matters might affect their own independence, and partly because persecution was considered harmful to the trade and commerce of the Netherlands. The moderate policy which they favoured in their capacity as members of the ruling Council of State, was also favoured to some extent by Margaret of Parma.

After an outbreak of Calvinist mob fanaticism in Antwerp in August 1566, symptomatic of growing Protestant power, Orange in his official capacity agreed upon another compromise, this time to allow the Calvinists freedom to preach openly in Antwerp, and so in effect granting Calvinism recognition equally with Catholicism. The Duchess disapproved of the compromise, but found herself obliged to implement a cautious policy of toleration in order to maintain religious order and restrain the anti-Spanish temper of the Catholic nobility under Orange. From 1566 we can discern the development of two important factors: first, the passing of revolutionary initiative to the Calvinist minority, who had been aided by the government's tolerant policy; secondly, the growing conviction of the Prince of Orange that the interests of the nobility and people of the Netherlands lay in freedom from persecution and consequently in religious coexistence.

A pamphlet published in 1566, and perhaps influenced by Orange, put the economic case for toleration succintly. Through persecution, claimed the author, 'trades which belong specially to the Low Countries have been driven into the hands of the English, French and other nations. And I do not mention innumerable other decent and experienced craftsmen who have sought shelter in foreign countries in order to enjoy freedom of conscience'. Although William of Orange was probably not a devout Catholic, it is more satisfactory to classify him as a *politique*, perhaps even a convinced adherent of freedom of conscience, than as one indifferent to religion. His writings and his public position throughout his life, as we shall see, opposed constraint in matters of faith and found in tolerance the best means of converting one's opponents.

Philip II refused to accept the existence of heresy in his domains, and in 1567 the Duke of Alba established himself in the Netherlands with the purpose of uprooting Calvinism. The imposition of an alien military government, whose methods threatened the security of the people of the Netherlands and not merely that of heretics, aroused the nobility to fierce opposition. Alba's Council of Troubles, nicknamed the Council of Blood, began a reign of terror which from 1567 to 1573, the period of the Duke's stay, condemned 12,302 people, of whom 1,105 were either banished or executed.

The policy of William of Orange

Orange now recognised that national independence was at stake. Writing to the Emperor Maximilian II in 1568, he condemned Alba's regime and claimed that 'this tyranny is exercised against everyone, irrespective of religion'. The result was that he felt compelled to embrace the cause of the Reformation in order to identify himself more closely with the active opposition; but he took care not to stand on a religious platform against the faith of the majority of his fellow-countrymen. On the one hand, therefore, he could in 1573 complain to the Reformed churches of East Anglia that they were not giving adequate help to their brethren in the Netherlands; and on the other he could write in 1576 to the Estates of Brabant, Flanders and Hainault to say, 'I wish to assure you that I do not wish to alter the status of the Roman Catholic religion'. He was unfortunate in having as allies rigid Calvinists who pursued a violent campaign of persecution of Catholics wherever they triumphed. William, however, wished to unite all faiths in a common national cause, and steps to promote this were taken in 1578, when the Calvinist-dominated provinces of Holland and Zealand under him made an anti-Spanish agreement with the Netherlands Estates General in the Pacification of Ghent.

The mutual toleration which the Pacification guaranteed had

now been accepted as necessary by many on both sides of the religious fence. As the new governor of the Netherlands, Don Juan of Austria, reported to Philip in 1577: 'Your Majesty should be firmly convinced of one thing which is deeply rooted in the minds of both the good and the bad: both desire freedom of conscience'. A leading part in this was taken by William, according to Don Juan: 'The Prince of Orange has always insisted on impressing on the people that freedom of conscience is essential to commercial prosperity'. Consequently when Calvinist zealots persecuted others, Orange was quick to react. In 1578 he wrote to the authorities at Middelburg, in favour of the Anabaptists who were being persecuted there. 'It is true that these men did not wish to fight in the army for their country', he argued, 'but from the financial point of view they have made our struggle possible. Have they not therefore deserved, like the others, to enjoy liberty of worship?' This must be one of the earliest examples of a European ruler defending conscientious objection. That same year he was writing to the magistrates of Bruges, condemning the intolerance of the Reformed in the city and demanding that the terms of the Pacification be observed: 'I desire nothing so much as to see everything conducted in such a way that no mishap or disunity befalls the nation'. The result of such pleas was William's plan for religious coexistence in the Netherlands.

The *Religionsvrede* or religious truce of 1578 was precipitated by Calvinist intolerance in Ghent. As presented to the Estates General, the plan proposed full equality between the Catholic and Reformed religions, the imposition of peace and an end to confessional strife, and some favourable concessions for Catholics, including the return of ecclesiastical property seized by the Reformed. Allegedly influenced by French and German examples, the *Religionsvrede* in fact resembled neither, for in France no toleration edicts had ever granted equality to the two faiths, and in Germany the peace of Augsburg had allowed only one religion in a territory, not two.

To support his policy William enlisted the aid of some gifted pamphleteers. One of these was the Huguenot leader Philippe du Plessis Mornay, who in 1578 applied to the Netherlands the *politique* doctrines then current in France. In a discourse which reflects the interest of the national cause against Spain, du Plessis Mornay stressed the need for 'not interfering with each other's freedom of conscience and religious practice in all these lands, since we all wish to live here in liberty'. Another defence of the *Religionsvrede*, appearing in 1579, was well in advance of its time in not merely advocating the complete separation of Church and State, but also in basing the right of religious liberty on natural law. This anonymous work, the *Discours contenant le vray entendement de la Pacification de Gand*, stated that 'it is not the business of legislators and political leaders to interfere in religion or to force anyone to profess one religion or another'. Such thorough support for the autonomy of religion must have been almost unique in its day.

Orange's plan was unprecedented in claiming equality for a minority religion. This would have annoyed Catholics as much as the knowledge of the ferocity of Calvinist minority rule over a Catholic majority in the northern provinces. As a result, the southern provinces gravitated towards Spain and signed a peace treaty at Arras in 1579. Simultaneously the northern provinces accepted federation in the Calvinist-dominated Union of Utrecht. Division along religious lines meant the end of toleration in either half of the country. Protestants in the south were not indeed subjected to the death-penalty, but their lot was made impossible. In the north, where the old religion still commanded a majority, the position of Catholics was not very different. William of Orange even favoured stronger measures against them, especially after the defection of the province of Groningen under its Catholic ruler, Rennenberg, to Spain in 1580. In the 1580s, and notably after the assassination of the Prince of Orange in 1584, open persecution of the Catholic majority in the United Provinces by the one-tenth of the population which was Protestant, led to a steady decline of the Catholic religion.

Partisans of liberty in the United Provinces

The sixteenth century in Holland ends with the failure of toleration, despite the sincere attempts of William of Orange to unite
his country against Spain regardless of religion. Wherever Calvinism triumphed, whether in the United Provinces or in Scotland,
religious liberty vanished.

The trend was not a lasting one. In Holland the closing years of
the sixteenth century witnessed an important reassessment of the
place of religion in society, provoked not only by the treatment of
Catholics but also by the freedom with which the controversial
works of Franck, Castellio and others were allowed to circulate.
The steady growth of a revisionist and liberal Calvinism which
came to question the theology and discipline of orthodoxy, is a
development which reaches its crisis in the great Arminian split,
discussed below.

Among the earlier Dutch proponents of unorthodox Calvinism
should be noted Hubert Duifhuis (1531–81), a pastor in Utrecht.
Religion for him consisted in the minimum of outward observances, and he governed his church on thoroughly democratic
lines. A firm opponent of excommunication and indeed of any
ecclesiastical discipline, he held that the State alone had the
authority to exercise coercion. This subordination of Church to
State was to become the key issue in the Arminian controversy.
Duifhuis' opposition to persecution in religion was absolute; the
persecution of Catholics he likewise opposed, and on one occasion
he warned the magistrates about this, saying, 'If you persecute
men on account of their faith, God will never prosper your
affairs'.

The first serious controversy on toleration was aroused by the
writings of Caspar Coolhaes (1536–1615), particularly his *Apologia*
(1580), which urged that 'we can and readily should tolerate all
those who still live in the darkness of papism and similar sects as
long as they do not commit acts of rebellion or other crimes which
public authority is in duty bound to punish'. Coolhaes, a citizen
of Leiden, was supported by the magistrates of the city, on whose

One of the most distinguished supporters of toleration to emerge from the Dutch war of independence: Dirck Coornhert was probably unique in supporting liberty not only for members of all religions but even for those who professed none.

behalf a tract was drawn up in protest against the tyranny of ministers who would 'bring this free Church under the yoke of a new papacy'. The author of the tract, Dirck Coornhert (1522–90), is noteworthy as one of the principal defenders of toleration in the sixteenth century.

From the beginning a supporter of the national revolt, Coornhert seems to have remained a nominal Catholic all his life, although his writings and thought show spiritualising tendencies. His love for liberty is revealed by the admission, made in 1580, that he 'found more truth, more piety and more edification in one page of Castellio's than in all the books written by Calvin and Beza'. When in 1581 the States of Holland prohibited Catholicism, Coornhert on behalf of the Catholics of Haarlem drew up a petition to William of Orange, without success. Writing in Dutch, in order to gain a wider public in his own country, Coornhert took up the pen against both Catholic and Protestant supporters of persecution. While supporting complete separation of Church and State, he believed that the State should preserve the civil peace between religions. The profundity of his belief in toleration can be measured by his apparent willingness to tolerate even atheists, a concession which very few were capable of making even by the end of the seventeenth century. This goes well beyond the largeness of his confession in 1578 that 'I own for brethren all those godly men who hold Christ for their cornerstone, whether they be priests, monks, Baptists, Reformed or Lutherans'.

The same prohibition of Catholicism which aroused Coornhert in 1581 also aroused liberal Calvinists. A Calvinist ex-burgomaster of Haarlem, Gerard Stuver, went to the Hague to protest that 'he was persuaded in his conscience that every Church ought to be allowed such an exercise of religion as she believed before God to be good and true; forasmuch as it was not only a violation of conscience to oblige any man to embrace a religion which he held to be false and pernicious; but it was also no less a violation to oblige any to forbear the public exercise of a religion which he in his conscience believed to be true and good'. Much the same sentiment was registered at the same time by the magistrates of Leiden, who protested at being obliged to persecute Catholics: 'As we intend not to offer violence to the conscience of any man, so likewise do we desire that in all our transactions we may remain masters of our own consciences. We cannot consent to use the very least force in matters of religion. We protest that we will not proceed against any man as a heretic'.

These examples of civil authorities protesting against pointless persecution are of some consequence. Not only were they, like the States of Holland later, attempting to free themselves from the yoke of Reformed theocracy. They were also concerned, as leaders of the commercial bourgeoisie, at the threat to economic life implicit in discrimination against a section of Dutch citizens. Both these reasons were prominent in the protests made in 1597 by Cornelis Hooft, burgomaster of Amsterdam, against the persecution of a weaver named Vogelsang who entertained individual theories about the Trinity. The aim of the war of independence, Hooft claimed, had been the securing of liberty and not lording

The Synod of Dort was of profound importance in Calvinist history. In Holland it raised vital theological and political issues, while abroad it led to a split in the world of Reformed theology, creating for the first time a school of liberal Calvinism.

The execution of the Grand Pensionary of Holland, Oldenbarnevelt, in 1619, set the seal on the victory of the strict Calvinist clergy and the royalist party in the United Provinces. Among the supporters of the defeated party who escaped abroad was Hugo Grotius.

over consciences. The war itself would not have been won 'had not the inhabitants, and among them a great many Romanists who abhorred the cruelty of the Spaniards, opened the gates to us themselves, in a firm persuasion that every man's conscience would be free; for which reason I cannot yet be convinced that we ought to do violence to the conscience of any man'. Hooft's proposal, therefore, was 'that none may be molested on account of conscience but all may be tolerated with Christian forbearance'. Subsequently, in January 1598, he again took up the defence of Vogelsang. The authorities were prosecuting him for blasphemy; yet, he said, 'that word blasphemy is extended so far that it is made to include Papists, Lutherans, Mennonites, enthusiasts, and, it seems, almost all that do not conform in every point to our own Church'. Hooft then made a telling point: 'It is very strange that those who so strenuously maintain the doctrine of predestination should insist upon persecution or forcing of conscience; for if their doctrine be true, no man can avoid that to which he is ordained'.

Arminianism and Erastianism

The issue of predestination lay ostensibly at the heart of the great controversy provoked by Jacob Arminius (1550–1609) when, as professor at the University of Leiden, he taught a less rigorous form of Calvinism than that officially received. His colleague and opponent, Gomarus, upheld the orthodox doctrine, which supported predestination. When followers of Arminius remonstrated in 1610 to the Grand Pensionary of Holland, Oldenbarnevelt, in favour of State action against the intolerance of the majority party, they began to be known as Remonstrants and their opponents as Counter-Remonstrants. The dispute, for all its theological fury, resolved itself into a struggle between the merchant oligarchy of wealthy Holland and the dynastic interests of the House of Orange–Nassau supported by the Counter-Remonstrant clergy. In 1618–19 the Calvinist Synod of Dort, held under the auspices of the orthodox theologians, expelled the Remonstrants from their Church and country, and enabled Maurice of Nassau to effect the overthrow of the regime in Holland and the execution of Oldenbarnevelt.

For a generation after the death of Arminius, the cause of the Remonstrants was bound up with that of toleration. For them liberty became a cardinal principle, primarily because they defended man's spiritual freedom against the apparently tyrannical doctrine of predestination. Beyond this, however, they were compelled to justify their own right to dissent. Their chief apologists were Uytenbogaert, leader of the party and counsellor to Oldenbarnevelt; and Simon Episcopius (1583–1643), professor at Leiden. Episcopius was an inflexible defender of religious liberty. In a speech to the Synod of Dort in 1618 he lamented divisions in the Church and urged the practice of a 'mutual tolerance'. Complete agreement, he said, was impossible: was there any place in Christendom where there was unanimity in religion? In 1629 he published his *Apologia pro confessione Remonstrantium*, which developed fully the Arminian point of view. Like his colleagues, he maintained that the State should rule the Church, but only in its exterior life; this principle, approximating in part to the theories of the sixteenth-century Heidelberg divine Erastus, was intended to protect the liberty of the Church against the theocratic tyranny of ministers. The Church, according to Episcopius, could exercise no coercive power beyond spiritual discipline, for coercive power was vested in the State. However, since the State governed only the exterior temporal life of the Church, it could not interfere in spiritual matters nor exercise force against conscience, so that the liberty of Christians was preserved. The individual had a right to believe, and to worship publicly, according to his own conscience. Voluntary association was a right, and permitted the existence of churches other than the State Church.

The Erastianism of the Remonstrants was that of a minority party looking to the State for protection against the majority. There was no obvious reason why a State as ruler of the Church should guarantee religious liberty: all experience hitherto in England and in Germany militated against it. But the qualifications made by Episcopius and Uytenbogaert (who differed to some extent on the role of the magistrate over the Church) delimited the spheres of activity assigned to ecclesiastical and civil authorities, and preserved the rights of conscience.

The Thirty Years War

While Calvinism in the United Provinces was suffering internal disruption, in the rest of Europe it was marching under the banners of the Elector Palatine and of the brilliant young Statthalter of the Upper Palatinate, Christian of Anhalt. Athwart the chief military routes in western Europe, and a focus of Protestant militancy in the Empire, the Palatinate suddenly became a major threat to peace when in 1618 its Elector accepted the throne of rebellious Bohemia. The Thirty Years War that resulted is no longer interpreted as an exclusively religious or purely German war. Spiritual considerations were lost in a struggle whose hallmarks became territorial devastation and human massacre. Through the chaos there emerged the beginnings of a consciousness that the Christian

O schaw doch wunder mein lieber Christ/
Wie der Bapst/Luther vnd Calvinist/
Einander in die Haar gefallen/
GOtt helffe den Verirrten allen.
Deß HErren Wort bleibt inn Ewigkeit

LUTHER.   PABST   CALVINUS

Einfalt.

Der HERR ist mein Hirt/mir wird
nichts mangeln. Psalm.23.

Churches should forgo their old enmities and unite against such common enemies as unbelief, impiety, and war. A German pamphlet of 1620 shows a print of an 'ecclesiastical brawl' in which the Pope, Luther and Calvin are attacking each other; below the print are some verses which end with the stanza:

> Lord Jesus, deign to look below
> And see how these three fall to blows:
> Come quickly, Lord, thy Church defend,
> And bring such quarrels to an end.

After the end of the war a German statesman, Hermann Conring, brought out in 1649 an edition of the writings of George Cassander and George Witzel, under the title *De sacris nostri temporis controversiis*. The introductory essay, by Conring, was

This expressive print of 1620 denounces clerical squabbles as alien to the life of the ordinary Christian who trusts in Christ alone as his shepherd. Significantly, all three major religions are equally condemned. A similar reaction against religious wars may be found in Grimmelshausen's *Simplicissimus*, the classic commentary on conditions during the Thirty Years War.

an appeal to his fellow-Catholics to extend the irenic work of the two Georges. He confessed an unwillingness to undo the whole work of the Reformation, and appealed to Catholics to realise that parties had always existed in the Church and that the reformers were only the last in a long tradition. 'Protestants are men: they are human beings like everyone else (*Homines sunt Protestantes: humani ab illis nihil est alienum*)', he felt it necessary to remind his coreligionists. The work looks beyond irenicism, however, to the vision of a united Church in a united Germany, when 'the wall which now, alas! divides the Churches, finally collapses, so that no longer in Germany will there be Rehoboam and Jeroboam, Jerusalem and Samaria, but all the faithful will have one voice, one heart, one baptism, one table, and one calling'.

Religious freedom made no immediate gains from the war, but the terms of the Peace of Westphalia (1648) were promising. The principle of *cuius regio eius religio* was confirmed, and so was the *jus reformandi*, or right of the prince to control religion. But substantial modifications were attached to both these. For the first time in Europe 'the liberty of conscience of each person' was guaranteed in an international treaty. What this meant was that everyone had the full right to such freedom of religion as he had enjoyed in 1624, and not even the change of a ruler's religion could now derogate from this. Only three religions were recognised by Westphalia – the Catholic, Calvinist and Lutheran; so that other sects, particularly those which were not tolerated in 1624, were still liable to expulsion from a German state. But the treaty laid down expressly that all dissidents were to be allowed 'with a free conscience to frequent privately their place of worship without being subjected to enquiry or disturbed; and shall not be prevented from taking part in the public exercise of their religion in their neighbourhood where and as many times as they wish'. Taken together, these clauses promised considerable freedom of religion in Germany. There were, for instance, no further attempts to make countries change their creed because their ruler had done so. In Brandenburg, where a Calvinist ruled over a largely Lutheran population; and in the Palatinate, where a Catholic ruled over a largely Reformed population, civil toleration had come to stay. But there was no way of assuring that rulers would interpret the clauses liberally, and particularly in the Habsburg territories unity of religion was firmly enforced.

At the end of this chapter on religious war, a brief note should be added about a champion of tolerance who gave his life in battle. This was George Niemirycz (1612–59), a Polish magnate of Ukrainian origin, who became a leader and defender of the Minor Church in its last difficult days in Poland. As a member of the Diet he was able to lead the campaign against official persecution, but in 1641, on account of his anti-Trinitarianism, he was convicted of blasphemy by the Supreme Court. Only the intervention of the liberal Catholic bishop of Kiev, Alexander Sokolowski, saved him. He was subsequently obliged to flee the country on the accession of the intolerant Catholic John Casimir as king. In exile he joined the Ukrainian Cossacks under Bogdan Khmelnitsky, whose daughter he married in 1657. The rest of his life was spent in an attempt to win freedom for the Ukraine from both Poland and Russia. In 1659, the year that Poland ratified the treaty recognising him as Chancellor of an autonomous Ukrainian duchy, he was killed defending the country against the Russians. For Niemirycz the struggle for a free faith became part of a larger struggle for human liberty.

7 The English contribution

The failure of toleration in England under Somerset was followed by the triumph of Protestantism, a triumph precipitated by the callous persecution undertaken by the authorities under Mary (1553–8). The heresy laws which Somerset had abolished were restored in 1555 by the Catholic Queen. The reaction, especially among the common people from whom most of the victims were chosen, against the fires of Catholicism and the Spanish alliance, did more than anything else to prepare the English for the sort of regime that Elizabeth (1558–1603) envisaged. Her national Church, created by the Act of Uniformity in 1559, was openly Protestant in theology; but its outward structure retained the old Catholic forms, and its enforcement was accompanied by very little positive pressure, so that controversy was muted and Englishmen were barely aware that a complete change in religion had been carried through. It is true that the number of Christians executed under Elizabeth was much the same as the number who suffered under Mary, but Elizabeth's persecution was protracted and discriminating and consequently had a smaller impact on opinion. Moreover, her policy was 'tolerant' in that she tried to include all shades of Christian opinion within the State Church, and was emphatic in subordinating theological differences to the necessity of a liberal comprehensiveness and unity.

Toleration was, despite this, not a distinctive feature of the Anglican Church. The Catholic population, which at the outset of the reign was still a substantial proportion, was subjected to penal laws which grew in intensity and ferocity as the reign went on and the menace from Catholic Spain grew greater. Elizabeth may have claimed not to wish to set a window into men's consciences, but the executions and repression suffered by English Catholics were a potent argument against the toleration of Protestants by Catholic powers in Europe. Under her 189 Catholics, the majority of them secular priests, were put to death; and some forty more died in prison. By the 1570s there had also grown up an uncompromising Protestant and sectarian opposition to the episcopal establishment: the members of these too suffered brutal persecution. This treatment of dissenters on both left and right was excused at the time by pleas of State security. To threaten the Erastian Church and organised religion was, in Elizabethan England as in Calvinist Geneva, to menace the foundations of society. The Jesuit Edmund Campion and the sectary Henry Barrow were, in England, both martyred by this argument at the hands of the State. Among the few on the Protestant side who opposed this policy is the surprising figure of John Foxe. The famous martyrologist, whose accounts of the persecution of Protestants kept alive for generations in the breasts of decent Englishmen a horror of Rome, objected also to persecution by his coreligionists. 'It is tyrannical to constrain by faggots', he wrote; 'consciences love to be taught. The most effective master of teaching is love'. This was written in 1557, under Queen Mary. But Foxe also pleaded in 1575 for the Anabaptists and in 1581 for Edmund Campion. He was a rare apostle of liberty.

It should not be forgotten that the opponents of the Anglican Church, whatever their persuasion, were scarcely more tolerant in principle. Cardinal Allen and the Jesuits Campion and Persons were concerned to point out that a Catholic could be a Catholic and still be completely loyal to the State; the State, they stressed, had no jurisdiction over consciences. But they nowhere spoke of general liberty of belief. The sectary Robert Browne tended to favour the separation of Church and State, but refused to countenance other truths than his own. When the Presbyterians in England under Thomas Cartwright argued for toleration of their ideas in the national Church, they were making no general appeal on behalf of heterodoxy. Cartwright himself supported the full rigour of the law being exercised against heretics: 'If this be bloudie and extreme . . . I am content to be so counted with the holie goste'.

Elizabeth succeeded in holding her Church together by alternate methods of liberality and repression, but ultimately failed to gain that comprehension which she desired. Ironically, it was from her repressive Church that some of the principal advocates of toleration in the next generation were to come.

The so-called Bullinger Goblet, dated 1560 and given by
Elizabeth of England to the Swiss reformer Henry Bullinger,
symbolises the Elizabethan policy of remaining on good terms
with European religious leaders. Despite such efforts, many
Protestants, particularly Calvinists, remained uneasy about
the religious policies of the Anglican leaders.

The beginnings of toleration in England

The position of Catholics became, in a Protestant country, the touchstone of religious liberty. James I (1603–25) professed an inclination to tolerance, and like all his Stuart successors was favourably disposed to the Catholics. In 1614 he told Parliament that no 'relygeone or heresye was evere exterpated by violense or the swoarde, nor have I evere judged it a way of plantyng truthe'. Later in 1621 he told them: 'I hold that we ought not to force the conscience of any one'. But English opinion forced him to act against Catholics, particularly after the Gunpowder Plot of 1605; and his own temperament was extremely hostile to the Calvinists in the Church of England, who went under the common name of Puritans. About thirty Catholics were executed during his reign, as well as some anti-Trinitarians. The great threat to the throne came not from these, however, so much as from the growing

The Papists' Powder Treason, a print of 1689 copying one of 1621, celebrates the deliverance of the English people from the Armada in 1588 and the Gunpowder Plot in 1605. Both events were used to spread the myth of Catholic disloyalty, which in turn became the excuse for persecution.

alienation of the Puritan section of the Church from Stuart policy. This radical opposition occurred at the same time as there grew up within the Church a body of liberal theologians, of whom the first was Hooker.

The earlier theorists of the Anglican establishment, particularly humanists like Thomas Starkey under Henry VIII, had supported the validity of the distinction between religious fundamentals and things indifferent (*adiaphora*), as a secure basis for national agreement on religion. Their contribution to a more liberal attitude was superseded by that of Richard Hooker (1554–1600), author of the *Laws of Ecclesiastical Polity*, and the first great apologist of Anglicanism. Though a supporter of civil intolerance, Hooker was willing to recognise that the essentials of salvation existed in all the major Christian Churches, including the Church of Rome, which he held to be a true Christian body despite its abominations. Even a pope, he conceded, could be saved. Hooker's historical and traditional approach modified the violent anti-popery of Protestants. Meanwhile other writers, often foreign, were contributing to the liberalisation of thought in the Anglican Church. The most prominent of these was Jacob Acontius, whom we have already discussed. Although his *Satan's Stratagems* was not translated into English until 1648, it was already known in England from the original Latin edition of 1564, and the author's presence in England during the reign of Elizabeth helped to make it better known. Under James I the literature of the Arminian dispute in Holland found a public in England, and Arminian writings helped to mould the thought of William Laud, created Archbishop of Canterbury in 1633 after a distinguished career in the Church. Though Arminianism helped to create a dialogue between orthodox Calvinists and Rome, it was not the reactionary movement that Puritan propagandists made it out to be. On the contrary, by their rejection of Calvinist predestination and their firm adherence to the principles of tolerance, the Remonstrants and their sympathisers in the Anglican Church opened the way for a dialogue between Anglicanism and the sectarians, a dialogue

A bishop preaching at Paul's Cross in the reign of James I, from a diptych (1616) by John Gipkyn. The King and Queen with Prince Charles and the court, the judges, Lord Mayor and civic authorities are in their respective galleries. The persecution of the Puritans under James I stimulated a great revolutionary movement in favour of religious toleration.

that was first made explicit in the writings of the Latitudinarians.

The Arminians were of profound importance in the liberalisation of English thought, and their influence stretches through the Latitudinarians to the Cambridge Platonists at the end of the seventeenth century. The three principal theorists of Latitudinarianism were Hales, Chillingworth and Falkland. Of these, John Hales (1584–1656), of Eton College, had been present at the Synod of Dort and had there supported the Remonstrants. Hales became one of the circle that met at the home of Lord Falkland in Oxfordshire, to discuss the state of the Church from a rationalist, tolerant viewpoint. Their tolerance made them support the adoption of a more liberal and less exclusive policy by the Church. Episcopacy was for them less important than a charitable comprehension of all parties within Anglicanism, and the authority of episcopacy and councils was of less consequence than, in Hales' words, 'reason illumined by the Revelation that comes to us from the Word of God'. For Hales, unity of opinion was impossible, but unity of individuals in spiritual charity was indispensable. William Chillingworth (1602–44), even more than Hales, was the principal apostle of Latitudinarianism. An Oxford don, and for a brief period a convert to Rome, Chillingworth returned to the Church of his birth in order to teach a startingly liberal interpretation of

ΜΟΝΩ
ΤΩ ΘΕΩ
ΛΟΞΑ

Allegorical print of Oliver Cromwell as champion and deliverer of England. The Greek inscription reads: 'To God alone be praise'. Cromwell was the first English ruler to maintain that toleration should be a fundamental of the constitution, but political instability destroyed his hopes of achieving it.

religion. Like Hales, he was thoroughly opposed to dogma, and even declined to formulate any so-called fundamental articles of religion. There was only one fundamental for Protestants, the Bible, and given this there need be no other disagreements among them, for each one was free to interpret Scripture as he wished. Scripture was to be read by the light of private reason, which was the sole arbiter of truth. If this principle was rationalist, it was also thoroughly tolerant, and allowed greater latitude to the various parties within the Anglican Church. By the same token, any Christian who used his reason rightly was capable of being saved, even in the Church of Rome. By sidestepping dogma and rejecting the minimum of fundamentals, Chillingworth achieved a system which offered complete toleration and the absence of religious persecution. However, Chillingworth also seems to have been an Erastian, and continued to allow the State control over the ordering of religion. This position, similar to that of the Remonstrants, offered few guarantees against persecution by the State.

The Latitudinarians were clearly hostile to Laud's policy of imposing uniformity on the Anglican Church. That policy had, by the late 1630s, contributed to the alienation of Church and Crown from the active group of liberals, Puritan or Anglican, in Parliament. Neither James I nor Charles I abstained from the selective persecution of religious opponents. The Puritans within the established Church bore the main brunt of intolerance, but Independents and other sectarians were also hunted down and imprisoned, while in 1612 two anti-Trinitarian heretics were executed for their beliefs, being the last Protestants in England to suffer for exclusively religious reasons.

The search for liberty in the Interregnum

The English Revolution which commenced in 1640 marshalled newly emerging forces in politics, commerce and religion against the oppressive regime of an authoritarian monarchy and a paternalist State. In their struggle against the Royalists, the upper gentry

Title-page by William Marshall for
The Dippers Dip't, a pamphlet against
the Anabaptists by Daniel Featley
(1645). The title shows the many
different sects of Anabaptists existing
by the mid-seventeenth century.

drew invaluable support from the little men who fought to preserve their individual freedoms; men like John Lilburne, for whom 'justice, liberty and freedome' were the only cause for which they had fought. As early as 1643, when the English Parliament was obliged to ally with the Scots in a Solemn League and Covenant in order to ensure its military survival, the issue of toleration came to the fore. The Presbyterian Scots wished to impose their Calvinist order on England, against the opposition on the parliamentary side of a core of Independents led by Oliver Cromwell and Sir Henry Vane the Younger. The Independents, drawn largely from the lesser gentry, became the leading opponents of Presbyterianism and supporters of a general toleration. One Scots observer claimed in 1644 that 'the great shott of Cromwell and Vane is to have a libertie for all religions, without any exceptions', and that Vane 'had reasoned for a full libertie of conscience to all religions'.

Independents like Cromwell were inclined to be as liberal as circumstances permitted. In 1643 Cromwell held that 'the State, in choosing men to serve them, takes no notice of their opinions; if they be willing to serve them, that satisfies'. This implied equality of religions in the eyes of the State. In 1654, when Cromwell had become Lord Protector, he stated firmly that 'liberty of conscience is a natural right; and he that would have it, ought to give it'. Such liberty, he said, was a fundamental of the constitution. Under his Protectorate the Catholics enjoyed greater peace than under the Stuarts. But his principal difficulty was in establishing universal toleration. Despite his good relations with some Anglican clerics he was not inclined to tolerate a Church that supported the Stuart monarchy. Nor was he willing to grant liberty to sectarians whose social doctrines were subversive of society and of the peace. To one sectarian Cromwell maintained stoutly, and correctly, that 'there was never such liberty of conscience as is now', but he was adamant in promising his first Protectorate Parliament in 1654 that 'liberty of conscience . . . abused for the patronising of villainies' would never be tolerated. His difficulty was that most of the

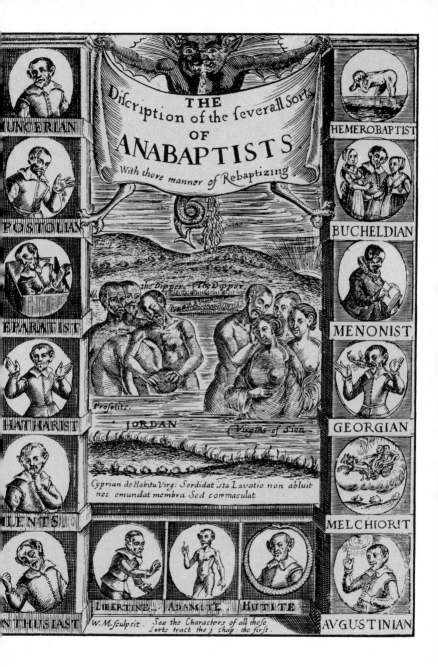

THE Discription of the severall Sorts OF ANABAPTISTS.
With there manner of Rebaptizing

LVNCERIAN

APOSTOLIAN

SEPARATIST

CHATHARIST

SILENTS

ENTHUSIAST

the Dipper   the Dipper

Proselits.

JORDAN   Virgins of Sion

Cyprian de Habitu Virg: Sordidat ista Lavatio non abluit nec emundat membra Sed commaculat

LIBERTINE   ADAMITE   HUTTITE

W. M. sculpsit.   See the Characters of all these Sorts tract the j chap: the first.

HEMEROBAPTIST

BUCHELDIAN

MENONIST

GEORGIAN

MELCHIORIT

AVGVSTINIAN

existing religions were identified with specific social doctrines, and that intolerance towards some of them was inevitable. Cromwell's early dream in 1648 of a great union of godly people, 'Scots, English, Jewes, Gentiles, Presbyterians, Independents, Anabaptists and all', was doomed to be unrealised so long as the sects were mutually intolerant and supported different forms of society.

Among Independents as a whole the progress towards toleration was slow and incomplete. In part this is because they were seldom in undisputed control of Parliament, and usually had to reckon with a Presbyterian majority. But the Independents were also themselves conservative, as we can see by the attitude of General Ireton and the New Model Army officers on social and religious questions. When Parliament in 1648 passed a blasphemy act laying down the death penalty for heresy and blasphemy against such dogmas as the Trinity and the Incarnation, the Independents gave their ready support to the Presbyterian majority. It was left to the dissenting sectaries, particularly the Levellers, to draw the conclusion that a universal toleration could be achieved only if political power passed to the people through universal suffrage. The Independents, moreover, were in the anomalous position of supporting the existence of a State Church (substantially the Anglican Church), as well as supporting religious toleration. The sectaries were thoroughly convinced that no State Church could coexist with liberty, and that the magistrate had no coercive authority in matters of religion. In the debates between Levellers and Independent officers in the winter of 1648–9, on the terms of the Leveller constitution *The Agreement of the People*, some Levellers went so far as to claim absolute liberty for all faiths, including Catholicism. This the majority of Independents were not inclined to concede.

In the period before the Protectorate the most important legislative measure promoting toleration was the 1650 Act for the relief of religious and peaceable people, which repealed all penal legislation from the time of Elizabeth onwards. Catholics were freed of all penalties for recusancy, but legislation against the

Mass and against priests was continued, although in practice Catholics were left unmolested in all their religious observances. The advance in liberal Independent thought with regard to the toleration of Catholics is shown most remarkably in the Parliamentary debates of May 1657 on a bill against Catholics. The bill had been inspired by the war against Spain, and went against the intentions of the Protector, who had promised France that he would be more amenable to recusants. When the movers of the bill proposed that Catholics take an oath against transubstantiation, there was widespread opposition, on the grounds that the oath violated liberty of conscience. Mr Bampfield protested that it resembled the old *ex officio* oath, by which dissenters had been forced by the Anglican authorities to denounce themselves; and that it was as bad as the Spanish Inquisition. Colonel Briscoe, from Cumberland, criticised the movers of the bill for practising liberty of conscience only with some sects and not with others. When the bill was eventually voted in June 1657, it was passed by 88 votes against 43. That one third of the members of Parliament should support toleration for Catholics was a significant advance in the history of Independency as well as in that of English Protestantism.

With regard to other faiths, the readmission of the Jews is usually taken as the highwater mark of toleration under Cromwell. More significant, however, is the fate of the left-wing sectaries. The Quakers, universally hated and persecuted as 'levellers against magistracy and property', to use the phrase of a member of the Protector's government, were dealt with leniently if it lay in Cromwell's power, and in October 1656 the government ordered the release of all Quakers imprisoned in four counties. The Unitarians, equally detested by other Christians, were treated gently in the person of John Biddle, who was twice arrested and twice freed after some intervention by Cromwell, although he went on to further imprisonment in 1655–8, and died eventually in prison after the Restoration. Revolutionary as the readmission of the Jews may now appear, there was at the time considerable

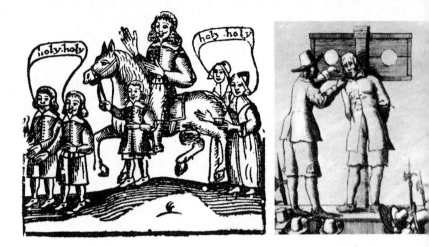

unanimity among evangelical Protestants that the only way to convert the Jews and thereby to accelerate the second coming of Christ, was to allow them back into England on liberal terms. Cromwell found less difficulty in getting his way here than in the apparently trivial instances of blasphemy during his regime.

The most severe test that Cromwell's policy of tolerance endured was the Nayler case. James Nayler, an adherent of the Quakers, began to be regarded by his followers as the Son of God and was brought before the House of Commons on a charge of heresy in 1656. His trial by a Committee of the House lasted seven days, at the end of which he escaped the death penalty when this punishment was rejected by 96 votes to 82. A motion to bore a hole through his tongue and brand his forehead passed by 113 votes to 59. The Lord Protector, and many members of Parliament, protested against the verdict on the grounds that there were no laws in existence against heresy, nor did Parliament have any jurisdiction over heresy. The large number of those who voted both against death and against mutilation is significant, and the rejection of the death penalty was certainly a victory for the Protector's policy.

In the debates Mr Bampfield, who was in 1657 to criticise the bill against Catholics, supported the death penalty on the grounds that the parable of the tares was addressed not to the magistrate but to private persons. Major-General Packer, on the other hand, in an eloquent speech against the death penalty, upheld the doctrine of

Three prints attacking the Messianic pretensions of James Nayler. One (*far left*) shows his triumphal entry into Bristol in October 1656, the incident which led to his prosecution for blasphemy. Another (*left*) shows the punishment meted out to him by order of parliament, an act of religious persecution of which Cromwell strongly disapproved. The third (*right*) compares the Quaker Nayler and the Greek Jew Sabbathai-Zevi as false Messiahs.

toleration: 'It is the strain of the Gospel all along, to use meekness and moderation . . . It matters not what people say, so we do our duty: that is, to give every man his native liberty, which is given in Holland, Poland, and other countries, a free exercise of their consciences'. Colonel Holland professed that 'the way to make the blessing of God upon a nation is to leave every man to the liberty of his conscience . . . I understand not any power the civil magistrate has to inflict censures'. After Nayler had been mutilated by order of the House, one member named Samuel Highland rose to make a long speech, 'how much the lives and liberties and estates of the people of England were concerned in our late judgment against Nayler. Better we had never been born than have taken that liberty to ourselves, to exercise such a power over the liberties of the people'.

The great debate on liberty

Highland's sentiments reflected those of the Protector. Religious liberty, and all civil liberty, would be in danger if there was arbitrary interference in the religion of individuals, however abhorrent their blasphemous tenets. The interdependence of liberty in Church and State was a primary concern of radical thinkers in seventeenth-century England. James Harrington in his *Oceana* (1656) maintained that 'a Government pretending to Liberty and yet suppressing Liberty of Conscience, must be a contradiction', and claimed in his *Political Aphorisms* that 'where Civil Liberty is intire, it includes Liberty of Conscience'. The great contribution of writers who were even more radical than Harrington was that they pursued liberty in religion only as part of the struggle for a freer and more democratic society. For the Levellers, as Haller observes, 'the toleration of religious differences was but a step toward the establishment of a state in which not alone religious differences but political opposition should not only be tolerated but admitted to a legitimate place and function in government'.

Among the Levellers William Walwyn and Richard Overton occupy an important place. Walwyn's *The Power of Love* (1643) asked that 'such opinions as are not destructive to humane society nor blaspheme the worke of our Redemption, may be peaceably endured and considered in love'. His *The Compassionate Samaritane* (1644) advocated full liberty of conscience and called for the repeal of all statutes directed against dissenters:

All times have produced men of severall wayes, and I believe no man thinkes there will be an agreement of judgement as longe as this World lasts. If ever there be, in all probability it must proceed from the power and efficacie of Truth, not from constraint.

Overton's *The Araignement of Mr Persecution* (1645) demanded full toleration for all faiths, even for the Jews, who are 'the apple of God's eye'. 'To force men and women against their consciences', he pointed out earnestly, 'is worse than to ravish the bodies of women and Maides against their wills'.

The Leveller protest was put in an even more radical way in 1649–50 by the Diggers, a visionary left-wing group whose spokesman, Gerrard Winstanley (1609–?), preached a thorough communism based on rationalism and liberty. Although Winstanley is of little political interest, since his movement collapsed into obscurity, he is important as an embodiment of both economic and religious radicalism, and in his writings the voice of the oppressed speaks out with a rare eloquence. In his *Truth Lifting up its Head above Scandals* (1648), he claimed that the authorities have rightful control over those 'servants' of theirs who are adherents of the national Church; they cannot, however, force the opinions either of these or of dissenters, 'but must leave both parties at liberty ... Neither can those servants say, we speak truths, and what differs from our constructions are errors; and so call upon the magistrate their master to punish such whom they brand for heretics. For all these things deny the Scriptures; and is contrary to the spirit of the Father'. In the scheme for a constitution drawn up in 1651 as *The Law of Freedom* and addressed to Cromwell, it was proposed as a law by the Levellers that 'no man shall be troubled for his judgment or practice in the things of his God, so he live quiet in the land'. This would seem to guarantee universal tolerance, even of sects which the Levellers hated; for as their *Letter to Lord Fairfax* professed in 1649:

As for spiritual teachings, we leave every man to stand and fall to his own master. If the power of covetousness be his master or king ... let him stand and fall to him. If the power of love and righteousness be his master or king ... let him stand and fall to him. Let the bodies of men act love, humility and righteousness one towards another, both in us and over us.

All sects, both good and bad, just and unjust, were therefore to be tolerated freely in a free commonwealth. Winstanley's courageous voice went unheard in his day, and the liberty he claimed for all was denied to him and to his followers.

Opposition to the Presbyterian regime that followed the 1643 Solemn League and Covenant between the English Parliament and the Scottish Covenanters, provoked several works on toleration. Henry Robinson (1605–73), an Independent merchant and administrator, denied liberty to Catholics because of their 'idolatry', but supported a full freedom for all others, in his *Liberty of Conscience* (1643). This tract is of considerable importance. Robinson decried exclusivism in religion, and held that we cannot know so much of the truth as to profess certainty, for truth is always in the process of evolving. Error helps the evolution of truth, for it provokes discussion. He condemned the 'murderous authority' of the Presbyterians, who would 'condemne the whole world into spirituall captivity, because their phansies tell them it is for Gods glory'. He questioned the power of the ruler in religion, and concluded that:

> There remaines no medium, either a liberty of conscience must be permitted us to enjoy our owne opinions in matters of religion, or else there is a necessity of being liable and subject against conscience, whensoever the civill powers which surely are no more infallible then ecclesiasticall, shall happen to enact or stablish any thing else.

Mention should also be made of Sir Henry Vane the Younger, always a very radical Independent, who based his support for civil liberty on freedom of conscience. His *A Healing Question Propounded* (1656) attacked State control over religion and upheld freedom of belief as a natural right.

Perhaps the most significant of the Independent supporters of tolerance was John Goodwin (1594–1665). An anti-Presbyterian who seems to have been influenced by Arminianism, Goodwin supported the complete separation of Church and State, and denied any authority of the ruler in matters of religion. The Presbyterian Baylie denounced him in 1644 for demanding 'a full liberty of conscience to all sects, even Turks, Jews, Papists'. Goodwin in turn became in 1644–6 a leading controversialist against the Scots. 'If presbytery be *jure divino*', he asked, 'why not Episcopacie? Why not Independencie?' For him, as for Castellio, the entire truth could not be known for certain, so that error was always possible, and persecution correspondingly lost its justification.

Toleration evolved rapidly during the Interregnum in England for several reasons. The Independent leaders, conservative as they might be in social matters, were willing to grant as much liberty as was consonant with their authority. Constant pressure was put on them by the democratic Levellers to accept a broad toleration as the *sine qua non* of a civil settlement; and Cromwell, despite his hostility to Leveller principles, did sincerely attempt to grant all godly men their liberty. The intolerance of the Presbyterians drove many Englishmen, notably Milton, to take up their pens in defence of both civil and religious liberty, and it became universally accepted by the end of the Protectorate that these two were interdependent. This, more than anything, explains why some men found it possible to oppose State persecution of Catholics, because they realised that a State which assumed coercive powers over one religion could assume them as easily over others.

Before passing from this scene we should grant Milton a word. His classic defence of the freedom of the press, *Areopagitica* (1644), also contains some observations relevant to religion. Some have decried enthusiasm among the sects, but, he says:

> What some lament of, we rather should rejoyce at, should rather praise this pious forwardness among men, to reassume the ill deputed care of their Religion into their own hands again. A little generous prudence, a little forbearance of one another, and som grain of charity might win all these diligences to joyn, and unite into one generall and brotherly search after Truth; could we but forgoe this Prelaticall tradition of crowding free consciences and Christian liberties into canons and precepts of men.

What appears as error, he says in echo of Gamaliel, should be allowed to exist: 'let (Truth) and Falsehood grapple; who ever knew Truth put to the worse, in a free and open encounter?' He goes on to say: 'How many other things might be tolerated in peace, and left to conscience, had we but charity'. For all his liberality, however, he refused to grant liberty to Catholics: 'I mean not tolerated Popery, and open superstition'.

The intellectual climate was no less responsible than political conditions for the growth of tolerant opinion. European writings played an enormous part. Walwyn was influenced by Montaigne, John Selden by Erastianism, the Latitudinarians by Acontius. A few rationalists, notably Sir Thomas Browne (1605–82), author of the *Religio Medici*, pursued the traditions of tolerant humanism. The biggest single foreign influence was that of the Dutch Arminians. From about mid-century there grew up at Emmanuel College,

Cambridge, a circle of rationalist Anglicans who came to be known as the Cambridge Platonists. Heirs to humanism and the Platonic revival of the Renaissance, the Cambridge circle also drew on the liberal and irenic doctrines of the Remonstrants through the contact between such people as Philip van Limborch in Holland and Henry More and Ralph Cudworth in England.

The religion of More, Cudworth, and their principal colleague Benjamin Whichcote (1609–83) was non-dogmatic, philosophic and irenic. The unity of Christians, and particularly of Protestants, was their chief care, and revelation became subordinate to reason. Heaven was open to all good men, even pagans. 'Nothing', claimed Whichcote, 'is desperate in the condition of good men; they will not live and die in any dangerous error'. Cudworth, preaching before the House of Commons in 1647, said that 'Christ was *Vitae Magister*, not *Scholae*: and he is the best Christian, whose heart beats with the truest pulse towards heaven; not he whose head spinneth out the finest cobwebs'. Whichcote went so far as to claim the irrelevancy of Churches and sects, and stated that for himself he belonged to no denomination ('*Non sum Christianus alicuius nominis*'), and was 'above all Sects'. To him also is due the celebrated declaration:

> Because I may be mistaken, I must not be dogmatical . . . I will not break the certain Laws of Charity, for a doubtful Doctrine or uncertain Truth.

By the Restoration it was accepted by virtually all informed Christian opinion in England that some toleration was necessary. The Anglican bishop Jeremy Taylor, in exile during the interregnum, wrote his *Liberty of Prophesying* (1647) to explain to his co-religionists that · liberty, even for Catholics, was necessary. (Unfortunately he modified his opinions after the Restoration). The Catholic John Austin was equally convinced of the need for toleration. Already thinkers like these were receiving support from the merchant community, which had reason to regret, especially after Cromwell's disastrous war against Spain, the consequences of confessional wars in an age of expanding commerce. One of the earliest writers to state their case was Henry Parker (1604–52), whose *Of a Free Trade* (1648), maintained, on Erastian principles, that it was the duty of the State to control religion and promote the religious liberty essential for unhindered trade. The stress on liberty, it should be noted, was incidental to Parker's main theme, a defence of the monopolistic Merchant Adventurers' Company; he was, in fact, defending unfree trade. But it was significant of the premium set on liberty that Parker should point out how the Adventurers had, by their promotion of trade to countries not normally tolerant, been able to gain for themselves and their countrymen greater freedom of belief and worship.

Henry Robinson, whom we have already noted, was one of the principal economic advisers to the Commonwealth. His religious persuasion in favour of toleration was complemented by his opposition, as a businessman, to religious restrictions on commercial liberty. Calling attention, as others were to do after him, to the tolerant policy of the United Provinces, he maintained that England too would prosper like the Dutch if it practised civil and religious liberty as the basis of free trade. With Robinson and Parker, we are at the threshold of a new approach to the old debate on freedom.

Conditions in the New World

The English contribution to toleration in the period before 1660 was as important across the Atlantic, in the new American colonies. The earliest settlers in north America were adherents of the established religion in England, and the first colonial charter, that granted to Virginia by James I in 1606, accepted the canons of the Anglican Church. Concurrent with persecution of Puritans in the mother country, repressive legislation was passed in Virginia, especially in 1642, after the outbreak of the revolution in England. The governor of Virginia, Sir William Berkeley, who was also one of the parties to the charter issued to the colony of Carolina in 1663, was a model of intolerance. In 1661 he said of conditions in Virginia: 'I thank God there are no free schools nor printing; and I hope we shall not have these hundred years: for learning has brought disobedience and heresy and sects into the world, and printing has divulged them and libels against the best government. God keep us from both!' Up to the end of the seventeenth century only Anglicanism was tolerated in Virginia, and the first dissenting minister to obtain freedom to preach under the terms of the 1689 Toleration Act, did so only in 1699. Carolina was in theory more tolerant, since its foundation charter promised 'freedom and liberty of conscience in all religious and spiritual things', but by the end of the century the Anglican Church alone was ensconced in power, although it represented only a minority of settlers.

The early Puritan settlers were implicitly in favour of religious liberty, the faculty denied to them in England. The Pilgrim Fathers, who arrived in the *Mayflower* in 1620, founded the Plymouth colony as a refuge for the persecuted, and tolerated both Quakers and extreme sectaries. In 1643 several members of the Plymouth legislature even proposed tolerating Catholics. Such a step would have been anathema to Plymouth's neighbour, the Massachusetts Bay colony, founded by settlers in 1630 on the basis of a charter granted the year before. The first governor of Massachusetts, John Winthrop, was a liberal and tolerant man, devoted to the cause of the colony. 'We doe not', he said on one occasion, 'challenge power over mens consciences, but when seditious speeches and practices discover . . . a corrupt conscience, it is our duty to use authority to reforme both'. Despite Winthrop, Massachusetts soon acquired a sinister reputation for Puritan intolerance and bigotry.

The structure of the colony in the mid-1630s approximated closely to 'a Theocracy, the best form of government in the Commonwealth as well as in the Church', to quote Boston's leading preacher, John Cotton. To Cotton we owe the sentiment that 'it was Toleration that made the world anti-Christian'. A generation later the president of Harvard University said: 'I look upon unbounded Toleration as the first-born of all abominations'.

Massachusetts clearly intended to defend orthodoxy, and did so in a series of celebrated cases.

The first clash arose over Roger Williams, whom we shall meet again. Arriving at Boston in 1631, Williams refused to join the official church, and was elected to an independent pulpit in Salem. After difficulties with the Massachusetts authorities, Williams was eventually expelled from the colony in 1635, and left for England to carry on his pamphlet warfare against John Cotton and tyranny. The second major case was the 'Antinomian' controversy centering around Mrs Anne Hutchinson and her doctrines on grace. Anne's teachings attracted wide support in Boston, particularly among the commercial and business classes, and also had the sympathy of Sir Henry Vane the Younger, who was governor for part of this period. Soon most of the Boston church adhered to Antinomianism, and the community was split between the business interest, which supported Anne, and the agricultural and gentry interests which supported John Winthrop. In 1637 Vane returned to England, and Cotton, who had for a time supported the Antinomians, was won back to the official church. A reaction now set in against Anne and her principal followers, who were banished. The narrow theological atmosphere of Boston was too much for a settler named Thomas Hooker, who set out in 1636 with his congregation to find greater liberty in Connecticut, where they founded the town

Cecil Calvert, second Lord
Baltimore, in the painting by G. Soest.
The map in his hand details the new
territory of Maryland, scene of the
first great experiment in religious
liberty in the western world.

of Hartford. For over a century thereafter Connecticut practised religious liberty, a circumstance helped by the fact that few sectaries came to live in the overwhelmingly Congregational colony, which received its charter in 1662.

The reign of intolerance in Massachusetts continued for most of the century. In 1659 four Quakers were put to death, and only in 1685 was the colony's charter revoked by the Catholic James II, who ordered the establishment of religious liberty. Even more extreme than Boston was the regime set up in 1638 by settlers from Massachusetts who went out to found the city of New Haven, where an absolute theocracy was proclaimed, on the grounds that 'the Scriptures do hold forth a perfect rule for the direction and government of all men in all duties, as well in the government of families and commonwealths as in matters of the Church'. After the English Restoration, New Haven was officially integrated into the liberal colony of Connecticut, and the theocracy ceased to exist.

The attainment of liberty: Lord Baltimore and Roger Williams

The first colony in the New World, and indeed in the history of the Christian world, to be established on the foundation of complete religious liberty, was that set up by the Catholic Lord Baltimore in Maryland. George Calvert, Lord Baltimore, converted to the Roman Church in 1624, made an application in 1630 to James I for a territory in America where his co-religionists might live at peace. The patent for Maryland was granted to his son Cecil Calvert, second Lord Baltimore, in 1632. When criticised by his fellow Catholics for accepting the principle of toleration, Baltimore was reassured by the English Jesuit provincial. Accordingly in 1632 the first expedition to the colony was made with 220 emigrants, of whom 128 were Protestants. The first law pronounced by the assembly of Maryland was unique. It declared that 'Holy Church within this province shall have and enjoy all her Rights,

'The Ark', the ship in which the Maryland colonists came over. From a relief at Hook Manor, Wiltshire.

liberties and Franchises wholly and without Blemish', but took care not to specify any particular Church! The governor, Baltimore's brother Leonard Calvert, was instructed to keep Catholics in their place and to 'cause all Acts of Romane Catholique Religion to be done as privately as may be, and that they instruct all the Romane Catholiques to be silent upon all occasions of discourse concerning the matters of Religion'. Church and State were, for probably the first time in Catholic history, completely separated. One law alone was to apply to clergy and laity alike, and Catholic clergy were given no privileged status. Cases are recorded of Catholics being prosecuted for offending the beliefs of Protestants.

This happy situation did not last long. As the Protestant settlers began to outnumber Catholics, Baltimore felt that stability might be assured if Protestants were given control of the administration. In 1648 he even replaced his brother with a Protestant governor. Puritan attitudes began to assert themselves. In 1649 a 'Toleration' Act was passed, restricting tolerance to Trinitarian Christians only. In 1652 the Protestants, in full control now of the government, overthrew Baltimore's regime, declared for Cromwell, and in 1654 replaced the 1649 Act with one denying toleration 'to popery, prelacy, or licentiousness of opinion'. Cromwell strongly disapproved of this move, and reinstated Baltimore. The trend was set, however, for the reaction against tolerance which distinguishes the end of the seventeenth century.

The principal exponent of liberty in seventeenth-century America was not the Catholic Baltimore but the Puritan Roger Williams (1603–83); for despite the great pioneering work of the former he enunciated no principles of tolerance and fought no battles to secure what was for him easily obtainable as a peer, the privilege of a proprietary colony. Williams, on the other hand, is in Atlantic history the first great defender of natural and religious liberty. His life in America, where he arrived in 1631 with his wife, was twice interrupted, in 1643–4 and in 1651–4, when he visited England.

After his expulsion from Massachusetts, Williams set out into the unsettled territory near Narragansett Bay, where he lived for extended periods with the Indians and began to study Indian languages. There in June 1636 he and his companions founded the town of Providence, which was the beginning of the colony of Rhode Island. He was one of the first Englishmen to look on the natives as the rightful owners of American territory and it was only after negotiating with them that he bought some land and settled it. He wrote at this time: 'Private interests, both with Indians and English, are many; yet these things you may and must do. First, kiss truth where you evidently, upon your soul, see it. Advance justice, though upon a child's eye. Seek and make peace, if possible, with all men'. Justice, for him, must be preserved equally between all races as between all religions.

In England in 1643 he began his writings against the tyranny both of John Cotton at Boston and of the Scottish Presbyterians in London. Of the Scots he asked in his *Queries of Highest Consideration* (1644): 'We query how you can profess and swear to persecute all others as schismatics, heretics, etc., that believe they see a further light and dare not join with either of your churches?'

In March 1644 Williams received from Parliament a charter for the territory of Rhode Island which he had purchased from the Indians. In July he published his famous *The Bloudy Tenent of Persecution for Cause of Conscience*. After decrying strife in the name of religion, Williams outlines his principles of toleration. He rejects even the doctrine of fundamentals in religion, on the ground that 'thousands and ten thousands' have differed on fundamentals since the time of Christ, and to define some articles as necessary for salvation would condemn all these to damnation. Heresy as a concept he rejects. 'This Greek word Hereticke is no

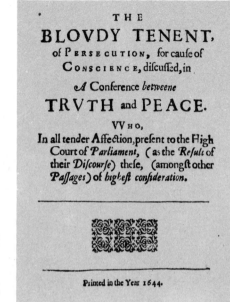

THE
BLOVDY TENENT,
of PERSECUTION, for caufe of
CONSCIENCE, difcuffed, in

A Conference *betweene*
TRVTH and PEACE.

VVHO,
In all tender Affection, prefent to the High
Court of *Parliament*, (as the *Refult* of
their *Difcourfe*) thefe, (amongft other
Paffages) of *higheft confideration.*

Printed in the Year 1644.

Roger Williams, author of *The Bloudy Tenent*, was a friend to liberty in every form. An opponent of Stuart despotism, of Presbyterian intolerance, of New England theocracy, and of Catholic oppression, he defended civil freedom and the rights of the Indians in America.

more in true English and in truth than an obstinate or wilfull person in the Church'. As to coercion in religion, 'there is a civill sword, called the sword of civill justice, which . . . cannot extend to spiritual and soul causes, spiritual and soule punishment, which belongs to that spirituall sword with two edges, the soule-piercing . . . Word of God'. Established religion is a disaster: 'Christianitie fell asleep in Constantine's bosome'. The State may well tolerate, for 'a false religion and worship will not hurt the civil state in case the worshipper break no civil law. And the civil laws not being broken, civil peace is not broken: and this only is the point in question'. This great treatise ends with the conclusion: 'That the doctrine of persecution for cause of conscience is most evidently and lamentably contrary to the doctrine of Christ Jesus, the Prince of peace. Amen'.

Cotton replied to Williams in *The Bloudy Tenent, Washed and Made White in the Bloud of the Lambe.* The latter, on his second visit to England, published his answer in *The Bloody Tenent yet More Bloody by Mr Cottons Endevour to Wash it White in the Blood of the Lambe* (1652). Only the year before this, in a letter to the governor of Massachusetts, Williams had protested against the persecution of dissenters and had defended his cause: 'I speak of Conscience, a persuasion fixed in the mind and heart of a man, which enforceth him to judge and to do so and so with respect to God, his worship. This Conscience is found in all mankind, more or less: in Jews, Turks, Papists, Protestants, pagans'.

One of the best known passages from Williams' writings occurs in his *Letter to the Town of Providence*, dated January 1655. In this letter he, as founder of the town, appeals to those citizens, most of them Baptists like himself, who objected to the military service essential to defend the town. Here Williams uses the image of a ship, whose passengers are completely free in all their activities, but whose crew must perform essential services or be punished. The imagery is particularly striking when it touches on toleration:

> There goes many a ship to sea, with many hundred souls in one ship, whose weal and woe is common, and is a true picture of a commonwealth ... It hath fallen out sometimes, that both Papists and Protestants, Jews and Turks, may be embarked in one ship; upon which supposal, I affirm that all the liberty of conscience that ever I pleaded for, turns upon these two hinges – that none of the Papists, Protestants, Jews or Turks, be forced to come to the ship's prayers or worship, nor compelled from their own particular prayers or worship, if they practise any. I further add, that I never denied that, notwithstanding this liberty, the commander of this ship ought to command the ship's course, yea, and also command that justice, peace, and sobriety, be kept and practised, both among the seamen and all the passengers.

The colony of Rhode Island, with its capital at Providence, did not have an easy life at the hand of its neighbours. Williams, however, was fortunate enough to receive support from the Commonwealth and Protectorate governments, and even after the Restoration, when a new royalist charter was granted in 1663, Charles II supported the policy of toleration. His charter laid down that, on the king's own decision, 'no person within the said colony, at any time hereafter shall be any wise molested, punished, disqualified or called in question for any difference of opinion in matters of religion'. Secure in this policy, the colony pursued its course in absolute liberty until the end of the century.

With the crowning achievement of Rhode Island we come to the end of a period in English history which witnessed an unprecedented increase in the total of civil and religious liberty available to freeborn Englishmen. The English contribution is unique. Alone of all European countries, England went beyond maintaining the rights of conscience, to the demand for personal and social justice as part of an inalienable liberty of which religious freedom was only a part. The forces producing a general acceptance of tolerance were varied: political compromise, religious indifference, the growth of sectarian opposition to established religion, the growth of rationalism, the rise of pacifism and opposition to force. But in the context of the social struggles of the seventeenth century perhaps the critical factor is the emergence to power of once inarticulate groupings, the seizure of the machinery of state by classes who were enabled for the first time to put into effect in government, commerce and religion a programme which appeared to them, and to others after them who were not necessarily from the same social sector, more in tune with the times and with elementary justice. To many Independents, as to most Levellers and sectarians, toleration was a *sine qua non* of just and godly authority; and by 1660 they had all learned to expect it as part of their political heritage.

8 Ebb tide of toleration

By the mid-seventeenth century toleration was hardly practised outside the English dominions. In pioneering Poland the Counter-Reformation had driven the Socinians out; in France the regime of the Edict of Nantes was crumbling. The Peace of Westphalia, despite its concessions to religious freedom, brought few practical gains in German territory. In Savoy the persecution of the Vaudois in 1655 seemed to promise a return to the worst epochs of religious oppression. Religious antipathy still appeared to be a potent force in Europe. Against this, however, must be set the factor of growing secularisation. Already in the Thirty Years War the alignment of parties had ceased to follow religious divisions. The Protestant armies of Sweden were financed by France, and after 1635 Lutheran Saxony had become an ally of Catholic Austria. Political considerations dwarfed confessional allegiances. The interests of absolutism and of commercial capitalism were alike impatient of religious divisions and restrictions, and each was to some extent responsible for an extension of toleration. It is not clear whether we can at this time speak of the secularisation of politics, but what is certain is that in several countries the interests of State were increasingly taken to be prior to those of faith. It is with the function of the State that this chapter is concerned, and with the extent to which State power was willing to concede civil and religious liberty.

Absolutism and religious liberty

As with enlightened despotism in the eighteenth century, absolutism in the seventeenth was usually content to be neutral before religious differences. The first of the Orange rulers in the United Provinces, Frederick Henry, allowed the Remonstrants to return to their country, and in 1630 a Remonstrant church was opened in Amsterdam, to be followed in 1632 by the foundation of a school that developed into a Remonstrant university. The relative tolerance that marked Orangist rule prepared the way for a slow revival of the Catholic religion.

In Brandenburg, which from John Sigismund (1608–19) onwards

had Calvinist Electors, toleration found one of its most distinctive expressions. Because of its geographically scattered holdings which stretched over the whole of northern Germany, the Electorate tended to include populations from all Christian denominations. In no territory was Calvinism a majority religion: the central Mark of Brandenburg was Lutheran, and both Cleves (on the Rhine) and East Prussia (beyond Poland) had mixed Catholic and Protestant populations. John Sigismund became a Calvinist in 1613; the year after this he issued an edict foregoing his *jus reformandi*, and allowing his subjects, contrary to the *cuius regio* principle, to differ from him in point of religion. The same policy was followed by Frederick William, the Great Elector (1640–88). Particularly after the territorial readjustments of the Peace of Westphalia, when some territories changed hands regardless of religion, it became imperative, as in the Calvinist Palatinate which went to a Catholic Wittelsbach ruler, to tolerate the majority religion in the State.

Frederick William was able to enforce tolerance because of his absolutist exercise of authority; but he also favoured an irenic policy in religion. A clear statement of this policy is available in the sermon preached before the Brandenburg Estates in 1653 by the court chaplain Stosch. After stating the need for toleration in place of religious strife, Stosch calls for unity between the Reformed and Lutherans, on the basis of agreement in essentials. The fundamental articles of belief, as laid down in the Bible, are common to both confessions: the Eucharist and predestination, although of importance, do not stand in the way of basic agreement. Evangelicals should also show charity and tolerance to Catholics.

The Elector wrote in 1645: 'We arrogate to ourselves no authority over the consciences of our subjects, but commit it to God alone'. He was committed in principle to tolerate all religions, regardless of the limits imposed later by the Treaty of Westphalia; for, he thought, it was 'unjust not to grant peace to peaceable people'. The aim of this liberal attitude was that his 'subjects might reach perfect unity in all points of the divine truth'. Far from believing that truth could be fully grasped in any religion, he considered that we can only see through a glass darkly and must therefore 'suffer one another till God should grant complete enlightenment'. No one religion was established in his dominions, but the Lutheran religion, being that of the majority, was given habitual precedence and preferential treatment in the Mark of Brandenburg. The limitations set on Catholicism allowed it to continue where it had existed, but not to expand. Thus although Catholics had rights of public worship in East Prussia, guaranteed by treaty with Prussia's overlord Poland, they were not allowed into Pomerania and Brandenburg proper. Nor were Jesuits allowed anywhere but in East Prussia. These were serious restrictions on the theoretical freedom proclaimed by the Elector, but they were probably necessary to eliminate confessional conflict in lands where the very presence of Papists and Jesuits may have aroused controversy.

French absolutism and Protestant freedom

Frederick William's regime involved a total separation of Church from State, but at the same time an absolute control over ecclesiastical affairs of all religions. French absolutism did not operate in this way. The creators of royal power in France were statesmen who could not conceivably base their religious policy on a separation of Church and State. On the other hand, they could and did guarantee the position of minority sects in the State, a policy enshrined in the Edict of Nantes. For three-quarters of a century and more the Edict remained in force as a symbol of religious concord within a Catholic State, at the very time that Protestant States refused all toleration to their Catholic populations.

Henry IV's settlement was bitterly disappointing to those Protestants who, like d'Aubigné, had sought equality and won only minority rights. Nevertheless the gains of Huguenots were immense. Equality before the law and eligibility for all public office, free public worship in selected localities, and the cession of specified fortress towns to the Reformed religion, were grants notable for their generosity. Not content with this, the more militant Protestants went to war for a brief period at the beginning of the reign of Louis XIII, but were soon obliged to recognise the *status quo. Politique* government came into its own. To balance his Catholic ministers, Henry the Great had his Huguenot minister Sully. Justice was administered impartially by tribunals on which both Catholics and Protestants were represented. Henry IV became for Frenchmen the symbol of national conciliation.

Under Cardinal Richelieu, who assumed power in 1624 under Louis XIII, *politique* government was perpetuated. Publicists, agents and colleagues of the Cardinal were chosen from the Huguenot party, particularly since French foreign policy during the Thirty Years War had a strong anti-Spanish and therefore pro-Protestant bias. 'Though divided in faith', Richelieu wrote in 1616, 'we remain united under one prince, for whose service no Catholic is so blind as to think a Spaniard better than a French Huguenot'. A strong opponent of the aggressive anti-Protestant attitude taken by the royal favourite Luynes during the Huguenot revolts in 1621, Richelieu was himself capable of acting firmly against religious separatism, and the desire to eliminate Protestant military power within France was from the start a cornerstone of his policy. The siege of La Rochelle (1627–8), which ended with the Peace of Alais, showed the Cardinal both firm and moderate towards his opponents among the militant Protestants. After La Rochelle he was encouraged by advisers to suppress the Protestant religion, but replied through Louis XIII that 'the conversion of the Reformed is a work we must await from Heaven'. At another time he observed: 'Diversity of religions may create divisions in the next world, but not in this'. This was typical of the statesman who had condemned the expulsion of the Moriscos from Spain in 1609 as the most barbarous act in human history.

Richelieu had shown that absolutism required not the elimination of dissident religions but the annihilation of their political autonomy. The quiescence of Protestants during the Frondes gave the young Louis XIV ample evidence of their loyalty: in 1652 he admitted explicitly that 'our subjects of the Reformed religion have given us incontrovertible proof of their affection and fidelity, which has pleased us very much'. Later, in 1666, the king maintained that 'those who profess the Reformed religion, being no less faithful than my other subjects, must not be treated with less consideration and kindness'. An era of concord between the two religions seemed to have been inaugurated. It should be noted in passing that the protagonists of absolutism, including Richelieu, were not tolerant by conviction. The great Cardinal at no time adopted other than political attitudes to the Protestants, and particularly after 1629 he began seriously to consider schemes of national reunion, not indeed for irenic motives, but to enhance his own prestige as head of a unified French Church.

His hopes were justified by the ecumenical mood that developed in France in the second half of the seventeenth century, signalling the liberalisation of French Calvinism but marking also the advent of indifferentism. Members of the upper classes became converted to the State religion because there lay the surest way to advancement. At the liberal Calvinist academy of Saumur, writers like Amyraut preached a universalism which undermined the dogmatic exclusivism of the Reformed Church. The Huguenots were outflanked both by Catholic control of the State and by Cartesian influence in the world of learning. Their irenicism was sincere, but also in part a counsel of despair. On the Catholic side there was a deepening charity. One prominent Huguenot lady claimed that 'not only do our adversaries take us for reasonable people, they also consider us Christians'. But there was also in Catholic quarters a new aggressiveness, which displayed itself in the Company of the Blessed Sacrament (1630–66), a vehicle of increasing intolerance among broad sections of the population.

The absolutism which Protestants accepted as their guarantee of security grew to become its greatest threat. Despite himself, Richelieu had set the trend, for by destroying the power of the

nobility and the feudal classes he weakened the supports of the Reform, who drew a substantial part of their power from the aristocracy. Of the 951 Protestant churches permitted in 1598, over a quarter, 257, were privately owned by the nobles; and in 1681 it was said of the Huguenots that 'nearly all those of this sect are nobles, merchants or artisans; there are very few from the lowest classes among them'. The collapse and defection of the aristocracy doomed the Reformed Churches, particularly after 1668 when their principal adherent, Turenne, embraced Catholicism in a sincere search for unity of faith. Turenne's conversion was followed by Bossuet's trumpet call, the *Exposition de la foi chrétienne* (1671), a book whose success helped to bring down the walls of Protestantism.

The Revocation of the Edict of Nantes

For all its initial importance, the Edict of Nantes was not a success, since its enforcement depended more on the voluntary tolerance of the Catholic population than on the goodwill of the government. Actual observance of the Edict probably ceased at the death of Henry IV in 1610. The period from 1610 to 1685 is that of the

One of a number of prints published in 1685 in Holland, depicting
atrocities that followed the Revocation of the Edict of Nantes in
that year. This one shows the transport of Huguenots to the galleys.
Criticism of the Revocation should be tempered by the fact that
France before 1685 was the only country in western Europe to have
constitutionally guaranteed toleration of religious minorities.

gradual revocation, bit by bit and piecemeal, of individual privileges contained in the Edict; so that the eventual date of the
revocatory Edict of Fontainebleau, 22 October 1685, has little
more than formal significance, and merely gave recognition to
what was already a *fait accompli*. Until the reign of Louis xiv
popular persecution, instigated probably by the clergy, was responsible for non-observance of the Edict. In 1651 the bishop of
Comminges addressed to the young king an appeal against 'this
unfortunate liberty of conscience, which destroys the liberty of the
true children of God'. In the years after this, and particularly
after the 1660s official support was given to persecution. In 1662
Protestant burials were forbidden in daylight hours. In 1669 all
cemeteries were put into Catholic hands. In 1679 the mixed-
membership judicial tribunals set up by the Edict of Nantes were
abolished. In 1680 all marriages between Protestants and Catholics
were declared invalid. Between 1679 and 1683 Protestants were
excluded from nearly all public professions up to and including
service in the royal household. Every year churches were closed
on various pretexts. At the end of 1684 a jury of theologians
informed Louis that he could legitimately revoke the Edict of
Nantes. In October the following year the perpetual and irrevoc-
able Edict was perpetually and irrevocably revoked.

To alienate a vast minority in the realm by open religious
persecution, threatened the internal security and welfare of the
country, and went against the policy of absolutism as practised
by the French crown since the time of Henry iv. Louis' reasons for
the Revocation – and the responsibility must be placed largely on
him – should be taken seriously. In August 1681 he had spoken of
'over a million Huguenots who remain in the realm'; by October
1685 he claimed to have effected the conversion of nearly one
million of this number. Consequently, to quote the preamble to the
Edict of Fontainebleau,

since the better and more numerous part of our subjects of the aforesaid
so-called Reformed religion has embraced the Catholic religion ... the
execution of the Edict of Nantes ... becomes useless.

Louis apparently believed that virtually no one remained to tolerate, so that toleration had lost its *raison d'être*. This self-deception is a measure of the extent to which absolute monarchy had lost contact with realities.

The reception given to the Revocation in France was unequivocally favourable. In the universal applause of French Catholics the only prominent voice to dissent was that of Condé. Protestant powers abroad, whose treatment of their own Catholic minorities had often been even more brutal, raised their hands in orror. and welcomed the 200,000 Huguenot exiles. Foreign Catholics tended to be critical. Queen Christina of Sweden considered the Revocation 'a false triumph'. The Pope gave his formal approval, but doubted the sincerity of Louis' motives and refused to celebrate a *Te Deum*. Both within and without the country, criticism soon arose of the violent measures, particularly the dragonnades, adopted by the government. Several bishops, notably Le Camus, bishop of Grenoble, denounced the dragonnades. and the bishop of Orléans obtained the removal of dragoons from his diocese. The intendant Daguesseau, a witness of the dislocation in the country, said ominously that 'both Catholicism and the State will feel the consequences of this more keenly in the future than either has yet experienced'. The Pope in 1688 said: 'We in no way approve these forced conversions, which are usually insincere'.

If the Revocation had stemmed the advance towards civil toleration in France, it also precipitated opposition to arbitrary power. Archbishop Fénelon of Cambrai, an ardent advocate of the decree but a conservative critic of Louis' absolutism, disapproved of coercion and wrote to the Elector of Cologne that 'force cannot persuade men'. In the widespread opposition of bishops, ministers and intendants to the employment of force in conversion, lay some hope for religious freedom in France. In 1689, 1692 and 1693 the famous engineer Vauban presented memoranda to the Crown, in which he pleaded for the restoration of the Edict of Nantes as a solution to the Huguenot revolt in the

Cévennes. 'Kings', he wrote, 'are certainly masters of the lives and goods of their subjects, but not of their opinions, for internal sentiments are beyond their jurisdiction'.

The resurgence of persecution

The eastern territories of Europe also witnessed at this time a resurgence of persecution provoked by government ineptitude and by national rebellion. Hungary had been one of the first countries in post-Reformation Europe to accept religious toleration. In the western (Habsburg) regions of Hungary the advance of the Reformation had been tolerated by the Emperors Ferdinand and Maximilian, and persecution commenced only under Rudolf. Opposition to his policy was expressed at the Hungarian Diet in 1604, but it was soon crushed by the intervention of the regent, the Archduke Matthias. Farther east, in the non-Habsburg part of Hungary known as Transylvania, which remained under Turkish protection from 1543 to 1691, the common interests of the noble class in their 'life on the marches', their struggle against the Turks, made them subordinate sectarianism to national security. Lutheranism had made great progress by the mid-sixteenth century, but the Catholic queen was obliged to keep the peace by decreeing at the Diet of Torda in 1557 that 'every one might hold the faith of his choice, together with the new rites or the former ones, without offence to any'. The acceptance of religious liberty was so general that in 1571 the Unitarian king, John Sigismund, was able to decree that the 'four received religions' of Transylvania – Catholicism, Lutheranism, Calvinism and Unitarianism – be put on an equal footing. John Sigismund's successor in 1571, Stephen Báthory, later king of Poland, maintained this tolerant policy. His nephew Sigismund started a Catholic reaction which led him in 1595 to exchange Turkish overlordship for Habsburg. This precipitated a revolt by the Hungarians, until in 1606 Stephen Bocskai won Transylvanian independence and re-established religious liberty. From 1604 to 1691 the kingdom had Calvinist

rulers. The most famous of these, Gabriel Bethlen (1613–29), upheld the liberties of his subjects, irrespective of race or religion. But towards the end of the century persecution of the Unitarians commenced. After the siege of Vienna in 1683, the prince of Transylvania offered to accept Habsburg suzerainty in return for preservation of the 'four received religions'. On these terms Leopold I was in 1690 elected ruler of Transylvania. Under him a Catholic reaction began to undermine the freedom of the kingdom.

In Habsburg Hungary the advent of the Counter Reformation led to spectacular successes for the Church of Rome, under the able leadership of Peter Pázmány, archbishop of Esztergom. A supporter of moderate methods, Pázmány opposed the use of force in effecting conversions. This moderate policy was followed, for political reasons, by the Emperor Ferdinand III, who in December 1645 concluded a peace treaty at Linz with the aggressive Transylvanian ruler Rákóczi. By this treaty, Hungary was guaranteed the benefits of religious liberty, and Protestant churches were returned to use. This settlement lasted less than a generation. Habsburg policy and the extension of German influence led in the

Contemporary illustration of a Turkish attack on the monastery of Sisak
in Croatia in 1592 repulsed by the monks. A year later the Turks were
heavily defeated when their siege of the monastery was relieved.
The ever-present threat of Turkish expansion throughout the sixteenth
and seventeenth centuries hardened feelings against non-Christians and
often helped towards toleration between different Christian communities.

1660s to the first stirrings of national revolt. The government
struck back in the first instance against national liberties, but
hand in hand with this went a calculated persecution of the
Protestant minority. German troops were sent in with the avowed
aim of crushing Hungarian independence. Hundreds of Calvinist
pastors were dismissed or deported, others were imprisoned.
Unable to suppress the Hungarian rebellion completely, largely
because of French aid to the insurgents, the Emperor in 1681
summoned the national Diet and accepted a compromise with the
ruling classes in Hungary. The privileges of the aristocracy and the
integrity of Hungary were recognised, but toleration of dissident
public worship was forbidden and the religion of the peasantry
was made to depend on their lords. The seventeenth century in
Hungary ended with the collapse of toleration and the consolidation of the noble class.

In Holland the heavy hand of orthodoxy was felt once again.
Pierre Jurieu, leader in exile of the French Huguenots, felt it his
duty to purge the Reformed Church of the dangerous liberal
doctrines that had been active in France long before the Revocation. At Rotterdam in 1686 a new synod was held, to affirm all
the decisions of the Synod of Dort and to expel dissidents. A fellow
exile, Pierre Bayle, observed in 1691 of these measures: 'God
preserve us from the Protestant Inquisition! Another five or six
years or so and it will have become so terrible that people will be
longing to have the Roman one back again'.

The intolerance of the English Restoration

The retreat from religious liberty was equally strong in the country
which had progressed most towards it. In England a government
of Independent gentry was replaced by one of Anglican gentry
and nobility. Elections to the Restoration Parliament gave a
majority to the two largest and most intolerant sects in the country,
the Presbyterians and the Anglicans. Faced with a breakdown of
government and the threat of yet more radical social and religious

adventures, the English ruling classes in 1660 chose the old mixture as before. And, as before, enthusiastic Anglicans claimed monopoly rights in their country by passing prohibitive legislation against all other Christian denominations. The collection of decrees known as the Clarendon Code flatly contradicted all Charles II's previous assurances. In the 1660 Declaration of Breda, made just before his return, he had promised that 'we do declare a liberty to tender consciences; and that no man shall be called in question for differences of opinion in matters of religion which do not disturb the peace of the kingdom'. In 1661, while awaiting implementation of Charles' promises, John Sturgion published *A Plea for Toleration*; and seven nonconformist ministers greeted the opening of the Cavalier Parliament that May with the publication of *Sion's Groans for the Distressed*.

These pleas were ignored in legislation that set up the religious monopoly of Anglicanism as strongly as ever. The reaction against Scottish bigotry and sectarian chaos made it an unsuitable time to advocate toleration. Political reasons governed this situation, since the fear of the Commonwealth was still strong in men's minds. Consequently the Conventicle Acts of 1664 and 1670 were directed explicitly against 'seditious sectaries and other disloyal persons who under pretence of tender consciences do at their meetings contrive insurrections'. There was little doubt that tender consciences deserved some toleration, but it must be of a kind that infallibly assured political security. Arguments both for and against toleration were therefore set in a political context, and the question revolved largely round the rights and powers of the magistrate.

The heritage of the Cambridge Platonists in the post-Restoration period, and the continuance of their doctrines by the large Latitudinarian party in the Church of England, helped to promote the cause of religious liberalism. The rise of a non-dogmatic approach to religion, and a new stress on the primacy of rationalism and morality, created a fundamental departure from tradition. The theologians of the Restoration period were reacting consciously against irrational enthusiasm based on devotion to doctrine. Latitudinarianism encouraged tolerance through an emphasis on the reason of individual men. Each man, by using his own reason, was to become the arbiter of his own belief and action; and the personal religion so achieved had inherent rights which could not be threatened by authority. The pretensions of both Church and State were a threat to the rights of reason, since they could imperil personal freedom and judgment. In this way the Latitudinarians worked towards a belief in the correctness of toleration as something necessary to preserve the dignity of rational man.

By their scepticism, they also undermined the acceptance of dogma. The Latitudinarian Joseph Glanvill held that the main function of reason was 'to destroy the confidence of assertions and establish a prudent reservedness and modesty in opinions'. The gospel of reason was such that even the fundamental articles so characteristic of irenic Christianity were dispensed with. The three points enumerated by Glanvill as being necessary to true religion contained no reference to any article of Christian revelation, and resembled a natural religion more than any other. Not surprisingly, the drift away from dogma was one that tended to naturalism and Deism, the latter being best expressed in John Toland's *Christianity not Mysterious* (1696).

Although tolerance and non-dogmatism marked the writings of Latitudinarians, who were before 1688 the most influential preachers in London, there is a curious equivocation in their personal attitudes. Stillingfleet, later Dean of St Paul's, in 1660 published his *Irenicum*, which encouraged a liberal attitude towards noncomformists, but two decades later he published considered attacks on granting legal toleration to dissenters. Glanvill went even further than dissenters in his rejection of dogmatic formulae, but could also state that 'to strive for toleration is to contend against all government; to allow the plea of conscience is to put an end to all laws'. John Tillotson, later archbishop of Canterbury, phrased his Latitudinarianism in the most generous way:

I had much rather persuade anyone to be a good man, than to be of any party and denomination of Christians whatsoever; for I doubt not but the belief of the ancient creed, provided that we entertain nothing that is destructive of it, together with a good life will certainly save a man, and without this no man can have reasonable hopes of salvation, no, not in an infallible Church, if there were any such to be found in the world.

The replacement of dogma by moralism may seem to have prepared the way for toleration. But the clergy were on the whole, and with few exceptions, supporters of the religious, social and political exclusivism of their Church. Stillingfleet in 1680, preaching on the 'Mischief of Separation', claimed that 'an universal toleration is that Trojan Horse which brings in our enemies without being seen'. Realising that acceptance of the general principle of toleration would mean conceding it even to Catholics, he preferred to oppose it, largely on political grounds. Tillotson was similarly concerned to enforce complete obedience to 'the established religion of a nation, though it be false'. Such complete Erastianism was again motivated by fear of political insecurity as a consequence of toleration. More particularly, the danger of the Catholic Duke of York succeeding Charles II as king aroused the forces in Church and State against any concession to non-Anglicans, for fear that concessions to Protestants would logically involve concessions to Papists. This explains the failure of Charles II's Declaration of Indulgence in 1672, a measure which suspended the penal laws and would have granted rights of public worship to Protestant dissenters and private worship to Catholics. The motives for the Declaration are interesting:

It being evident by the sad experience of twelve years, that there is very little fruit of all those forcible courses . . . we do now accordingly issue out this our royal Declaration, as well for the quieting the minds of our good subjects in these points, for inviting strangers in this conjuncture to come and live under us, and for the better encouragement of all to a cheerful following of their trades and callings . . . as also for preventing for the future the danger that might otherwise arise from private meetings and seditious conventicles.

Parliament's firm opposition to the Declaration resulted in the imposition of even stronger sanctions on the Catholic population. Happily the pressure for milder courses continued. On the non-conformist side John Owen and John Sturgion led the propagandists. Owen's *Indulgence and Toleration Considered* (1667) pointed out that not even in the Roman Church was there absolute uniformity. Persecution, he said, will impoverish the country. The State certainly has an interest in preserving man's civil loyalties; 'but as for Religion, it is the Choice of Men', and does not concern the government. His *A Peace Offering in an Apology and Humble Plea for Indulgence and Liberty of Conscience* (1668), repeated most of the classic arguments in favour of religious freedom.

On the Anglican side, Herbert Croft, bishop of Hereford, published anonymously in 1675 his *The Naked Truth*, which urged relief for dissenters. Gilbert Burnet, later bishop of Salisbury, was one of the more consistent supporters of toleration, and went farther than most of his colleagues towards appreciating the need for mildness, even to Catholics. 'I have long looked on liberty of conscience', he was to write in his classic *History of My Own Time*, 'as one of the rights of human nature, antecedent to society . . . and our Saviour's rule, of doing as we would be done by, seemed to be a very express decision to all men'.

William Penn and the struggle for minority rights

Among the most eminent advocates of tolerance was the Quaker leader William Penn (1644–1718). His *The Great Case of Liberty of Conscience* (1670) was dated from Newgate prison, where he was then a prisoner. The position of Quakers was at the time analogous to that of the Anabaptists in the sixteenth century. Hated and despised by all established religions, and bitterly persecuted by both Calvinists and Anglicans, the Quakers led all other sects in the number of their martyrs in both Old and New England. It is estimated that in the five years of the Protectorate alone, nearly 2000 Quakers were imprisoned and 21 died in gaol. The links

THE

GREAT CASE

OF

Liberty of Conſcience

Once more Briefly

Debated & Defended,

BY THE

Authority of *Reaſon, Scripture,* and
Antiquity :

Which may ſerve the Place of a General Reply to
ſuch late Diſcourſes, as have Oppos'd a
Tolleration.

The Authour *W. P.*

*For whatſoever ye would that men ſhould do unto you, that do you unto
them,* Matth. 7. 22.
Render unto Cæſar, *the things that are* Cæſars ; *and to* God, *the
things that are* Gods, Matth. 12. 27.

Printed in the Year, 1670,

William Penn's *The Great Case of Liberty of Conscience* was a socially conservative defence of toleration by the most eminent member of a radical and despised sect. His struggle culminated in the foundation of Pennsylvania as a state open to men of all creeds.

between Quakers and Levellers were fairly close, and the Leveller leader Lilburne joined them before his death. It appears also that several members of the even more radical Diggers, including Winstanley, joined the sect. The social conscience of the Quakers made them potentially as subversive in matters of State as their doctrine of the 'inner light' made them revolutionary in matters of religion: so at least many contempories thought.

For an outstanding man like Penn, son of a famous admiral, propertied and socially acceptable, to join the Quakers, was of inestimable benefit to the sect. His influence, whether personal or through the pen, brought them eventual respite in England and a home abroad in America.

In *The Great Case*, Penn defined liberty of conscience to mean the right of public worship. Persecution, he said, erred in five ways: it intruded on faith and conscience, which are the domain of God alone; it overturned Christianity by contradicting the meekness of Christ and the spiritual nature of his kingdom; it went against the Scriptures, which oppose restraint; it was detrimental both to natural rights and to the free use of reason; and it went against the true interests of government, which is not served by force, since 'force never yet made either a good Christian or a good subject'. Penn then developed an argument which he was to amplify in later writings. Liberty is a natural right as much as property is, and both these rights are guaranteed by civil society, and by the ancient laws of England. 'We are persuaded that no Temporary Subsequential Law whatever, to our Fundamental Rights (as this of Force on Conscience is) can invalid so essential a part of the Government, as an English Liberty and Property'. Intolerance is both illegal and unconstitutional, since the original contract between people and government laid down no condition that all the people must conform in religion in order to share civil rights. 'To conclude, Liberty of Conscience we ask as our undoubted Right by the Law of God, of Nature, and of our own Country'. Five years later, in 1675, Penn issued his *England's Present Interest Discovered*. Here again he emphasised that civil rights are prior to all demands of religious conformity, and that liberty of conscience is a property to which all Englishmen are entitled. 'A Man may be a very good English Man, and yet a very indifferent Church-man', he wrote, stressing the separate interests of Church and State. The interesting feature of these arguments for religious liberty are their rationalist and secular nature, as well as their social conservatism. The difference from the religious radicalism of earlier periods could not be more forthright.

The cause of toleration under Charles II was unfortunately adopted by the Earl of Shaftesbury to promote the interests of the Whig party, and when Shaftesbury discredited himself by his vendetta against the Duke of York and the Crown, toleration crumbled into the mass of Whig rubble. Penn, who had been a

This pleasant print of 1699 shows a Quaker general assembly presided over by George Whitehead and William Penn. By this date the Quakers could benefit from the substantial religious (though not civil) liberty offered by the 1689 Toleration Act, which granted them freedom of worship and released them from the obligation to take the oath when testifying in court.

strong supporter of the Whigs, now decided to approach the Crown and ask for a grant of land in America as payment of a government debt to his late father. The territory granted him by charter became known as Pennsylvania, and provided at last a haven of liberty for his persecuted coreligionists. In England Penn found moreover that the new king (since 1685) was sympathetic to his aims.

The succession of a Catholic king in England augured well for toleration. Absolutist in belief, and a would-be absolutist in practice, James II was determined not to let Parliament or the Church stand in his way. At the same time, he appears to have been a sincere believer in liberty of conscience, and not to have desired it exclusively as a means of promoting the Catholic interest. When in October 1687 he issued a Declaration of Indulgence suspending all penals laws against dissenters, he professed that:

We cannot but heartily wish, as it will easily be believed, that the people of our dominions were members of the Catholic Church; yet we humbly thank Almighty God it is, and has of long time been our constant sense and opinion (which upon divers occasions we have declared) that conscience ought not to be constrained, nor people forced in matters of mere religion. It has ever been directly contrary to our inclination, as we think it is to the interest of government, which it destroys by spoiling trade, depopulating countries, and discouraging strangers, and finally, that it never obtained the end for which it was employed. And in this we are the more confirmed by the reflection we have made upon the conduct of the four last reigns.

For after all the frequent and pressing endeavours that were used in each of them, to reduce these kingdoms to an exact conformity in religion, it is visible the success has not answered the design; and that the difficulty is invincible.

The reasoning is lucid and the honesty unequivocal. Penn, a long-standing friend of the new king, could testify to James' sincerity. In 1673, when Duke of York, the latter had told the Quaker leader 'that he looked upon us as a quiet industrious people, and though he was not of our judgment yet he liked our good lives'. When a delegation of Quakers, Penn amongst them, went to thank James for the Declaration of Indulgence, the king said: 'Some of you know (I am sure you do, Mr Penn) that it was always my Principle, that Consciences ought not to be forced, and that all men ought to have the Liberty of their Consciences'.

Penn's personal testimony to James' integrity was emphatic:

Whatever Practices of Roman Catholicks we might reasonably object against (and no Doubt but such there are), yet he has disclaimed and reprehended those ill Things by his declared Opinion against Persecution, by the Ease in which he actually indulges all Dissenters, and by the Confirmation he offers in Parliament for the Security of the Protestant Religion and Liberty of Conscience. And in his Honour, as well as my own Defence, I am obliged in Conscience to say that he has ever declared to me, *It was his Opinion*. And on all Occasions, when Duke, he never refused me the repeated Proofs of it, as often as I had any poor Sufferers for Conscience-sake to solicit his Help for.

The Quakers, led by Penn and Robert Barclay, had formed an alliance for toleration between sectaries and Papists. While such an alliance might conceivably succeed under a Catholic king, it could not fail to horrify the landed and trading interest. Penn's *Good Advice to the Church of England, Roman Catholic, and Protestant Dissenter* (1687) was a passionate plea in support of the Declaration of Indulgence. The true enemies of liberty, he affirmed, were not the small minority of Catholics, but the entrenched majority of Anglican Tories. Catholics were no intrinsic danger, and, in any case, 'Violence and Tyranny are no natural Consequences of Popery, for then they would follow everywhere, and in all places and times alike'. The argument unfortunately carried little conviction to those English Protestants who felt that they saw in the 1685 Revocation of the Edict of Nantes, the natural consequences of the Papist tendency to persecute. Moreover, the high-handed way in which James was attacking the privileges of the Tory oligarchies alienated potential supporters of the Crown, who turned for help to William of Orange. The Declaration had one important effect. It compelled Anglicans to recognise the necessity of freedom for dissenters, if these were ever to be attracted away from James II. In November 1687 William of Orange and his wife Mary, daughter of the English king, issued a declaration from Holland in which they supported complete liberty of worship for dissenters and the retention of penal laws against Catholics, but with their right to full liberty of conscience assured. Such a promise was exactly what was needed to swing support away from James.

The retreat from liberty in the English-speaking world

After the king's overthrow in 1688, the new rulers of England, William and Mary, put their views into effect in the 1689 Toleration Act. For all its importance in granting liberty to non-conforming Protestants, the Act was reactionary in tone and content, and fell far short of contemporary ideals. In order to placate the English upper classes, William and Mary omitted to fulfil even the terms of their 1687 declaration. Unlike James' Declaration, the 1689 Act was prefaced by no doctrine of tolerance; the motives for it were too plainly political. Not a single old law against religious liberty was repealed or suspended; instead dissenters were granted relief by being *exempted* 'from the Penalties of certaine Lawes'. All the penal laws were held to be in force, particularly against Catholics and Unitarians, who received no relief whatsoever despite the promises of 1687. Toleration was extended to Baptists, and Quakers were tolerated if they made a declaration in place of the required oath against transubstantiation.

It is true that the Toleration Act opened up a new era in English political and economic life, and prepared the way for Protestant supremacy in the West. But it represented a step away from the ideals propounded by Penn and his predecessors. When Sir John Reresby said on the eve of the 1688 Revolution that 'most men were now convinced that liberty of conscience was a thing of advantage to the nation', he may have been reflecting a substantial body of sincere opinion, but the fight for adequate toleration was only just beginning. Dissenters were still excluded from public office by their religion, and a generation was to pass before their religious liberty was expanded into civil equality. In America, the Toleration Act destroyed what liberty of religion had existed up to 1689.

In Anglican Virginia, the Act brought no change for ten years, the first dissenting minister in that colony being licensed only in 1699. Eleven years later, in 1710, the governor wrote that 'this government is in perfect peace and tranquillity, under due obedience to royal authority and a gentlemanly conformity to the Church of England'. In Carolina, this conformity went further: the Anglican Church was formally established there in 1704 and all non-conformists were disfranchised. In Plymouth the Act brought little change, since sects were freely tolerated; the colony was in 1691 incorporated by charter into the colony of Massachusetts. The new charter specified that 'forever hereafter there shall be liberty of conscience allowed in the worship of God, to all Christians (except Papists)'. This was a step back from the government appointed in 1685 when the old charter of Massachusetts had been revoked. On that occasion James II had ordered full liberty of conscience to be practised in the colony.

The most important retrogressions from toleration occurred in the crown and proprietary colonies. New Amsterdam, which was captured from the Dutch in 1664, remained in English hands despite a temporary reversion to its former owners in 1673–4. Renamed New York, it was granted by Charles II to his brother the Duke of York. James here made his first display of practical tolerance. It was announced that 'in all the territories of His Royal Highness liberty of conscience is allowed . . . nor shall any person be molested, fined, or imprisoned for differing in judgment in matters of religion, who professes Christianity'. A Christian church was to be established in each parish of the colony, and all the churches, of whatever denomination, were to come under the direct control of the civil authority. After the territory's recapture in 1674, James sent the following instructions to Governor Sir Edmund Andros:

You shall permitt all persons of what Religion soever, quietly to inhabitt within the precincts of your jurisdiccon, without giveing them any disturbance or disquiet whatever for, or by reason of, their differing opinions in matters of Religion: Provided they give noe disturbance to ye publique peace, nor doe molest or disquiet others in the free exercise of their religion.

The toleration established under James continued undisturbed during his rule in England, and the Catholic governor of that time, Thomas Dongan, proved himself an outstanding servant of the colony. All this changed in 1691, when Governor Henry Sloughter was sent out by William and Mary. Unitarian and Catholic Christians were denied civil and religious toleration, and all nonconforming Protestants were excluded from office.

New Netherland between the Hudson and Delaware rivers, renamed New Jersey at its conquest by the English in 1664, was likewise granted to the Duke of York, and full religious liberty was established there under his regime. After the recapture of New Netherland in 1674, the western part of New Jersey came under Quaker proprietorship. The new owners, who included William Penn, in 1677 decreed that 'no man . . . upon earth hath power or authority to rule over men's consciences in religious matters; therefore, it is . . . ordained, that no person or persons whatsoever within the said province . . . shall be . . . called in question . . . for the sake of his opinion . . . or worship towards God in matters of religion'. Four years later, in 1681, the first assembly of west New Jersey issued a law that 'liberty of conscience in matters of faith and worship shall be granted to all people within this Province'.

The eastern part of New Jersey had meanwhile been sold, on the death of its proprietor in 1680, to a group in which Quakers preponderated but which included Catholics as well as Presbyterians. After the 1688 Revolution New Jersey lost its Quaker character, and its charters, for both the eastern and western portion, were surrendered to the Crown in 1702. The colony became thereafter a royal province.

Penn's experience with the New Jersey colony inspired him to

press for a proprietary grant. This was issued by charter in March 1681, and Penn was given territory to the west of the Delaware river. Pennsylvania, as it came to be called, was a colony based throughout on civil and religious liberty. Penn himself arrived in America in October 1682 and visited the site of the capital being built for him at Philadelphia, the city of brotherly love. Like Roger Williams before him, he was anxious to live in amity with the Indians, from whom he formally purchased the land already granted to him by charter. The new colony rapidly became wealthy and populous, at peace with its Indian neighbours and internally secure. One of the principal attractions of Pennsylvania to immigrants from Europe was its very wide religious freedom. All

An anti-Quaker pamphlet of 1701
by Francis Bugg, a former Friend,
who later became an implacable
adversary of the Society.
He wrote a series of tracts
attacking the Quakers.

Christians of whatever denomination, that is all who 'profess faith in Jesus Christ' and confessed 'one Almighty and Eternal God', were enfranchised and could hold office. Even Catholics were in this category. Complete freedom of conscience and worship was assured to all. But Penn, despite his own inclinations, was obliged to accept certain restrictions on liberty. Non-Christians, though free to live in Pennsylvania, were denied the franchise and could not hold office. After the Toleration Act there were further restrictions on liberty, and all Catholics and Unitarians were disqualified from office. It was in vain that Penn resisted these changes.

The retreat from freedom in America was, of course, linked directly to events in England. The English government was able to interfere virtually at will in the constitutions and charters of its colonies, so that the interests of proprietors such as Baltimore (whose charter was annulled by William III) and Penn were set aside in the interests of Protestant supremacy. The effect of this must, however, not be exaggerated. Rhode Island seems to have practised complete religious liberty throughout the colonial period, and in some colonies observance of the law would not have been as rigorous as in England. Moreover, Catholics, Unitarians and non-Protestants were a small minority in America, and the evil done to them can fairly be set against the good done by the Toleration Act in those colonies which were set free from the control of Puritan oligarchies.

9 The theory of toleration

By the middle of the seventeenth century the greatest exponents of toleration had had their say. W. K. Jordan claims with justice that 'the theory of religious toleration stood substantially complete in 1660'. The liberal Calvinists in Holland, the Latitudinarians in England, the colonial pioneers in America, had together formulated a set of principles which were not appreciably enlarged upon in the second half of the century. The fact that only a minority of people actively supported toleration, and that the principles drawn up by religious leaders were seldom put into full effect by politicians, is of minor consequence. Governments and governing classes are invariably behind the times in their political philosophy, and it was enough for the moment that in the West as a whole the most prominent theorists were in favour of toleration.

In the West: but it would be fairer to limit this to the Protestant West alone. In continental Europe no influential body of Catholic thought had taken up the mantle of the humanists and irenicists of the post-Reformation epoch. Catholic governments in France and Hungary had towards the end of the century recommenced the severe persecution of Protestants, and in Catholic Italy and Spain dissent was almost completely stifled. Only in the Anglo-Saxon countries, where adherents of Rome were a crushed minority, did Catholics become open supporters of tolerance, and some of them, like John Austin (1613–69) in England, expressed their arguments in theoretical form.

To attribute the decline of tolerance at the end of the seventeenth century to absolutist government, an argument often applied to Louis XIV, is misleading and unfair. In France, as we have seen, the absolutist structure relied largely on toleration, so that absolutism by itself is not a sufficient explanation of the Edict of Fontainebleau. In Brandenburg, again, absolutism thrived on the necessary toleration of dissenting minorities. The one truly absolutist Stuart king, James II, was precisely the one who had given incontrovertible evidence, both in America and in England, of his support for universal toleration. In the United Provinces the rule of the authoritarian House of Orange coincided with an era of greater freedom for the large Catholic minority. It would be true – and paradoxical – to say that absolutism was in the long run the friend of toleration, since by asserting its authority and control over the majority Church it subordinated Church to State and prevented the former from exercising undue coercion against dissenting minorities.

The recrudescence of persecution in the later seventeenth century shows clearly that practice lagged behind theory, for the leading philosophers in Europe tended to agree that a large measure of toleration was not only advisable and just but also right. Among those who shared this belief were Althusius, Spinoza, Pufendorf and Thomasius.

The Politics of Althusius

One of the first theorists to accept toleration as a cornerstone of political practice was Johannes Althusius (1557–1638). Born in Westphalia, he ended his days as the chief magistrate of Emden in the United Provinces. This post, which he held from 1604 till his death, gave him the experience on which to base his political judgments. Although he was a staunch member of the Reformed Church, and a critic of the Remonstrant party, Althusius in his *Politica methodice digesta* (1603) set down principles which offer a good illustration of the liberal policy pursued by Dutch magistrates in the seventeenth century.

Althusius supports an established Christian Church, but is far from giving it a theocratic position: 'Clergymen have been subjected to the power of kings, except in those matters that are proper to them . . . the preaching of the Word and the administration of the sacraments'. The interaction of Church and State is close, and while the magistrate directs the clergy on all matters of external order, the clergy direct the magistrates in questions of ecclesiastical censures and things pertaining to salvation. All Church assemblies, councils and visitations are directed by the magistrates, who have the duty of enforcing the decrees of synods. 'The

correction and reformation of the Church from all error, heresy, idolatry, schism and corruption pertains to the magistrate . . . The administrator ought to establish and permit only one religion in his realm, and that the true one. He shall expel all atheists and all impious and profane men'.

The last sentence in fact covers a wide range of persons. Althusius opposes toleration for 'epicureans, sectaries, heretics, seducers, profaners of the Sabbath, despisers of the true religion, magicians, soothsayers, perjurers, idolaters', and so on. But despite this he is willing to allow religious dissidents. 'A pious magistrate can in good conscience permit Jews to live in his dominion and territory, and to dwell and engage in business with the faithful'. They may have synagogues if they do not insult the official Christian religion. As for Catholics, 'the magistrate can in good conscience permit them to live within the boundaries of the realm if the pious do not partake of their superstitions'. But they are not to have churches.

The Exchange or Bourse at Amsterdam was built in 1608–11. It became the key to Holland's commercial and political operations, and negotiated business with all nations and all faiths, including Catholics and Jews. The success of this tolerant policy did not go unobserved in other countries.

Heresies in general may be tolerated so long as they have not been authoritatively condemned and are not politically subversive: heresies of the latter kind 'should be severely attended to by the magistrate with exile, prison or the sword'. So far Althusius reflects the *status quo*, and his last observation prepares the way for the political persecution of the Remonstrants.

He goes on, however, to deliver an unqualified condemnation of intolerance. 'A magistrate in whose realm the true worship of God does not thrive should take care that he does not claim imperium over that area of the faith and religion of men that exists only in the soul and conscience. God alone has imperium in this area ... Those who err in religion are to be ruled not by external force or by corporal arms but by the sword of the Spirit ... If they cannot be persuaded by the Word of God, how much less can they be coerced by the threats of punishments of the magistrate'.

Though Althusius condemns persecution on principle, he appears to be more concerned by the very utilitarian consideration that persecution produces civil unrest. 'Heretics, so far as they are delinquent in external actions, are to be punished just as much as any other subjects. But if the magistrate invades the imperium of God, exceeds the limits of his jurisdiction, and arrogates to himself imperium over the consciences of men, he shall not do this evil with impunity. For because of this action, seditions and tumults, which persecution is wont to cause, will arise in his realm ... Today in France, Belgium, Hungary, Poland and other realms persecution causes disorders, tumults and seditions. But where there are no persecutions, there everything is peaceful, even though there are different religions ... Whoever therefore wishes to have a peaceful realm should abstain from persecution'. It should be clear, claims Althusius, that 'the magistrate who is not able, without peril to the commonwealth, to change or overcome the discrepancy in religion and creed, ought to tolerate dissenters for the sake of public peace and tranquility, lest the entire realm, and with it the household of the Church, be overthrown'.

This position represents accurately the practice of many Calvinist magistrates in Holland. While on the one hand condemning toleration of 'false' religions, on the other they gave extensive freedom to dissenting Christians because it promoted trade and social stability.

Theorists in Holland and Germany

In his *Tractatus Theologico-Politicus*, published at Hamburg in 1670, the Dutch Jew Baruch Spinoza (1632–77) accepted as his basic premise that the liberty of the individual is the foundation of the constitution of States. Correspondingly, the end of the State is the promotion of the liberty of subjects, for to subvert their liberty would be to subvert the State. In religious matters, individuals have complete freedom of conscience: 'the right of judging and interpreting religion [is] lodged with each individual man, because it is his own peculiar and private business'. But Spinoza advocates thorough Erastianism in the government of religion: 'No one, save by the authority of the sovereign or government, has any right of administration in ecclesiastical affairs'. The State must therefore be the peace-keeper in religion, by not favouring one sect over another. Only the State can act as a policeman: 'Liberty of opinion must of necessity be conceded, and men so governed that though they notoriously think differently from one another, they may still live together in peace and amity'. Taking as his example the struggle between Remonstrants and Counter-Remonstrants in his native Holland, he stressed that the State must remain impartial between both. If there is to be a State Church it must be totally controlled by the State, except in matters of inward faith; but the State must not discriminate between religions. Coexistence should take as its model Amsterdam, where 'men of every nation and creed and sect live together in the utmost harmony'.

Samuel Pufendorf (1632–94), the German jurist, whose *De habitu religionis christianae ad vitam civilem* was published at Bremen in 1687, was one of the principal theorists of natural law

Gerard Dou's beautiful portrait of Rembrandt's mother reading a Bible emphasises the pre-eminent position in seventeenth-century Europe enjoyed by Holland as a refuge for Protestant refugees and as a unique centre of unrestricted and free printing.

in the seventeenth century. In his *De habitu* he stressed a point we have already seen outlined by Penn, namely that the original contract which first set up civil society did not involve any surrender of one's religious beliefs. The magistrate, Pufendorf maintained, has no authority over faith and opinion: 'The Magistrate is no more concerned in the different ways whereby men worship God, and may do so without injuring one another, than he is in the different tenets and opinions which they hold in physics or any other science. And yet there is no question but if men under pretence of religion shall disturb the peace of the government, shall raise rebellions or hatch treasons, they are to be restrained and punished by the civil powers. It is no part of the prince's duty to prosecute those who differ from him in religion'.

Pufendorf supported the separation of Church and State, but only to the extent that the State was not to interfere in matters of faith. For the rest, he approved of an established Church in which the State could appoint ministers and summon synods. He was clearly an Erastian who considered secular authority the best guarantee of liberty. Dissenting sects would of necessity be tolerated, for 'mere external force and civil compulsion can fill the Church with none but hypocrites'. There was no inherent danger in variety of religions, and 'difference of opinions in religion does not of itself, and in its own nature, tend to disturb the public peace and quiet'.

Finally, some mention should be made of Christian Thomasius (1655–1728), whose writings owe a great deal to John Locke. A native of Leipzig, and later professor then rector of the University of Halle, Thomasius devoted several treatises to the question of religious error. Of these perhaps the best known is his *Das Recht evangelischer Fürsten in theologischen Streitigkeiten* (1696), in which he deals with the problems of Church and State. All religious dissidents, he maintained, should be tolerated if they do not disturb the public peace. The principal exception to this are Catholics, who cannot be tolerated in so far as they have a loyalty to a foreign prince, and believe that faith cannot be kept with non-Catholics. In his *Disputatio an haeresis sit crimen*? (1697) he argued that the only criteria for judging religious error were the Scriptures and reason. Reason showed that heresy was an error not of the will, but of the understanding; it was consequently not a crime, and not liable to punishment.

The evidence of these theorists points unmistakeably to a general acceptance of the principles of religious liberty in learned circles. The countries which followed such principles were still few in number. Prominent among them was Holland, as shown by the currency of the phrase 'an Amsterdam of religions' to mean a universal toleration. By the time of the visit of the English ambassador Sir William Temple in 1672 it was recognised that all sects, even Catholics, lived there in greater freedom than in most other Protestant countries. Temple had this to say of the position of Catholics:

What was not provided for by the Constitutions of their Government was so, in a very great degree, by the Connivance of their Officers, Who, upon certain constant Payments from every Family, suffer the exercise of the Roman-Catholick Religion in their several Jurisdictions ... This, I suppose, has been the reason that though those of this Profession are very numerous in the Country, among the Peasants and considerable in the Cities; and not admitted to any publick charges; Yet they seem to be a sound piece of the State.

He went on to report that 'of all other Religions, every Man enjoys the free exercise in his own Chamber, or his own House, unquestioned and unespied'; and that 'no man can here complain of pressure in his Conscience'. Finally, as though to defend the United Provinces from the charge that active religion had declined there, Temple concluded: 'Religion may possibly do more good in other places, but it does less hurt here'. To him and to the English, moreover, the great interest of relative toleration in Holland was that it coincided with Dutch commercial supremacy in Europe. Was there perhaps some connection between religious liberty and success in business?

Economic motives for toleration

The question had long been mooted with reference to the Jews. In Catholic Spain it had become axiomatic that finance thrived with Jews, and that the Dutch heretics had managed to flourish because Jewish finance had entrenched itself in Amsterdam. Olivares, prime minister of Philip IV of Spain from 1621 to 1643, in his last bid to save a crumbling empire had seriously entertained plans to invite the Jews back to Spain and so undo the irreparable harm of their expulsion in 1492. The price of toleration would be small compared with the presumed benefit to Spain. His proposal never bore fruit, but there was nothing novel about the toleration of Jews. Most Catholic countries had tolerated them, and it was a commonplace often repeated by advocates of religious liberty that the city of Rome, which would not suffer Christian heretics, allowed complete freedom to its Jewish community, no doubt for financial reasons. The growing trade rivalry between England and Holland in the seventeenth century made England emulate Holland's policy towards Jews, and Cromwell was the first to take the momentous – and for him, economically satisfying – step of inviting them back into England.

The expansion of commercial capitalism, particularly in Europe's two principal maritime powers, Holland and England, was a powerful factor in the destruction of religious restrictions. Trade was usually a stronger argument than religion. Catholic Venice in the sixteenth century was reluctant to close its ports to ships of the Lutheran Hanseatic traders. The English wool interest spent the first half of the seventeenth century in energetic opposition to the anti-Spanish policy of the government. By the Restoration in 1660 it was widely held that trade knows no religious barriers; the important corollary that followed from this was that the abolition of religious barriers would promote trade. Sir Anthony Ashley Cooper (later Lord Shaftesbury) in 1668 presented a memorial to Charles II in which he used the trade factor to support his plea for greater liberty to dissenters. In 1669 the House of Lords reported 'that ease and relaxation in ecclesiastical matters will be the means of improving the trade of this kingdom'. Sir William Petty came to the conclusion in his *Political Arithmetic*, which was written in the 1670s but published in 1690, 'that for the advancement of trade, if that be a sufficient reason, indulgence must be granted in matters of opinion'. The argument simply becomes a discussion of the political and economic role of the trading classes.

The Anglican opponents of toleration distrusted the motives of liberals. It was true, wrote John Goodman, that trade benefited the nation, but by fostering contacts between different nations and cultures it also brought 'latitude of conscience' and indifference to religion, so that merchants were a threat to orthodoxy. In a sermon delivered at Trinity House in 1681 the chaplain to the Earl of Berkeley complained that 'it is to be feared that the great outcry for liberty of trade is near of kin to that of liberty of conscience, which to our sorrows we have experienced was only a politick fetch of a party to lay all in common'. Samuel Parker in his *A Discourse of Ecclesiastical Politie* (1669) declared that "tis notorious that there is not any sort of people so inclinable to seditious practices as the trading part of a nation'.

With toleration questioned in such terms, it was obviously advisable to defend freedom as a concomitant of economic progress and security for property. One nonconformist minister, John Collinges, pointed out that the bourgeoisie was a propertied class and that trade, far from threatening society, 'necessarily requires the freedom and security of all who are of any considerable fortunes'. Henry Robinson, who had been one of the first to stress the necessary link between liberty in religion and liberty in trade, emphasised that property was most secure when civil peace had been achieved by the granting of an unqualified toleration that would eliminate all the sectarian quarrels which hindered trade. The merchant class, many members of which were now of the aristocracy of the nation, should be granted full social and political equality with the old landed aristocracy of the country. Such equality would only come when Dissent, which predominated among the merchants, was granted full toleration. England could

LE ROY DE FRANCE.
l'Nóme immortel Chef de la S.te Ligue .

Mon soleil parsa force eclaira l'heretique .
Il chassa tout d'un coup les brouillards de Calvin:
Non pas par un Zele divin ,
Mais afin de cacher ma fine Politique .

L'EVESQUE DE MEAUX .
Secretaire du Conseil de la S.te Ligue .

Bellarmin . du Perron auec leur controuerse .
Contre les protestans n'ont pas fait fort grand fruict :
Un traict de ma plume sans bruit ,
Les enuoye tous a la renuerse .

then look forward to a period of commercial greatness.

Spokesmen of the commercial class like Robinson and his colleague Henry Parker, both of whom wrote their pleas for toleration before the Restoration, were the real begetters of the theory, taken for granted by Petty and others after 1660, that material prosperity betokened the divine approval. Surely it was no coincidence, Protestant travellers felt, that the poverty of Catholic Spain and Italy resulted from their intolerant religion, and that the growing wealth of England flowed from its liberal attitude to dissent, particularly after 1689. Further support for this argument came after the Revocation of the Edict of Nantes.

It was universally agreed at the end of the seventeenth century that the Revocation had helped to ruin France, and controversialists of the day fed the argument with evidence of their own. The anonymous author of *Les soupirs de la France esclave* (1689) painted a picture of widespread decay and disaster. Half a century later Antoine Court in his *Lettre d'un patriote sur la tolérance civile des protestants de France* (1756) traced all France's ills back to the loss of its Protestants. In fact, as now seems likely, the Revocation was only one, and not necessarily a disastrous, factor in the

LE ROY IACQUE DÉLOGE.

J'avois fait un ragoust pour tout l'Angleterre:
sans que ie me suis trop hasté.
J'aurois demon renom rempli toutte la terre;
Mais un ORANGE a tout gâté.

Caricatures by Cornelius Dusart from *Héros de la Ligue* (1691) attacking the political Catholicism of Louis XIV (*left*) and his associates, who here include Bossuet (*centre*) and James II of England (*right*). In fact, the results of the Revocation of the Edict of Nantes proved that toleration was a more profitable political course than persecution.

stagnation of the French economy. In any case, only ten per cent of France's two million Protestants left the country. The émigrés, however, were welcomed in countries which prided themselves on being more liberal. Brandenburg, in particular, benefited from the influx. To the Brandenburg authorities, persecution of minorities seemed foolish when these could make valuable contributions to the economy. Benjamin Raule, the Elector's adviser in commercial affairs, emphasised in 1684 to his master the benefits available if 'your Highness takes advantage of these troublous times, when religious persecution is rife in neighbouring countries, and imports groups of foreigners from England, France and Holland . . . into your lands and cities, so nearly destitute of good merchants. Such aliens are almost always merchants and traders'. In 1685 the Brandenburg government passed the Edict of Potsdam, inviting Huguenot refugees into its territory. The immigrants were undoubtedly useful, though their contribution to industry in the Electorate was negligible. It should be noted that this immigration policy was not intrinsically a tolerant one, since the settlers welcomed by the Calvinist Elector were almost exclusively Calvinists from Holland, Switzerland, Piedmont and the Palatinate.

Irenicists in the late seventeenth century

The gradual acceptance of economic motives for tolerating dissidents. may be linked to the growth of secularism in everyday life and in politics. At its highest level, secularism expressed itself in the conscious indifference of governments to religious confessions. The absolute rulers of the late seventeenth century were devoted primarily to the interests of the secular State, and tended to adopt a permissive attitude to all sects that did not disturb society. At the same time trading communities in both Catholic and Protestant countries came to accept the dogma that religious affiliations were irrelevant to the maintenance and promotion of commerce. Despite retrogressive developments in several countries, the general mood by the end of the seventeenth century was one of hope and, in a few instances, irenicism.

Frederick I's patronage aided the irenic efforts of Daniel Jablonski (1660–1741) in Prussia. Part of Jablonski's education was in England: there he took up schemes for the reunion of all Protestant Churches on the basis of fundamental articles: despite this, his emphasis was not so much on doctrinal agreement as on mutual toleration. To Frederick such schemes, futile though they turned out to be, were of value in trying to promote greater unity in a kingdom divided both territorially and religiously.

A more promising enterprise, launched at roughly the same time, occupied the attention of Elector Ernst Augustus of Hanover. The man to whom the Elector gave his confidence was Gottfried Wilhelm von Leibniz (1646–1716). The great philosopher, concerned at the disunity of Europe and sectarian strife in Christendom, had made it his concern to promote a union of the Churches in Germany and perhaps in Europe. Hanover was the ideal centre for this attempt, to which Protestant theologians and the See of Rome gave full approval. Leibniz was first brought to Hanover at the instance of the Catholic Elector Johann Friedrich, whose Lutheran successor in 1679, Ernst Augustus, was as keenly interested in reunion. His principal helpers in the enterprise were the irenically-minded Catholic Cristobal de Rojas y Spinola,

General of the Franciscan order and later bishop of Wiener–Neustadt; and the Lutheran abbot of Lockum, Gerhard Molanus. In 1683 Spinola spent several months in Hanover with Protestant theologians, the result of their endeavours being the *Regulae circa christianorum omnium ecclesiasticam reunionem*, which was to serve as a basis for further discussion.

The year after this, Leibniz drew up his own suggestions for the debate. It was not enough, he wrote in his *Des méthodes de réunion*, to begin with simple toleration; moreover 'the method of dispute or discussion is useless . . . [and] it seems also that the way of compromise is a dead end'. One way remained. Both Catholics and Protestants had at one time agreed to recognise a truly ecumenical Council of the Church. Trent had not been such a Council. Therefore the avenue still lay open for one that would reconcile the parties. For himself, Leibniz was willing to make substantial concessions to Rome, such as accepting papal supremacy. The dream of reunion – it was hardly more than that – bears witness to the continuance in Germany of the great tradition of Witzel and Cassander. Leibniz wrote to a correspondent in 1691: 'You are right to judge me a Catholic at heart; I am even one openly . . . But the essence of Catholicity is not external communion with Rome. The true and essential communion, which makes us members of Jesus Christ, is charity'.

He was an indefatigable correspondent. Among those who wrote to him was the Catholic Landgrave of Hessen–Rheinfels, a sincere irenicist who condemned persecution everywhere and who even welcomed Huguenots into his territory after the Revocation of the Edict of Nantes, a measure he denounced as 'unchristian, against every rule of charity'. Leibniz's greatest hopes, however, rested on his correspondence, from 1691 onwards, with Bossuet. As the most influential prelate of the most autonomous section of the Catholic Church, Bossuet was essential to all plans of reunion. But in the end he proved to be an uncompromising conservative. His firm stand disappointed Leibniz and gradually alienated him from Rome. In addition the aggressive foreign policy of France threatened international goodwill among the European powers. In 1699 the Hanoverian court ordered Leibniz to suspend the dialogue with Bossuet. With this all practical hopes of reunion collapsed.

The exchanges were nonetheless symptomatic of a mood of understanding between the opposing sides. It is significant that the Hanoverian efforts were being made in spite of the ferocious persecution of Protestants in France. In Germany at this time the non-dogmatic principles of pietism, and the move towards fraternity and toleration, were well established; and were happily able to surmount the sectarian hostility shown in Catholic France and Austria. For pietists spiritual fellowship counted more than denominational divisions. The 'separatist' wing of pietism, led by Ernst Hochmann (1670–1721), organised the publication of tracts to further the unity of all Christian Churches, including that of Rome. One of the most prominent representatives of the school, Gerhard Tersteegen of Mulheim, confessed that:

> I believe and am certain that among the Roman Catholics, as well as among the Lutherans, Reformed, Mennonites and so forth, and indeed in all the various opinions and usages of these parties, no less than among the Separatists, souls can attain to the highest level of holiness and union with God.

It was Holland, however, that led the liberal world as the principal republic of letters in the seventeenth century. It was the only nation in Europe where writing and publishing was free and flourishing. Amsterdam alone was reputed to have some four hundred printers and booksellers. If a work were forbidden anywhere else, it could be printed in Holland. The blaze of controversy, the outpourings of journalism, found their finest expression here. It was here in the 1680s that two exiles, one from England, one from France, prepared the two most important defences of toleration to be penned in this century.

The achievement of John Locke

John Locke (1632–1704), a fellow of Christ Church, Oxford, and for some time an associate of the Earl of Shaftesbury, fled to Holland in 1683 when the political reaction against Shaftesbury began to reach out against his other Whig associates. In Utrecht he found the security which allowed him to devote his time to writing. He began to set down methodically the ideas which he had been working on for some time: these formed the beginning of his *Essay Concerning Human Understanding*. At the same time he drew up a Latin version of a work he had begun in the 1660s: this was published in 1689, after his return to England. The same year a translation came out in English, entitled *A Letter Concerning Toleration*. It was followed by two more letters on the same subject, in 1690 and 1693.

The *Letter Concerning Toleration* was neither as original nor as liberal as defences of toleration penned by other European writers who had preceded Locke. Its main arguments were laboured restatements of old positions. The importance of the work, however, lay less in its originality than in its influence. As the work of the most powerful philosopher of the century, a citizen of rationalist Europe and prophet of the 1688 revolution in England, Locke's words commanded an audience and a respect which made them apparently the final word on the subject. All the great safeguards of conscience outlined by past thinkers are in Locke written up into immutable principles of reason. To the disciples of reason Locke's formulations were unexceptionable because eminently rational. To the propertied classes of England in 1689 Locke was decisive because his principles allowed a liberty that satisfied both the Tory gentry and the Whig oligarchies, both Anglican establishment and nonconformist Dissent.

Locke begins his *Letter* by esteeming 'toleration to be the chief characteristical mark of the true church', since sufferance of those who disagree in religion is both 'agreeable to the Gospel of Jesus Christ and to the genuine reason of mankind'. He then goes on to define once and for all the separate spheres of Church and State:

'I deem it above all things necessary to distinguish exactly the business of civil government from that of religion ... The care of souls cannot belong to the civil magistrate, because his power consists only in outward force: but true and saving religion consists in the inward persuasion of the mind'.

'A church', he says, 'I take to be a voluntary society of men, joining themselves together of their own accord, in order to the publick worshipping of God'. Whereas, however, in the formation of a State, which is also a voluntary society, men surrender some of their natural rights by contracting to obey the rule of the majority, in the formation of a Church men surrender no natural rights, so that the Church has no coercive power over its members beyond expulsion (or 'excommunication'). A Church therefore has no coercive power over its members, just as 'no private person has any right to prejudice another person in his civil enjoyments'. Nor has one Church rights over any other: 'this is the fundamental and immutable right of a spontaneous society, that it has power to remove any of its members who trangress the rules of its institution: but it cannot ... acquire any right of jurisdiction over those that are not joined with it'.

All Churches being thus rendered harmless to their own members and to each other, it remains to ensure that the State does not impose its will in religious matters. 'The civil power can either change everything in religion, according to the prince's pleasure, or it can change nothing. If it be once permitted to introduce anything into religion, by the means of laws and penalties, there can be no bounds to it'. Locke reiterates that the magistrate must, in view of this danger, have no power in matters of faith and conscience. In one of his most eloquent passages he says: 'Although the magistrate's opinion in religion be sound and the way that he appoints be truly evangelical, yet if I be not thoroughly persuaded thereof in my own mind, there will be no safety for me in following it. No way whatsoever that I shall walk in against the dictates of my conscience, will ever bring me to the mansions of the blessed'.

Locke has two chief practical arguments against intolerance. He claims that persecution has always been ineffective, and has never produced conformity or unity. He also repeats the argument that our certainty in religious matters is limited, and that our knowledge of truth is never so complete as to entitle us to claim that we are right and others are wrong. Even revelation is not as certain as may at first appear. For Locke the claims of different sects to have differing revelations renders them suspect, and 'it still belongs to reason to judge of the truth of . . . a revelation, and of the signification of the words wherein it is delivered'. Reason therefore becomes the criterion of judgment, and one that allows common discussion and the removal of differences. 'We should do well to commiserate our mutual ignorance and endeavour to remove it in all the gentle and fair ways of information; and not instantly treat others ill, as obstinate and perverse because they will not renounce their own and receive our opinions'. In so far as a sect holds to the basic tenets of the Bible, it is technically Christian and must not be shunned: 'He that denies not anything that the Holy Scriptures teach in express words, nor makes a separation upon occasion of anything that is not manifestly contained in the sacred text; however he may be nick-named by any sect of Christians, and declared by some, or all of them, to be utterly void of true Christianity; yet in deed and in truth this man cannot be either a heretick or schismatick'.

There was, however, to be no unlimited toleration. Locke outlines three exceptions, two of which were generally accepted at the time, and one of which was at best conservative. The first exception is that sects which subvert society cannot be tolerated: 'No opinions contrary to human society, or to those moral rules which are necessary to the preservation of civil society, are to be tolerated by the magistrate'. This principle could obviously be interpreted so broadly as to cover all heterodox sects, and by itself undermined much of Locke's stand for tolerance. Again, 'those are not at all to be tolerated who deny the being of God. Promises, covenants, and oaths, which are the bonds of human society, can have no hold upon an atheist'. This exception is akin to the first.

Finally, 'that church can have no right to be tolerated by the magistrate which is constituted upon such a bottom, that all those who enter into it do thereby *ipso facto* deliver themselves up to the protection and service of another prince'. This exception is not only conservative, in that it is less liberal than the position of Penn, Williams and others; it is also, like the exception of atheists, a curious example of *a priori* prejudice which could have been dispelled by personal contact with atheists or Catholics. Admittedly, as Locke points out, the tendency of Catholics to claim for themselves a toleration which they did not grant to others, deprived them of the right to be tolerated. More important than this, however, for Locke as for all English Protestants, was the consideration that Catholics might be a fifth column for French aggression. Particularly after the Revocation of the Edict of Nantes, English Catholics would have to resign themselves to the penal laws.

Despite the limits on Locke's doctrine of tolerance, his position reflected fairly accurately that of the Toleration Act, so that he came to be accepted as the philosopher of religious liberty. The spread of his philosophical ideas, and his essentially rationalist attitude to religion, gave the *Letter* added authority as the classic statement on the subject of toleration.

The liberal Calvinist school and Pierre Bayle

Locke's distinguished fellow-exile in Holland was Pierre Bayle (1647–1706). This illustrious French Calvinist professor of philosophy lost his teaching post in 1681 when all Protestant academies were suppressed in France. He went abroad and took up a chair of philosophy at Rotterdam. Never so widely acclaimed as Locke for his writings on tolerance, Bayle nevertheless went further than the English philosopher in his struggle for the absolute freedom of faith and intellect. His writings spring directly out of the controversies in international Calvinism at the end of the seventeenth century, and it is with these that we must begin.

Although the Synod of Dort, which opened in 1618, was able to squeeze the Arminians out of the ranks of Calvinism, it did not and could not signal a return to the old illiberalism. Some of the orthodox delegates to the Synod, particularly those from England and Bremen, held themselves free to give a liberal interpretation to the decrees passed by it. In France the date 1618 was doubly important to the Reformed, for it was the year of the installation of the Scotsman John Cameron as professor of theology at the Academy of Saumur, a liberal institution founded by Du Plessis Mornay in 1604. Cameron's appointment marked the beginning of a revolution in French Calvinism. His disciple Moïse Amyraut, later rector of the Academy, expanded Cameron's doctrines out of a theological into an ethical and rationalist framework which modified the strictness of traditional Calvinism without ever becoming unorthodox. In 1664 a Cartesian scholar was appointed to the chair of philosophy at the Academy. Saumur, now a supporter of the new philosophy, became a centre of controversy over the question of toleration.

In 1670 the pastor D'Huisseau published an irenic work on *La réunion du christianisme*. He was supported by the Academy as well as by an ex-professor of the Academy, one Claude Pajon, now a pastor in Orleans. Both Huisseau and Pajon were denounced by Huguenots on the grounds that they were rationalists, Arminians and even Socinians. Huisseau was deprived of the ministry and his book condemned. Pajon survived, to die in 1685 just before the Revocation of the Edict of Nantes. French Calvinists were split into liberal and conservative wings that continued their controversy even beyond the Revocation. A synod in exile at Rotterdam in April 1686 condemned Pajonism as contrary to orthodoxy. Re-thinking of attitudes had, however, gone too far to be checked so easily. In 1684 at Rotterdam the Frenchman Basnage de Beauval published his *Tolérance des religions*, the first important Huguenot defence of toleration as a principle, and this at a time when the Revocation was imminent. Basnage rejected exclusivism in religion, and held that we are not so certain of the full truth that we can persecute others for their differences. Good faith, even in an erroneous conscience, must be respected in all fellow human beings. Heresy itself is not necessarily evil, since its mere existence activates the orthodox position: 'Heresies were ordained by God to the benefit of his Church'.

Basnage was, however, ill equipped to draw up a systematic defence of toleration. This task was fulfilled the year after the Revocation by Bayle in his *Commentaire philosophique sur ces paroles de Jésus-Christ: Contrains-les d'entrer*. The work was published anonymously, and claimed to be a translation from the English. Despite this subterfuge, Bayle was soon recognised as the author of one of the major philosophic works of the century. The reception given to it by Huguenots was largely hostile. Their leader in exile, Pierre Jurieu, an old friend of Bayle and now a pastor in Holland, wrote in reply his *Traité des deux souverains . . . contre la tolérance universelle* (1687), which was virtually an apology for the Revocation by one of its most eminent victims. In Holland Jurieu set in motion ecclesiastical machinery against the protagonists of tolerance. In 1690 a synod at Amsterdam condemned the propositions 'that reason and piety demand the civil and ecclesiastical toleration of all heresies; [and] that the magistrate has no right to employ his authority to crush idolatry and prevent the progress of heresy'. Subsequently the work of Gédéon Huet, *Apologie pour les vrais tolérants* (Dordrecht 1690), had several of its propositions condemned, among them the statement that 'no heretic is really guilty before God, save he who is convinced in his conscience that his dogmas are false'. Jurieu's fulminations were ultimately of little effect. By the end of the century Huguenots had been compelled by the circumstances of their own persecution to find reasons for the disavowal of all persecution. The force of their reassessment of the question of toleration made its mark on the Calvinist world. The Grand Pensionary of Holland, Fagel, can be found at this time claiming that 'everyone is free to follow the motions of his conscience, and to try and force men to adopt the dominant religion is to trespass on the rights of God'.

Bayle's *Commentaire* not only sets the seal on all preceding discussions of tolerance: it also points the way ahead to a universal acceptance of intolerance as being both ethically and rationally wrong. His text is the classic one taken by Saint Augustine from the parable of the supper (Luke 14: 23), where the master tells his servants to force the guests to come in – *compelle intrare*.

'To refute this absolutely', says Bayle, 'I rely on this principle of natural light, that any literal meaning which includes an obligation to commit crimes, is false'. He goes on to say: 'a literal meaning which renders vain the complaints of the early Christians against their persecutors, is false. But this is the literal meaning of these words, *compelle intrare*, therefore it is false'. The point of this argument is that all modern Christians would be subject to persecution if the text were valid against the early Christians, a conclusion no Catholic or Protestant would willingly hold.

One of the fundamentals of Bayle's exposition is his so-called scepticism, namely his view that we are unable to attain absolute certainty and truth. No philosophical system, as he pointed out in his *Dictionnaire historique et critique*, can give us the absolute truth or should pretend to do so; each gives only a portion of the truth. Were absolute truth in evidence, it would be received as such by all men; but it is notorious that they disagree even on apparent fundamentals. We are not therefore bound to accept without question what is not absolutely true, and must make allowances for those people to whom even falsehood wears the appearance of truth. There are adherents of false as well as of true principles: both sincerely believe theirs to be the truth, and they must be respected. 'The conscience which is in error has the same rights as that which is not'. Whatever its principles, conscience must be obeyed, for 'the erroneous conscience should secure for error the same prerogatives that the orthodox conscience secures for truth'. On this subjective basis, all faiths have an 'inalienable right' to full liberty. To try to force conscience is the gravest of crimes, for 'conscience is for each man the voice of God's law, known and accepted as such by he who has this conscience; so that to violate this conscience is to violate the law of God'.

By these principles both Catholics and Protestants must tolerate and be tolerated. What, however, if someone were to claim that his conscience obliged him to persecute others? Must he not follow his conscience? Bayle's answer in effect is that the conscience is itself subject to reason. This brings us to Bayle's fundamental rationalism. The essential criterion for toleration, over and above conscience, is 'reason speaking through the axioms of natural light or metaphysics'. Like Locke, Bayle brings revelation to the bar of reason: 'Every dogma which is not verified and registered in the supreme court of Reason and natural light, can have only shaky authority'. Reason therefore must govern the place of religion in society.

The practical freedom which Bayle grants to religion is virtually absolute. Catholics tend to persecute where they are the majority, therefore the State should restrict their activities; but they are nevertheless entitled to complete freedom of belief and worship. To tolerate many sects in one state may hold some danger for the unity of the state, but this is better than to suffer the civil strife and bloodshed which attempts to impose unity would bring. Muslims should be tolerated if they accept the political constitution of the State; after all, they respect Christ as a great prophet. Socinians and extreme sectarians should also be tolerated. With conscience and reason as the decisive criteria, no one faith can claim a monopoly, and all faiths are entitled to exist in civil society.

To emphasise that his treatise is meant to have general validity and not simply to be an attack on Louis XIV, Bayle devotes considerable space to a criticism of his fellow-Calvinists. Their persecution of Anabaptists is immoral, since these are the least harmful of all the sects. Even more reprehensible is their persecution of Catholics: 'Not content with establishing the security and even the superiority of the Reformed religion in their state over all other religions, as they were entitled to do, they abolished all other public worship and inflicted penalties on those who could not in conscience abandon the faith of their fathers or conform to the plan of reformation approved by the sovereign'. In later works Bayle continued this controversy. His anonymous *Réponse d'un nouveau converti à la lettre d'un réfugié* (1689) cited as evidence of Protestant intolerance not only Servetus but also the case of Nicolas Antoine, who was convicted of Judaism and strangled and burnt at Geneva in 1632. He also accused the Huguenots of nurturing a 'spirit of rebellion' against the French authorities: this criticism was directed against Jurieu, who was at the time promoting disaffection in France among Huguenots who had nominally conformed.

Bayle's reputation, limited in his lifetime, grew immeasurably after his death. The eighteenth-century *philosophes* greeted in him the initiator of the age of reason, and for unbelievers everywhere his scepticism became the new orthodoxy. In a sense, his writings on toleration did not deal fully with the problem, for they were written from a standpoint of complete theological indifference; but his contribution was one that even believers could accept to some extent, and was consequently of outstanding importance in the struggle to obtain greater freedom for man in society and in the pursuit of truth.

10 The growth of liberty

The eighteenth and nineteenth centuries in the West were devoted to the piecemeal application of those principles of toleration whose rise has been traced through the sixteenth and seventeenth. In the later period toleration ceased to be a religious issue in Protestant countries, thanks to the decay of dogma and the general acknowledgment of liberal rationalism; instead, minority problems were treated on a political or racial level. Protestant England, for example, continued to repress Catholic Ireland for reasons ostensibly political and economic, but also implicitly and psychologically religious. Liberty in the liberal epoch became a word much used on Protestant lips, and in contrast the countries of Catholic Europe were dismissed as areas of superstition and despotism; the former, it was claimed, acted on no principles but those of reason, while the latter acted from motives of bigotry and intolerance. The conflict between liberal (usually English, Dutch or German) Catholics and conservative (usually Latin) Catholics over the proclamation of the dogma of papal infallibility in 1870 revealed starkly to the world that Rome was indeed the symbol of reaction in a world which was otherwise progressing towards fuller liberty.

Rome and religious freedom

For a historian of toleration the position of the Roman Church is intrinsically more interesting than that of the Protestant Churches. In the case of the latter, religious liberty arose not so much because of the fundamental tenets of the Reformation, as because of the subversion of dogma by various rationalist influences and because of the acceptance by bourgeois societies of free religion as a concomitant of free trade. In Protestant countries, therefore, toleration tended to increase in proportion to the decrease of dogmatic belief. Could it have increased with no decline in Christian belief? The example of the Catholic countries would seem to prove that rigid orthodoxy is incompatible with religious liberty. Not surprisingly, Catholicism itself came to be regarded as incompatible with freedom. Substance was lent to this belief by the pronouncements of nineteenth-century popes. Gregory XVI in his encyclical *Mirari vos* (1832) stated that 'from the most foul well of indifferentism flows that absurd and erroneous opinion, or rather delirium, of liberty of conscience . . . But what death is worse for the soul than the freedom to err? as Augustine once asked'. Writing in 1888, in his encyclical *Libertas Humana*, Leo XIII went some way towards liberalising the traditional stand, but even he rejected any idea that Church and State should be separate, and condemned liberty of worship as 'no liberty, but its degradation'.

The Catholic Church thus pursued a completely different line of development, and the writings of Locke and Bayle, which were authoritative in most of Protestant Europe, found no echo south of the Alps or the Pyrenees. What should be stressed is that political conditions were largely responsible for this. The civil liberties available to the population in northern Europe and in America were denied to the inhabitants of Spain, Sicily and the papal states. Consequently, while American Catholics were committed from the first to a separation of Church and State and the guarantee of democratic liberties, in theocratic Rome supporters of a separation were viewed as heretics. Cardinal Gibbons of Baltimore declared in 1887 that 'our Catholic forefathers suffered so much during the last three centuries for the sake of liberty of conscience that they would rise to condemn us if we made ourselves the advocates or defenders of religious persecution'. These sentiments, until very recently, could not have been uttered in many parts of the Catholic world.

In view of the traditional conservatism of the Roman Church, the teachings of Pope John XXIII and the deliberations of the Second Vatican Council constitute nothing less than a revolution, particularly since their acceptance of universal toleration has not been accompanied by any repudiation of dogma. John XXIII's encyclical *Pacem in Terris* (1963) outlines unequivocally the basic rights of man, and states: 'Also among man's rights is the right to be able to worship God in accordance with the right dictates of his own conscience, and to profess his religion both in private and in public'.

Any doubts about the tenor of this sentence are swept away by the contents of the decree on religious liberty issued by the Vatican Council:

This Vatican Council declares that the human person has a right to religious freedom. This freedom means that all men are to be immune from coercion on the part of individuals or of social groups and of any human power, in such wise that no one is to be forced to act in a manner contrary to his own beliefs, whether privately or publicly, whether alone or in association with others, within due limits. The Council further declares that the right to religious freedom has its foundation in the very dignity of the human person as this dignity is known through the revealed word of God and by reason itself.

The Council goes on to declare:

In all his activity a man is bound to follow his conscience, in order that he may come to God, the end and purpose of life. It follows that he is not to be forced to act in a manner contrary to his conscience.

Family prayers, from an Austrian nobleman's
account of life in the country (1682).
The personal devotion of pietists
and others towards the end of the
seventeenth century gradually led
to more tolerant attitudes.

At the same time the Council admitted that the Church, by its
intolerance in the past, had frequently violated the laws of charity
and justice:

In the life of the People of God as it has made its pilgrim way through the
vicissitudes of human history there has at times appeared a way of acting
that was hardly in accord with the spirit of the Gospel, or even opposed to it.

For the first time, therefore, in its long history, the Church has
approved of religious freedom in the most positive and universal
terms. Christians of all persuasions are united today in accepting
the validity and necessity of freedom of conscience and worship.

'The bonds of mutual love'

In general, the mainstream of both Protestant and Catholic
thought has been hostile to religious liberty. It is unfortunate for
convinced Christians that liberty has been more often associated
with non-Christian influences than with Christian. Religious
enthusiasm in the case of Protestants, and religious conservatism
in the case of Catholics, has invariably produced the most extreme
intolerance. Liberalisation has often had to rely on non-dogmatic
religion, secular philosophy and anticlerical politics. In some
countries, freedom of belief was assured only by the arbitration
of the State, so that only an essentially neutral and possibly non-
Christian power could keep the peace between Christians. Others,
however, went farther than this. The *politiques* elevated the State
above religion, the Remonstrants subjected the Church to the
magistrate, Erastians like John Selden in England proclaimed that
'all is as the State pleases'. One immediate result of this was that
absolutism became for many the principal guarantee of religious
parity. For a period this solution worked. But to rely on the
arbitrary will of the magistrate for toleration was, for Christians,
to put their heads in the lion's mouth, as Protestants discovered at
the Revocation of the Edict of Nantes.

State toleration, in other words. was no real toleration. It operated on no principles save that of *raison d'état*. It presupposed a State Church, and therefore presented a constant threat to minority rights. Where it was operated by an absolutist ruler it guaranteed no civil rights and could therefore hardly guarantee rights of conscience. The usual Christian alternative to all this was simple. Church and State should be completely separate and autonomous. The Churches should operate mutual tolerance on the basis of charity. The magistrate should concern himself only with the civil character of Christians, and by ensuring the natural rights of all he would automatically protect religious interests. This was the position ultimately adopted by most sectarians and minority Churches. It was not a secularist solution, for it still assumed that the magistrate was a Christian. But it was naturally violently rejected by the established religions in both northern and southern Europe, with the result that by the end of the seventeenth century few countries were on their way to achieving a secure religious freedom, although, paradoxically, the theory of toleration had by then attained its fullest exposition.

It would be difficult, even through the two centuries we have covered, to discover a progressive development of religious liberty. Each age and society has its own intolerant enthusiasm, and the intolerance of proletarian movements in recent history has been a logical reaction against the complacent freedoms of bourgeois society. Religion is still discriminated against and persecuted, in Communist Russia, in Catholic Colombia, and in Protestant Ulster. Yet the limitation of freedom here is not so much a positive repression of conscience, as a reflection of the lack of liberty in society as a whole, a fact which underlines the necessary connection between social development and toleration. A developing society operating on illiberal political principles cannot possibly recognise toleration for all faiths. The hierarchy in Spain finds it more difficult to support liberty of conscience than the hierarchy of the United States, just as the French bishops in 1685 found it impossible to accept principles which many of their Anglican colleagues at the same date took for granted. The battle to maintain elementary freedoms is obviously a constant one, and carries no assurance of success, for the gains of a past age may be wiped out in the present. In this uncertain situation a student of the history of toleration may well echo the closing words of John XXIII in *Pacem in Terris*: 'May Christ inflame the desires of all men to break through the barriers which divide them, to strengthen the bonds of mutual love, to learn to understand one another and to pardon those who have done them wrong. Through His power and inspiration may all peoples welcome each other to their hearts as brothers, and may the peace they long for ever flower and ever reign among them'.

Chronological table
to collate some events and writings mentioned in this book

Events	Writings
	1516 Thomas More's *Utopia* Machiavelli's *The Prince*
1517 Luther's 95 Theses	
1521 Diet of Worms. Excommunication of Luther	
1523 Zwingli reforms Zürich	1523 Luther *On Secular Authority*
	1524 Hubmaier's *Concerning Heretics* Erasmus *On Free Will*
1525 The Peasant War	1525 Luther *On the Unfree Will*
1530 The Confession of Augsburg	
	1531 Servetus's *Errors concerning the Trinity*
1533 Geneva adopts the Reformation 1533–5 Anabaptist rule in Münster	
1536 Death of Erasmus	1536 Calvin's *Institutes of the Christian Religion*
1541 Contarini at the Diet of Regensburg	
1545 Opening of Council of Trent 1553 Execution of Servetus	
	1554 Castellio's *Concerning Heretics*
1555 Peace of Augsburg 1556 Abdication of Charles the Fifth 1560 L'Hospital as Chancellor of France	
	1561 Cassender's *De officio pii*

Events	Writings
1563 End of Council of Trent	1563 Ochino's *Dialogues*
	1564 Acontius's *Satan's Stratagems*
1565 Foundation of Minor Church in Poland	
1572 Massacre of Saint Bartholomew	
1573 Confederation of Warsaw	
1578 Religious truce in Netherlands	
	1580 Coolhaes's *Apologia*
1584 Assassination of William of Orange	
	1594 Publication of Socinus's *De Jesu Christo Servatore*
1598 Edict of Nantes	
	1603 Althusius's *Politics*
1605 Catechism of Raków	
1609 Twelve Years Truce between Spain and Netherlands	
1610 Assassination of Henry IV of France	
1618 Beginning of Thirty Years War and of Synod of Dort	
1620 Sailing of the *Mayflower* to America	
	1623 Comenius's *Labyrinth of the World*
	1628 Przypkowski's *De pace*
1629 Richelieu makes Peace of Alais with Protestants	1629 Episcopius's *Apologia*
1632 Foundation of colony of Maryland in America	
1640 Beginning of English Revolution	

Events	Writings
	Writings
Events	1641 Grotius's *Annotata*
	1643 Robinson's *Liberty of Conscience*
	1644 Williams's *The Bloudy Tenent of Persecution*
1648 Peace of Westphalia ends Thirty Years War	
1653 Cromwell as Lord Protector of England	
	1658 Zwicker's *Irenicum Irenicorum*
1660 English Restoration	
	1667 Owens's *Indulgence and Toleration*
	1670 Penn's *The Great Case.* Spinoza's *Tractatus Theologico-Politicus*
1685 Revocation of Edict of Nantes	
	1686 Bayle's *Commentaire Philosophique*
1687 James II's Declaration of Indulgence	1687 Pufendorf's *De habitu religionis*
1688 Overthrow of Stuart dynasty	
1689 Toleration Act in England	1689 Locke's *Letter concerning Toleration*
1715 Death of Louis XIV	

Bibliographical note

The principal sources for a study of toleration are the original writings cited in the text of this book. To repeat their titles here would be superfluous. The following list consists of some of the more useful secondary works on the subject. A detailed bibliography dealing principally with the sixteenth century is given in the classic work by Lecler. For the seventeenth century there is no comparable study available. It will be appreciated that the author has inevitably used more books in English than in other languages where the literature on toleration is also considerable.

Lord Acton, *The History of Freedom and other Essays*, London, 1907.

Roland H. Bainton, *Studies on the Reformation* (Collected Papers in Church History, Series II), Boston, 1963.

G. Bonet-Maury, *La liberté de conscience en France depuis l'Edit de Nantes jusqu'à la Séparation (1598-1905)*, Paris, 1909.

Gerard Brandt, *History of the Reformation in and about the Low Countries*, 4 vols., London, 1721.

Ernst Cassirer, *The Platonic Renaissance in England*, London, 1953.

Sandford H. Cobb, *The Rise of Religious Liberty in America*, New York, 1902.

Rosalie Colie, *Light and Enlightenment. A study of the Cambridge Platonists and the Dutch Arminians*, Cambridge, 1957.

C. R. Cragg, *From Puritanism to the Age of Reason*, Cambridge, 1950.

Lucien Dubois, *Bayle et la tolérance*, Paris, 1902.

Paul Fox, *The Reformation in Poland*, Baltimore, 1924.

M. Freund, *Die Idee der Toleranz im England der grossen Revolution*, Halle, 1927.

William Haller, *Tracts on Liberty in the Puritan Revolution 1638-1647*, 3 vols., New York, 1934.

William Haller, *Liberty and Reformation in the Puritan Revolution*, New York, 1955.

Paul Hazard, *The European Mind 1680-1715*, London, 1953.

Philipp Hiltebrandt, *Die kirchlichen Reunionsverhandlungen in der zweiten hälfte des 17 Jahrhunderts*, Rome, 1922.

J. Huizinga, *Erasmus of Rotterdam*, London, 1952.

G. J. Jordan, *The Reunion of the Churches. A Study of G. W. Leibnitz*, London, 1927.

W. K. Jordan, *The Development of Religious Toleration in England*, 4 vols., London, 1932-40.

Stanislas Kot, *Socinianism in Poland*, Boston, 1957.

W. E. H. Lecky, *History of the Rise and Influence of the Spirit of Rationalism in Europe*, 2 vols., London, 1865.

Joseph Lecler, *Toleration and the Reformation*, 2 vols., London, 1960.

F. Lezius, *Der Toleranzbegriff Lockes und Pufendorfs*, Leipzig, 1900.

A. Malagrin, *Histoire de la tolérance religieuse*, Paris, 1905.

Perry Miller, *Roger Williams: his Contribution to the American Tradition*, New York, 1953.

R. H. Murray, *Erasmus and Luther: Their Attitude to Toleration*, London, 1920.

Jean Orcibal, *Louis XIV et les protestants*, Paris, 1951.

Nicolas Paulus, *Protestantismus und Toleranz im 16 Jahrhundert*, Freiburg, 1911.

Giovanni Pioli, *Fausto Socino. Vita, opere, fortuna*, Guanda, 1952.

Frank Puaux, *Les Precurseurs français de la tolérance au XVIIe siècle*, Paris, 1881.

Walter Rex, *Essays on Pierre Bayle and Religious Controversy*, Hague, 1965.

Francesco Ruffini, *Religious Liberty*, New York and London, 1912.

R. Rouse and S. C. Neill (edd.), *A History of the Ecumenical Movement 1517–1948*, London, 1954.

Richard Schlatter, *The Social Ideas of Religious Leaders 1660–1688*, London, 1940.

Warren C. Scoville, *The Persecution of Huguenots and French Economic Development 1680–1720*, Berkeley, 1960.

A. A. Seaton, *The Theory of Toleration under the Later Stuarts*, Cambridge, 1911.

William W. Sweet, *Religion in Colonial America*, New York, 1943.

Ernst Troeltsch, *The Social Teaching of the Christian Churches*, 2 vols., London, 1931.

H. C. Vedder, *Balthasar Hubmaier*, New York and London, 1905.

Karl Völker, *Toleranz und Intoleranz im Zeitalter der Reformation*, Leipzig, 1912.

Earl Morse Wilbur, *A History of Unitarianism: Socinianism and its Antecedents*, Harvard, 1946.

George H. Williams, *The Radical Reformation*, London, 1962.

Acknowledgments

I am extremely grateful to Professor E. G. Rupp and to the Rev. Dr T. M. Parker for their helpful comments on the typescript of this book. For all errors of omission and commission I, of course, remain solely responsible. I am grateful to Mr Colin Haycraft for some valuable suggestions, and am particularly indebted to Mr Michael Raeburn for his work in choosing and editing illustrations to fit a rather difficult text. My wife, who typed the entire text, occupies as always a special place in this catalogue of obligations.

Acknowledgment is due to the following for illustrations (the number refers to the page on which illustration appears): 9, 104, 140 André.Held; 14 Alinari; 16, 60 *right* Bildarchiv der österreichischen Nationalbibliothek; 19 Museu Nacional de Arte Antiga, Lisbon, photo Royal Academy of Arts; 25, 35 William Speiser; 31, 42, 57, 72, 114 Ullstein Bilderdienst; 40 Wartburg-Stiftung, Eisenach; 44 Lutherhalle, Wittenberg; 45, 146, 154, 155, 158, 164, 168, 174 *right*, 208 British Museum; 47, 163 Schweizerisches Landesmuseum, Zürich; 48 Musée Historique de la Réformation, Geneva; 88 *top*, 115 Deutsche Fotothek, Dresden; 88 *bottom* Staatsbibliothek Berlin, Bildarchiv Handke; 92 Bildarchiv Foto Marburg; 102 Národní Museum, Prague; 126 Dr Waclaw Urban; 135 *top* Musée Condé, Chantilly, photo Giraudon; 135 *bottom* Bibliothèque Nationale, Paris, photo Giraudon; 140 Musée Cantonal des Beaux-Arts, Lausanne; 166 Society of Antiquaries, London; 174 *left*, 175, 214 Society of Friends Library; 183 Hariette Merrifield Forbes; 184 Enoch Pratt Free Library, Baltimore; 186 J. Fowler Smith; 221 Rijksmuseum, Amsterdam. All other illustrations were photographed from originals in the British Museum by John R. Freeman.

H.K

Index

World University Library

Some books published or in preparation

Economics and Social Studies

The World Cities
Peter Hall, *London*

The Economics of Underdeveloped Countries
Jagdish Bhagwati, *Delhi*

Development Planning
Jan Tinbergen, *Rotterdam*

Leadership in New Nations
T. B. Bottomore, *Vancouver*

Key Issues in Criminology
Roger Hood, *Durham*

Human Communication
J. L. Aranguren, *Madrid*

Education in the Modern World
John Vaizey, *Oxford*

History

Ancient Egypt
Werner Kaiser, *Berlin*

The Emergence of Greek Democracy
W. G. Forrest *Oxford*

Muhammad and the Conquests of Islam
Francesco Gabrieli, *Rome*

The Crusades
G. Widengren, *Uppsala*

The Medieval Economy
Georges Duby, *Aix-en-Provence*

The Ottoman Empire
Halil Inalcik, *Ankara*

The Rise of the Working Class
Jurgen Kuczynski, *Berlin*

The Left in Europe
David Caute, *Oxford*

Chinese Communism
Robert C. North, *Stanford*

Religion and Philosophy

Christianity
W. O. Chadwick, *Cambridge*

Monasticism
M. D. Knowles, *London*

Judaism
J. Soetendorp, *Amsterdam*

The Modern Papacy
K. O. von Aretin, *Göttingen*

Sects
Bryan Wilson, *Oxford*

Language and Literature

A Model of Language
E. M. Uhlenbeck, *Leyden*

French Literature
Raymond Picard, *Paris*

Russian Writers and Society 1825–1904
Ronald Hingley, *Oxford*

Satire
Matthew Hodgart, *Sussex*

The Arts

Primitive Art
Eike Haberland, *Mainz*

The Language of Modern Art
Ulf Linde, *Stockholm*

Aesthetic Theories since 1850
J. F. Revel, *Paris*

Art Nouveau
S. T. Madsen, *Oslo*

Academic Painting
Gerald Ackerman, *Stanford*

Palaeolithic Cave Art
P. J. Ucko and A. Rosenfeld, *London*

Twentieth Century Music
H. H. Stuckenschmidt, *Berlin*

Psychology and Human Biology

Eye and Brain
R. L. Gregory, *Cambridge*

The Ear and the Brain
Edward Carterette, *U.C.L.A.*

The Variety of Man
J. P. Garlick, *London*

The Psychology of Attention
Anne Treisman, *Reading*

The Biology of Work
O. G. Edholm, *London*

Psychoses
H. J. Bochnik, *Hamburg*

Child Development
Philippe Muller, *Neuchâtel*

Man and Disease
Gernot Rath, *Göttingen*

Zoology and Botany

Animal Communication
J. M. Cullen, *Oxford*

Mimicry
Wolfgang Wickler, *Starnberg*

Migration
Gustaf Rudebeck, *Stockholm*

The World of an Insect
Rémy Chauvin, *Strasbourg*

Biological Rhythms
Janet Harker, *Cambridge*

Primates
François Bourlière, *Paris*

Lower Animals
Martin Wells, *Cambridge*

Conservation
C. Delamare Deboutteville, *Paris*

Physical Science and Mathematics

Energy
Etienne Fischhoff, *Paris*

Mathematics Observed
H. Freudenthal, *Utrecht*

The Quest for Absolute Zero
K. Mendelssohn, *Oxford*

Particles and Accelerators
Robert Gouran, *C.E.R.N., Geneva*

What is Light?
A. C. S. van Heel and C. H. F. Velzel, *Delft*

Waves and Corpuscles
J. A. e Silva and G. Lochak, *Paris*
Introduction by Louis de Broglie

Earth Sciences and Astronomy

Anatomy of the Earth
André Cailleux, *Paris*

The Electrical Earth
J. Sayers, *Birmingham*

Climate and Weather
H. Flohn, *Bonn*

The Structure of the Universe
E. L. Schatzman, *Sorbonne*

Applied Science

Words and Waves
A. H. W. Beck, *Cambridge*

The Science of Decision-making
A. Kaufmann, *Paris*